Three-Wheelers
Ultimate Portfolio
1909-1952

Compiled by R M Clarke

ISBN 9781855208384

BROOKLANDS BOOKS LTD.
P.O. BOX 146, COBHAM,
SURREY, KT11 1LG. UK
sales@brooklands-books.com

MR3UP

Printed in China

Brooklands Books

ROAD TEST SERIES

Abarth Gold Portfolio 1950-1971
Alfa Romeo Giulietta Gold Portfolio 1954-1965
Alfa Romeo Giulia Berlina Lim. Edit. Extra 1962-76
Alfa Romeo Giulia Coupes Lim. Edit. Ultra 1973-76
Alfa Romeo Alfasud 1972-1984
Alfa Romeo Alfetta Gold Portfolio 1972-1987
Alfa Romeo Spider Ultimate Portfolio 1966-1994
Alfa Romeo Spider & GTV Perf. Port. 1995-2005
Allard Limited Edition Ultra
Alpine Renault Ultimate Portfolio 1958-1995
Alvis Gold Portfolio 1919-1967
AMC Rambler Limited Edition Extra 1956-1969
AMX & Javelin Gold Portfolio 1968-1974
Armstrong Siddeley Gold Portfolio 1945-1960
Aston Martin Gold Portfolio 1921-1947
Aston Martin Ultimate Portfolio 1948-1968
Aston Martin Ultimate Portfolio 1968-1980
Aston Martin Ultimate Portfolio 1981-1993
Aston Martin Ultimate Portfolio 1994-2006
Audi Quattro Gold Portfolio 1980-1991
Audi Quattro Takes On The Competition
Audi TT Performance Portfolio 1998-2006
Austin-Healey 100 & 100/6 Gold Port. 1952-1959
Austin-Healey 3000 Ultimate Portfolio 1959-1967
Austin-Healey Sprite Gold Portfolio 1958-1971
Bentley & Rolls-Royce Portfolio 1990-2002
Berkeley Sportscars Limited Edition
BMW 6 & 8 Cyl. Cars Limited Edition 1935-1960
BMW 700 Limited Edition 1959-1965
BMW 1600 Collection No. 1 1966-1981
BMW 2002 Ultimate Portfolio 1968-1976
BMW 6 Cylinder Coupes & Saloons Gold P. 1969-1976
BMW 316, 318, 320 (4 cyl.) Gold Port. 1975-1990
BMW 320, 323, 325 (6 cyl.) Gold Port. 1977-1990
BMW 3 Series Gold Portfolio 1991-1997
BMW M3 Ultimate Portfolio 1986-2006
BMW M5 Gold Portfolio 1980-2003
BMW 5 Series Gold Portfolio 1988-1995
BMW 6 Series Ultimate Portfolio 1976-1989
BMW 7 Series Performance Portfolio 1977-1986
BMW 7 Series Performance Portfolio 1986-1993
BMW 8 Series Performance Portfolio
BMW X5 Limited Edition Extra 1999-2006
BMW Alpina Performance Portfolio 1967-1987
BMW Alpina Performance Portfolio 1988-1998
BMW Z3, M Coupe & M Roadster Gold Port. 1996-02
Borgward Isabella Limited Edition
Bristol Cars Portfolio
Buick Performance Portfolio 1947-1962
Buick Muscle Portfolio 1963-1973
Buick Riviera Performance Portfolio 1963-1978
Cadillac Performance Portfolio 1948-1958
Cadillac Performance Portfolio 1959-1966
Cadillac Eldorado Performance Portfolio 1967-1978
Cadillac Allante Limited Edition Extra
Impala & SS Muscle Portfolio 1958-1972
Corvair Performance Portfolio 1959-1969
El Camino & SS Muscle Portfolio 1959-1987
Chevy II & Nova SS Gold Portfolio 1962-1974
Chevelle & SS Gold Portfolio 1964-1972
Camaro Muscle Portfolio 1967-1973
Blazer & Jimmy Limited Edition Extra 1969-1982
Blazer & Jimmy Limited Edition Extra 1983-1994
Camaro Performance Portfolio 1993-2000
Chevrolet Corvette Gold Portfolio 1953-1962
Chevrolet Corvette Sting Ray Gold Port. 1963-1967
Chevrolet Corvette Gold Portfolio 1968-1977
High Performance Corvettes 1983-1989
Chrysler Imperial Gold Portfolio 1951-1975
Valiant 1960-1962
PT Cruiser Performance Portfolio
Citroen Traction Avant Limited Edition Premier
Citroen 2CV Ultimate Portfolio 1948-1990
Citroen DS & ID 1955-1975
Citroen DS & ID Gold Portfolio 1955-1975
Citroen SM Limited Edition Extra 1970-1975
Shelby Cobra Gold Portfolio 1962-1969
Crosley & Crosley Specials Limited Edition
Cunningham Automobiles 1951-1955
Datsun Roadsters Performance Portfolio 1960-71
Datsun 240Z & 260Z Gold Portfolio 1970-1978
DeLorean Gold Portfolio 1977-1995
De Soto Limited Edition 1952-1960
Dodge Limited Edition 1949-1959
Dodge Dart Limited Edition Extra 1960-1976
Dodge Muscle Portfolio 1964-1971
Charger Muscle Portfolio 1966-1974
ERA Gold Portfolio 1934-1994
Facel Vega Limited Edition Extra 1954-1964
Ferrari Limited Edition 1947-1957
Ferrari Limited Edition 1958-1963
Ferrari Dino Limited Edition Extra 1965-1974
Ferrari 308 & Mondial Ultimate Portfolio 1975- 85
Ferrari 328 348 Mondial Ultimate Portfolio 1986-94
Ferrari F355 & 360 Gold Portfolio 1995-2004
Fiat 600 & 850 Gold Portfolio 1955-1972
Fiat Dino Limited Edition
Fiat 124 Spider Performance Portfolio 1966-1985
Fiat X1/9 Gold Portfolio 1973-1989
Ford Consul, Zephyr, Zodiac Mk. I & II 1950-1962
Ford Zephyr, Zodiac, Executive Mk. III & IV 1962-1971
High Performance Capris Gold Portfolio 1969-1987
Capri Muscle Portfolio 1974-1987
High Performance Fiestas 1979-1991
Ford Escort RS & Mexico Limited Edition 1970-1979
High Performance Escorts Mk. II 1975-1980
High Performance Escorts 1980-1985
High Performance Escorts 1985-1990
Ford Thunderbird Performance Portfolio 1955-1957
Ford Thunderbird Performance Portfolio 1958-1963
Ford Thunderbird Performance Portfolio 1964-1976
Ford Fairlane Performance Portfolio 1955-1970
Ford Ranchero Muscle Portfolio 1957-1979
Edsel Limited Edition 1957-1960
Ford Galaxie & LTD Gold Portfolio 1960-1976
Falcon Performance Portfolio 1960-1970
Ford GT40 & GT Ultimate Portfolio 1964-2006
Ford Torino Performance Portfolio 1968-1974
Ford Bronco 4x4 Performance Portfolio 1966-1977
Ford Bronco 1978-1988
Shelby Mustang Ultimate Portfolio 1965-1970
Mustang Muscle Portfolio 1967-1973
High Performance Mustang IIs 1974-1978
Mustang 5.0L Muscle Portfolio 1982-1993
Mustang 5.0L Takes On The Competition
Ginetta Cars Limited Edition Ultra 1958-2007
Goggomobil Limited Edition
Honda S500 • S600 • S800 Limited Edition 1962-1970
Honda CRX 1983-1987
Honda S2000 Performance Portfolio 1999-2008
Hudson Performance Portfolio 1946-1957
International Scout Gold Portfolio 1961-1980
Isetta Gold Portfolio 1953-1964
ISO & Bizzarrini Limited Edition Ultra 1962-1974
Jaguar and SS Gold Portfolio 1931-1951
Jaguar XK120 • 140 • 150 Gold Portfolio 1948-1960
Jaguar C-Type & D-Type Gold Portfolio 1951-1960
Jaguar E-Type Ultimate Portfolio 1961-1975
Jaguar XJ6 Series I & II Gold Portfolio 1968-1979
Jaguar XJ6 Series III Perf. Portfolio 1979-1986
Jaguar XJS Gold Portfolio 1975-1988
Jaguar XJ-S V12 Ultimate Portfolio 1988-1996
Jaguar XK8 & XKR Performance Portfolio 1996-2005
Jeep CJ-5 Limited Edition 1960-1975
Jeep CJ-5 & CJ-7 4x4 Perf. Portfolio 1976-1986
Jeep Wagoneer Performance Portfolio 1963-1991
Jeep J-Series Pickups 1970-1982
Jeepster & Commando Limited Edition 1967-1973
Jeep Cherokee & Comanche Pickups P. P. 1984-91
Jeep Wrangler 4x4 Performance Portfolio 1987-99
Jeep Cherokee & Grand Cherokee 4x4 P. P. 1992-98
Jensen Interceptor Ultimate Portfolio 1966-1992
Jensen - Healey Limited Edition 1972-1976
Kaiser - Frazer Limited Edition 1946-1955
Lagonda Gold Portfolio 1919-1964
Lancia Aurelia & Flaminia Gold Portfolio 1950-1970
Lancia Fulvia Gold Portfolio 1963-1976
Lancia Beta Gold Portfolio 1972-1984
Lancia Stratos Limited Edition Extra
Lancia Delta & integrale Ultimate Portfolio
Land Rover Series I, II & IIA Gold Portfolio 1948-71
Land Rover Series III 4x4 Perf. Portfolio 1971-1985
Land Rover 90 110 Defender Gold Portfolio 1983-94
Land Rover Discovery Perf. Port. 1989-2000
Lamborghini Performance Portfolio 1964-1976
Lamborghini Performance Portfolio 1977-1989
Lamborghini Gold Portfolio 1990-2004
Lincoln Gold Portfolio 1949-1960
Lincoln Continental Performance Portfolio 1961-1969
Lincoln Continental 1969-1976
Lotus Sports Racers Portfolio - covering 1951-1965
Lotus Seven Gold Portfolio 1957-1973
Lotus Elite Limited Edition 1957-1964
Lotus Elan Ultimate Portfolio 1962-1974
Lotus Elan & SE 1989-1992
Lotus Europa Gold Portfolio 1966-1975
Lotus Elite & Eclat 1974-1982
Lotus Elise & Exige Gold Portfolio 1995-2005
Marcos Coupés & Spyders Gold Portfolio 1960-1997
Maserati Cars Performance Portfolio 1957-1970
Maserati Cars Performance Portfolio 1971-1982
Maserati Cars Performance Portfolio 1982-1998
Maserati Cars Ultimate Portfolio 1999-2007
Matra Limited Edition 1965-1983
Mazda Miata MX-5 Performance Portfolio 1989-1997
Mazda Miata MX-5 Performance Portfolio 1998-2005
Mazda Miata MX-5 Takes On The Competition
Mazda RX-7 Gold Portfolio 1978-1991
McLaren F1 • GTR • LM Sportscar Perf. Portfolio
Mercedes 190 & 300 SL 1954-1963
Mercedes S & 600 Limited Edition Extra 1965-1972
Mercedes S Class 1972-1979
Mercedes S Class Limited Edition Extra 1980-1991
Mercedes 230 • 250 • 280SL Gold Portfolio 1963-1971
Mercedes-Benz SLs & SLCs Ultimate Port. 1971-89
Mercedes SLs Performance Portfolio 1989-1994
Mercedes G-Wagen Gold Portfolio 1981-2005
Mercedes 190 Limited Edition Extra 1983-1993
Mercedes CLK & SLK Limited Edition 1996-2000
Mercedes AMG Gold Portfolio 1983-1999
Mercedes AMG Ultimate Portfolio 2000-2006
Mercury Gold Portfolio 1947-1966
Mercury Comet & Cyclone Lim. Edit. Extra 1960-75
Cougar Muscle Portfolio 1967-1973
Messerschmitt Gold Portfolio 1954-1964
MG Gold Portfolio 1929-1939
MG TA & TC Gold Portfolio 1936-1949
MG TD & TF Gold Portfolio 1949-1955
MGA & Twin Cam Gold Portfolio 1955-1962
MG Midget Gold Portfolio 1961-1979
MGB Roadsters 1962-1980
MGB MGC & V8 Gold Portfolio 1962-1980
MGC & MGB GT V8 Limited Edition
MGF & TF Performance Portfolio 1995-2005
Mini Gold Portfolio 1959-1969
Mini Gold Portfolio 1969-1980
Mini Gold Portfolio 1981-1997
High Performance Minis Gold Portfolio 1960-1973
Mini Cooper Gold Portfolio 1961-1971
Mini Moke Ultimate Portfolio 1964-1994
Mini Performance Portfolio 2001-2006
Starion & Conquest Performance Portfolio 1982-1990
Mitsubishi 3000GT & Dodge Stealth P.P. 1990-1999
Morgan Three-Wheelers Ultimate Portfolio 1909-1952
Morgan Four-Wheelers Ultimate Portfolio 1936-1967
Morgan Ultimate Portfolio 1968-1990
Morgan Ultimate Portfolio 1991-2009
Nash Limited Edition Extra 1949-1957
Nash-Austin Metropolitan Gold Portfolio 1954-1962
NSU Ro80 Limited Edition
NSX Performance Portfolio 1989-1999
Oldsmobile Limited Edition Premier 1948-1963
Oldsmobile Muscle Portfolio 1964-1971
Cutlass & 4-4-2 Muscle Portfolio 1964-1974
Opel GT Ultimate Portfolio 1968-1973
Opel Manta Limited Edition 1970-1975
Pantera Ultimate Portfolio 1970-1995
Panther Gold Portfolio 1972-1990
Plymouth Limited Edition 1950-1960
Plymouth Fury Limited Edition Extra 1956-1976
Barracuda Muscle Portfolio 1964-1974
Plymouth Muscle Portfolio 1964-1971
High Performance Firebirds 1982-1988
Firebird & Trans Am Performance Portfolio 1993-00
Pontiac Fiero Performance Portfolio 1984-1988
Porsche Sports Racing Cars UP 1952-1968
Porsche 917 • 935 • 956 • 962 Gold Portfolio
Porsche 912 Limited Edition Extra
Porsche 365 Ultimate Portfolio 1952-1965
Porsche 911 1965-1969
Porsche 911 1973-1977
Porsche 911 SC & Turbo Gold Portfolio 1978-1983
Porsche 911 Carrera & Turbo Gold Port. 1984-1989
Porsche 911 Ultimate Portfolio 1990-1997
Porsche 911 Takes On The Competition 1990-1997
Porsche 911 Ultimate Portfolio 1998-2004
Porsche 914 Ultimate Portfolio
Porsche 924 Gold Portfolio 1975-1988
Porsche 928 Gold Portfolio 1977-1995
Porsche 928 Takes On The Competition
Porsche 944 Ultimate Portfolio
Porsche 968 Limited Edition Extra
Porsche Boxster Ultimate Portfolio 1996-2004
Railton & Brough Superior Gold Portfolio 1933-1950
Range Rover Gold Portfolio 1970-1985
Range Rover Gold Portfolio 1985-1995
Range Rover Performance Portfolio 1995-2001
Range Rover Takes on the Competition
Riley Gold Portfolio 1924-1939
Rolls-Royce Silver Clould & Bentley S Ultimate Port.
Rolls-Royce Silver Shadow Ultimate Port. 1965-80
Rover P4 1949-1959
Rover 2000 & 2200 1963-1977
Studebaker Ultimate Portfolio 1946-1966
Studebaker Hawks & Larks Lim. Edit. Premier 1956-66
Avanti Limited Edition Extra 1962-1991
Subaru Impreza Turbo Limited Edition Extra 1994-00
Subaru Impreza WRX Performance Port. 2001-2005
Sunbeam Alpine Limited Edition Extra 1959-1968
Sunbeam Tiger Limited Edition Extra 1964-1967
Suzuki SJ Gold Portfolio 1971-1997
Vitara, Sidekick & Geo Tracker Perf. Port. 1988-1997
Toyota Land Cruiser Gold Portfolio 1956-1987
Toyota Land Cruiser 1988-1997
Toyota Supra Performance Portfolio 1982-1998
Toyota MR2 Ultimate Portfolio 1984-2006
Toyota MR2 Takes On The Competition
Triumph TR2 & TR3 Gold Portfolio 1952-1961
Triumph TR4, TR5, TR250 1961-1968
Triumph TR6 Gold Portfolio 1969-1976
Triumph Herald 1959-1971
Triumph Vitesse 1962-1971
Triumph Spitfire Gold Portfolio 1962-1980
Triumph 2000, 2.5, 2500 1963-1977
Triumph GT6 Gold Portfolio 1966-1974
Triumph Stag Gold Portfolio 1970-1977
TVR Performance Portfolio 1986-1994
TVR Performance Portfolio 1995-2000
TVR Performance Portfolio 2000-2005
VW Beetle Gold Portfolio 1935-1967
VW Beetle Gold Portfolio 1968-1991
VW Bus Camper Van Perf. Portfolio 1954-1967
VW Bus Camper Van Perf. Portfolio 1968-1979
VW Bus Camper Van Perf. Portfolio 1979-1991
VW Karmann Ghia Gold Portfolio 1955-1974
VW Scirocco 1974-1981
VW Golf GTI Limited Edition Extra 1976-1991
VW Corrado Limited Edition Premier 1989-1995
Volvo PV444 & PV544 Perf. Portfolio 1945-1965
Volvo 120 Amazon Ultimate Portfolio
Volvo 1800 Ultimate Portfolio 1960-1973
Volvo 140 & 160 Series Gold Portfolio 1966-1975
Forty Years of Selling Volvo
Westfield Performance Portfolio 1982-2004

RACING & THE LAND SPEED RECORD

The Land Speed Record 1898-1919
The Land Speed Record 1920-1929
The Land Speed Record 1930-1939
The Land Speed Record 1940-1962
The Land Speed Record 1963-1999
Can-Am Racing 1966-1969
Can-Am Racing 1970-1974
Can-Am Racing Cars 1966-1974
The Carrera Panamericana Mexico - 1950-1954
Le Mans - The Bentley & Alfa Years - 1923-1939
Le Mans - The Jaguar Years - 1949-1957
Le Mans - The Ferrari Years - 1958-1965
Le Mans - The Ford & Matra Years - 1966-1974
Le Mans - The Porsche Years - 1975-1982
Le Mans - The Porsche & Jaguar Years - 1983-91
Le Mans - The Porsche & Peugeot Years - 1992-99
Mille Miglia - The Alfa & Ferrari Years - 1927-1951
Mille Miglia - The Ferrari & Mercedes Years - 1952-57
Targa Florio - The Porsche & Ferrari Years - 1955-1964
Targa Florio - The Porsche Years - 1965-1973

RESTORATION & GUIDE SERIES

BMW 2002 - A Comprehensive Guide
BMW 02 Restoration Guide
BMW E30 - 3 Series Restoration Bible
Classic Camaro Restoration
Engine Swapping Tips & Techniques
Ferrari Life Buyer's Portfolio
Land Rover Restoration Portfolio
PC on Land Rover Series I Restoration
Lotus Elan Restoration Guide
MG 'T' Series Restoration Guide
MGA Restoration Guide
PC on Midget/Sprite Restoration
PC on MGB Restoration
Mustang Restoration Tips & Techniques
Practical Gas Flow
Restoring Sprites & Midgets an Enthusiast's Guide
SU Carburetters Tuning Tips & Techniques
PC on Sunbeam Rapier Restoration
The Great Classic Muscle Cars Compared
Weber Carburettors Tuning Tips and Techniques

MILITARY VEHICLES

Complete WW2 Military Jeep Manual
Dodge WW2 Military Portfolio 1940-1945
German Military Equipment WW2
Hail To The Jeep
Combat Land Rover Portfolio No. 1
Land Rover Military Portfolio
Military & Civilian Amphibians 1940-1990
Off Road Jeeps Civilian & Military 1944-1971
US Military Vehicles 1941-1945
Standard Military Motor Vehicles-TM9-2800 (WW2)
VW Kubelwagen Military Portfolio 1940-1990
WW2 Allied Vehicles Military Portfolio 1939-1945
WW2 Jeep Military Portfolio 1941-1945

ROAD & TRACK SERIES

Road & Track on Aston Martin 1962-1990
Road & Track on Austin Healey 1953-1970
Road & Track on BMW Cars 1966-1974
Road & Track BMW M Series Portfolio 1979-2002
R & T BMW Z3, M Coupe & M Roadster Port. 96-02
R & T Camaro & Firebird Portfolio 1993-2002
R & T on Cobra, Shelby & Ford GT40 1962-1992
Road & Track on Corvette 1968-1982
Road & Track on Corvette 1982-1986
Road & Track on Corvette 1986-1990
Road & Track Corvette Portfolio 1997-2002
Road & Track Dodge Viper Portfolio 1992-2002
Road & Track on Ferrari 1975-1981
Road & Track on Ferrari 1984-1988
Road & Track Ferrari V-12 Portfolio 1992-2002
Road & Track Ferrari F355 360 F430 Portfolio 95-06
Road & Track on Fiat Sports Cars 1968-1987
Road & Track on Jaguar 1950-1960
Road & Track on Jaguar 1961-1968
Road & Track on Jaguar 1968-1974
Road & Track on Jaguar 1974-1982
Road & Track on Jaguar 1983-1989
R & T Jaguar XJ-S - XK8 - XKR Portfolio 1975-2003
Road & Track MX-5 Miata Portfolio 1989-2002
Road & Track on Mercedes 1952-1962
Road & Track on Mercedes 1963-1970
Road & Track on Mercedes 1971-1979
R & T Mercedes SL - SLK - CLK Portfolio 1990-2003
Road & Track on MG Sports Cars 1949-1961
Road & Track on MG Sports Cars 1962-1980
Road & Track Mustang Portfolio 1994-2002
Road & Track Nissan 300ZX & 350Z Portfolio 1984-03
Road & Track on Porsche 1951-1967
Road & Track on Porsche 1968-1971
Road & Track on Porsche 1972-1975
Road & Track on Porsche 1975-1978
Road & Track on Porsche 1979-1982
Road & Track on Porsche 1985-1988
Road & Track Porsche 928 Portfolio 1977-1994
Road & Track Porsche 911 Portfolio 1990-1997
R & T on Rolls Royce & Bentley 1950-1965
R & T on Rolls Royce & Bentley 1966-1984
R & T on Toyota Sports & GT Cars 1966-1984
R & T on Triumph Sports Cars 1967-1974
R & T on Triumph Sports Cars 1974-1982
Road & Track on Volkswagen 1951-1968
Road & Track on Volkswagen 1968-1978
Road & Track on Volvo 1957-1974
Road & Track on Volvo 1977-1994
Road & Track - Best of PS
Road & Track - Peter Egan Side Glances 1983-92
Road & Track - Peter Egan Side Glances 1992-97
Road & Track - Peter Egan Side Glances 1998-02
Road & Track - Peter Egan Side Glances 2002-06

CAR AND DRIVER SERIES

Car and Driver on BMW 1957-1977
Car and Driver on Corvette 1978-1982
Car and Driver on Corvette 1983-1988
Car and Driver on Ferrari 1955-1962
Car and Driver on Ferrari 1963-1975
Car and Driver on Mustang 1964-1973
Car and Driver on Porsche 1955-1962
Car and Driver on Porsche 1963-1970
Car and Driver on Porsche 1970-1976
Car and Driver on Porsche 1977-1981
Car and Driver on Porsche 1982-1986

HOT ROD 'ENGINE' SERIES

Chevy 265 & 283
Chevy 302 & 327
Chevy 348 & 409
Chevy 396 & 427
Chevy 454 thru 512
Chevy Monster Big Blocks
Chrysler Hemi
Chrysler 273, 318, 340 & 360
Chrysler 361, 383, 400, 413, 426 & 440
Ford 289, 302, Boss 302 & 351W
Ford 351C & Boss 351
Ford Small Block
Ford Big Block

MOTORCYCLES

To see our range of over 70 titles visit www.brooklands-books.com

14/07Z81960

Acknowledgements

Brooklands Books has been publishing 'road test' books such as this on a wide range of makes and models for over 50 years. This is the first of four soft covered books tracing the history of the Morgan company over its first hundred years. This book covers the company's three-wheelers and the following three books their four-wheeler models. Compiling it has been an enjoyable and nostalgic journey as the first car I owned, whilst serving in the R.A.F. in 1952, was a 1931 Family Four. Over the following two years it accompanied me to England, Wales and Scotland plus Northern and Southern Ireland. Also, my first careful steps into publishing, in the mid-fifties, was an 'owners handbook' for this car.

The Morgan company has been one of the true survivors of the British motor industry. Its fortunes have been judiciously guided through two world wars and numerous booms and busts by four generations of the Morgan family and is now in the sure hands of Charles Morgan. Their latest road cars are a testament to his drive and energy and the creativity of those on his team.

The purpose of this book is to trace Morgan's history through the pages of contemporary magazine articles for the 100 years from 1909. Some of the pages are not of the quality we would have liked and for that we apologise. They have, it must be remembered, been taken from up to 99 year-old magazines, mostly printed on newsprint quality paper and some, from necessity, are copies of copies. It is however the information that we believe to be of interest, which is our reason for including them.

A work of this nature relies on the help and co-operation of many people and organisations. First and foremost our thanks goes to Mr Charles Morgan who generously loaned us 35 wonderful scrapbooks, initally started by his great grandfather the Rev. H.G. Morgan and then continued by his grandfather, 'H.F.S.' the first managing director of the company. Over a hundred pages of this book were sourced from this collection. The staff at Malvern - Matthew Parkin, Beverley Moore, Jayne Dobson and many others all helped in their own way to make this a valuable work of reference. We are also indebted to members of the The Morgan Three-Wheeler Club and especially Graham Joseph for photographs of his 1930 maroon JAP powered Super Aero which can be seen on our back cover and also to Dr. John Alderson, the well-known author of a number of books on Morgans, who kindly wrote the informative introduction that follows.

None of our 'road test' series could or would exist if it were not for the understanding and generosity of the publishers of the world's leading motoring and motorcycling journals, who for over 50 years, have allowed us to include their invaluable copyright stories. We are sure that Morgan owners will wish to join with us in thanking the managements of the following magazines for their ongoing support: *Autocar, Car South Africa, Classic & Sports Car, The Cyclecar, Light Car, The Light Car and Cyclecar, Modern Motor, Motor, The Motor Cycle, The Motor Cycle & Cycle Trader, Motor Cycling, Motor Sport, NZ Classic Car* and *Performance Car*.

R.M. Clarke

The Morgan Works - 1919

Introduction

HFS Morgan was running a garage in Malvern Link with his early business partner Leslie Bacon when he decided to design and build a single seater three-wheeler in 1909 just for his own interest.

It had many special features, including all independent suspension, the front two wheels using his own design of sliding axles, this system still being in use by the Company today.

When the prototype was registered CJ743 in June 1910 it weighed just 3 cwt. ensuring an excellent power to weight ratio, a feature of all Morgan products ever since.

In 1912 the Morgan Motor Company was founded to manufacture three-wheelers, which by now were available as two-seaters. At this time the motor car was only for the rich, but those who disliked the motorcycle could buy a cyclecar, a cheap three or four-wheeled vehicle powered by a motorcycle type engine. Many of these were crude with dubious engineering, and HFS Morgan, supported by his wife Ruth, took part in all the forms of competition open to them to show that the Morgan three-wheeler was better than the opposition. This association with motor sport has continued throughout the Morgan Company's existence.

One of the first supporters of the Morgan in competition was W G McMinnies, who raced Morgans with great success including winning the French Cyclecar Grand Prix in 1913. As he was also the editor of "The Cyclecar" he gave the Morgan a great boost in his race write up. HFS Morgan was able to set in motion plans to greatly increase production, building in stages a new factory in Pickersleigh Road in Malvern Link.

After the First World War demand for Morgans was high, and HFS supplied several different body styles to suit the keen public. Several racers extracted amazing power from the vee-twin engines, enabling races to be won and world speed records to be broken.

It all began to decline when Herbert Austin introduced a large car in miniature, namely the Austin Seven, which was much more suitable to the family buyer than the cyclecar. Other car manufacturers soon followed Austin's lead.

HFS attempted to update his three-wheelers to take account of the buying trends, introducing a three speed and reverse gearbox in 1931, and then a chassis to take a four-cylinder Ford engine (the F-Type) in 1933. Despite these innovations production did not pick up and the last vee-twin Morgans were assembled just after the Second World War. The F-type continued until 1952. It was finally killed off by the post-war British government insisting on high volumes being exported to get steel quotas, and the three-wheeler was not easy to sell abroad.

Today the Morgan three-wheeler has a fanatical following, with many humbling much larger vehicles in historic motor racing.

Dr J Alderson

Brooklands Books

Contents

Brooklands Books

Contents - Continued

Morgan - An Overview of the First 100 Years
by Charles Morgan

Interestingly enough each Morgan design reaches the end of its life cycle after about 30 years, except in the case of the Morgan Plus Eight, which reached the ripe old age of 40! Of course there are minor improvements to each design made every few years or so but the basic concept of a Morgan design remains much the same.

The first Morgan era was of course the age of the Threewheeler. HFS Morgan designed a fun car, the Morgan Runabout, for people with little money but a sense of adventure. He had a huge business success and in the 1920s the Morgan factory in Malvern was making 2500-3000 cars a year with a smaller number being built in France under the Darmont Morgan brand. Nevertheless each year production was always sold out in advance as customers were desperate for small cars. The Morgan was popular because it was one of the best and most reliable light cars you could buy. Stripped down a Morgan Threewheeler also made a successful racing car. In 1913 a Morgan won the French Cyclecar Grand Prix and at Brooklands in the 1920s the JAP V twin engined Morgans were as fast as a Blower Bentley, completing a lap of the banked circuit at an average speed of over 100mph. Numerous records were broken in Morgan Threewheelers, notably by Gwenda Stewart at Brooklands and Monthlery. In spite of this success on the racetracks, during the 1930s Morgan Threewheeler sales fell off a cliff. By 1935 there were only 300 orders for the cars. The reason for this was the arrival of mass produced cars from Ford, Morris and Austin costing a similar price but offering more features for the money.

So HFS Morgan had to come up with something new. He did this in 1936 and announced the Morgan Four Four, a light sports car with four wheels and a four cylinder Coventry Climax engine. HFS had established the Morgan design philosophy with his Three-wheeler and subsequently for the next 100 years all Morgans have had a high power to weight ratio and lots of torque. So Morgans have always been fun to drive and capable of winning races in their class. Right from the start the Morgan Four Four was making its name in competition and finished well at Le Mans in 1938 and 1939.

With the interruption of War the second Morgan era did not really start until 1940 but it lasted until 1970. These were Morgan's "Heritage Years", when the company established its reputation as a successful sports car manufacturer. The slogan was, "Race on Sunday, sell on Monday" and the Morgan was successful in Rallies and Races in more or less standard form. The Morgan was typical of a breed of cars built for motoring enthusiasts who wanted to combine a car to get to work in with a bit of motor racing at the weekend. In the right amateur hands the Morgan could take on International competition and notably achieved a class win against the works teams at Le Mans in 1962. The car also achieved great success in the USA where success in sports car racing led to many sales of the Morgan Plus Four. The end of this period saw the birth of the Morgan Plus Eight, a light car fitted with a small block aluminium V8. The Plus Eight was the perfect example of a "wolf in sheep's clothing" with its long bonnet and elegant flowing wings but rumbling exhaust. The car became a best seller in Germany.

Although the Morgan Plus Eight was to become an enduring design, only ending production in 2004, the third Morgan era really began in the 1970s when the increasing importance of making vehicles safer, more efficient and more economical forced Morgan to make many changes to the design of its chassis and drivetrain. Between 1970 and 2000 the company met demanding new standards on a modest budget with the help of a talented and flexible workforce and the support of loyal suppliers. During this time most of the low volume car manufacturers failed to meet this challenge and slowly disappeared.

A further challenge for Morgan during this period was to improve quality and the efficiency of its manufacturing processes. The Japanese car makers in the 1970s and 1980s were proving that quality and efficiency were synonymous and car makers that failed to learn this lesson had a hard time surviving. Only a few of the 50 British independent motor manufacturers that were in business after the war have survived and of course Morgan is one of them.

The end of this era saw the birth of the Morgan Aero Eight. Testing and development had led the company into many new technologies such as electronic engine management, superformed body panels and an adhesively bonded aluminium chassis. The Aero Eight was the first car to use Alcan's Aluminium Intensive Vehicle technology that has subsequently been adopted by most of the luxury sports car industry to create a stiff but lightweight structure. The Aero Eight also marked the start of a successful collaboration with BMW giving Morgan access to some of the most advanced powertrain technology in the world. In spite of the cost of developing a new car the company kept some of its "gung ho" spirit alive and the Aero Eight production car was originally developed on the race track. The Morgan Aero Eight has competed at Le Mans in 2002 and 2004 and a three car team is now competing in the International FIA GT3 Series, frequently coming in the top ten finishers.

In 2009, during the Centenary year, a new era for Morgan begins. Environmental responsibility is the key message. Morgan has a head start with some existing green credentials. The modest weight of all Morgan sports cars make them economical and low polluting. The current Morgan Four Four emits only 139 gms CO_2/km which already puts it under the imposed limit for car manufacturers of 140 gms CO_2/km in 2012. Simple and efficient design using the latest Computer Aided Design software, the use of recyclable raw materials and water based paint all give Morgan a very low carbon footprint. Morgan also uses the latest electronic technology and fits efficient engines and gearboxes from Ford and BMW to give the lowest pollution levels. The AeroMax is the lightest V8 coupe in the world and emits just 260 gms CO_2/km in spite of accelerating to 60 mph in 4.5 seconds and reaching a maximum of 170mph. With the LIFECar Morgan is proposing a potential design revolution, a zero emission high performance sports car.

Morgan is now a vibrant exciting company with a great history behind it. The company can definitely learn from this history and I hope the reader of these transcripts gets a powerful glimpse of some of that history. In the last 100 years Morgans have created much passion and the company has had its supporters and its detractors. But all would agree that although a very small company Morgan has made a big contribution to the history of the sports car and the company intends to continue to do this in the future by being innovative, independent and exciting, just as it has been in the past.

The Morgan Three-Wheeler Runabout
1909-1952

The man who guided the destinies of the Morgan car for so nearly the fifty-years of its history - H.F.S. Morgan, was born at Stoke Lacy Rectory, Hereford, in 1881. His father was the late Rev. Prebendary H.G. Morgan, and he married Ruth the daughter of the late Rev. Archibald Day, formerly Vicar of St. Matthias, Malvern Link.

'H.F.S.' as he was known, to his loyal workers and personal friends

1907 - The Morgan motor works in Malvern.

was educated at Stone House, Broadstairs; Marlborough College and the Crystal Palace Engineering College. He began his career as the 18 year old pupil of Mr. W. Dean, Chief Engineer of the G.W.R. Railway Works at Swindon where he eventually worked as a draughtsman in the drawing office for some seven years.

Whilst making his own modest contributions to the history of steam, H.F.S.'s loyalties were divided between the locomotive and the motor car.

After a hair raising first drive in a 3$^{1}/_{2}$ h.p. Benz car that ran away with him down the 1 in 6 gradient of a hill between Bromyard and Hereford and from which he emerged intact but with damages to his car that cost his father about £28 for repairs, H.F.S. Morgan saved hard for three years.

The object of his saving was, not unnaturally, the purchase of a motor vehicle - an Eagle Tandem. Previously he had hired his cars including the ill fated Benz from a Mr. Marriot, the first motor trader in Hereford. The Eagle

1909 - Mr. Stephenson-Peach at the tiller of the car that H. F. S. Morgan built in Malvern College

1910 - The single-seater show car at Olympia

was a Three-wheeler, fitted with an 8 h.p. water cooled De Dion engine and it was from his experiences with this machine and a 7 h.p. two cylinder car called "The Little Star", that his first idea of making his own three-wheeler came.

When he left the G.W.R. drawing board in 1906 at the age of 25 he opened a garage and motor works in Malvern Link from where, in addition to his experimental work, he ran a most successful Bus Service with special 10 h.p. Wolseley 15 seaters from Malvern Link to the Wells and later from Malvern to Gloucester. At this time he was district agent for Wolseley and Darracq.

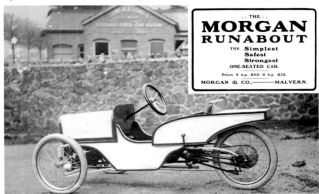

1911 - The single-seater show car as displayed at Olympia

It was during this period that he bought a 7 h.p. Twin Peugeot engine, intending to build a motor cycle. Although be was a keen cyclist - his dislike for motorised two-wheel transport prompted him to build the Peugeot engine into a light Three-wheeled, tubular chassis which he had already designed - a decision which, unknown to him, was to change the destinies of his company for the next 50 years ......the first Morgan Three-wheeler had been born!

With very little facility for machine work in the garage, most of this was done in the Malvern College Workshops under the kindly eye of the late Mr. Stephenson-Peach, then Engineering master at Malvern and Repton Colleges.

This very first model was completed in 1909 and was called the Morgan Run-about. (With, perhaps, as many thoughts of the running about between garage and college that heralded its final completion as for the more obvious connotation!).

The first machine was successful, largely due to its rigid frame, light weight and a factor almost unheard of in that day and age - in

1912 - The erecting shop

1912 - The prototype 4-seater.

1912 - The successful Morgan-JAP powered single-seater racer.

dependent front suspension! Another important factor contributing to the machine's success was undoubtedly the unusual power to weight ratio of 90 brake h.p. per ton which enabled this little vehicle to hold its own with any car being produced, at that time.

1913 - H.F.S. Morgan

Just how finely balanced are the wheels of fate and fortune can be judged from the fact that at this time there was no intention of marketing the vehicle, only after much favourable comment for the little machine whenever it was seen, was the decision made to build a few. With capital for some machine tools and the extension of the Malvern garage provided by his father, H.F.S. Morgan began manufacture in 1910. A Patent was granted, the Patent drawings being produced, at that time, by a bright youth who afterwards became the famous Sir John Black of the Standard Motor Company.

The Morgan name made its very first appearance at the Olympia Motor Show in 1910. The two Three-wheelers, both single-seaters fit-ted respectively with 8 h.p. twin and 4 h.p. single cylinder J.A.P. engines, created great interest and secured some 30 orders, but it soon became apparent that for the vehicles to be successful they would have to become two-seaters.

It was whilst the two-seater version was in preparation that H.F.S. Morgan entered his single-seater Three-wheeler in the well-known London-Exeter-London Reliability Trial gaining a Gold Medal - the highest possible award.

1912 -The Rev. H.G. Morgan

Two seaters made their first appearance at the 1911 Olympia Show. They were fitted with 8 h.p. engines.

At this time the orders received were many more than Mr. Morgan could cope with at Malvern and he approached several large Manufacturers to make them for him. It was, no doubt, fortunate that they turned the proposition down, for, with the help of deposits on orders he was able to purchase more machine tools and make further extensions to his garage.

1913 - Show Cars (top left) Sporting   (top right) Commercial   (bottom left) Grand Prix   (bottom right) De Luxe

The Morgan Runabout at the summit of the Worcestershire Beacon, 1,395 ft. above sea level. The three-wheeler was driven up this remarkable climb non-stop from Ludlow with its full complement of passengers. Has any other passenger-machine achieved this feat?

On the Way to Farlow Bank.

Last Wednesday morning, then, saw me once more aboard, accompanied by the photographer and bound for Farlow Bank, the dread test hill of the forthcoming Midland Quarterly Trial. It was cold work as we sped along the Kidderminster road, taking the left-hand turn for Stourport and Bewdley. Having passed safely through Stourport, we were hurtling along when. lo and behold, around a corner ahead of us appeared another three-wheeler, an A.-C. by the look of it, on the wrong side of the road. The driver did not see me until I hallooed, when he gave a wicked swerve over to his proper side of the road, whilst the Morgan mounted the bank. We bumped down safely and did not overturn, and, looking back, beheld the other man disappearing into the distance no worse for his fright.

At an early hour in Bewdley we ran across a party of motorcyclists who had come over from Birmingham. One rode a two-speed Douglas, another a two-speed Enfield, and a third a Triumph. "Are you coming to Farlow?" we shouted. "Yes," came the answer; "we'll follow you." We arrived first at the celebrated bank, and stuck just above the second corner, through my having forgotten to pump up pressure in the petrol tank. On extremely steep hills, when the petrol supply is low, it is quite possible that the petrol will not flow by gravity from the tank to the carburetter, which is placed right forward in front of the engine, and for this eventuality the pressure pump is fitted. At the next attempt the machine went up solo with the back wheel wobbling and racing in the loose gravel. Then I made an even more perilous descent, with low gear engaged, compression down, and with back wheel brakes screaming under the strain. However, the Morgan came down safely and then went up again, this time with plenty of pressure and the passenger aboard.

We then retraced our steps to see the motorcyclists perform. The Douglas two-speeder got up with a hot engine at the first attempt, a jolly good performance, though the rider knew the hill. The Triumph man apparently considered discretion the better part of valour, for he made no attempt while we were there. The Enfield rider made many and exciting trials. First he went up round the corner so fast that he skidded and was only prevented from gyrating off down the hill by his crankcase coming into contact with the near bank His next trial was even more thrilling, for he turned a complete circle in the loose gravel and faced down the hill, leaving a circular skid track on the surface of the road. At last, after several other equally exciting and amusing (for the spectator) attempts he managed to make a clean ascent, and then we left him rejoicing. From the summit of Farlow we proceeded viâ Doddington to Ludlow, over a most delightfully wild moorland road ascending to a great height by well-engineered gradients. On the left there was a sharply-sloping descent into the valley, whilst all along that side of the road were white stones, presumably to guide travellers at night by showing them the edge of the road. Far away on the left we could see the Malvern Hills, with the Worcestershire Beacon towering supreme above the valley and the town of Malvern.

A long and dangerous descent into Ludlow followed, and after a stop to inspect the castle bridge and quaint archway we made ahead for Tenbury, taking the main road in preference to the more direct cross-country route. It was during the next four miles of narrow, twisting country lanes that we really found out the charm of the runabout. Its pick-up around corners, its instant acceleration as soon as the throttle was opened can only be compared to that of a well-tuned motor-bicycle engine. Cars are not in it. Life, vim, "devil," if I may use a slangy term, form the nucleus of the Morgan's charm, in conjunction with great smoothness, steadiness, and comfort. We made excellent time to Tenbury, when we lost our way, eventually stopping at a cul de sac and having to

Speed and Sport on a Morgan (contd.).

retrace our tracks for a mile or more. Then we took the Worcester road, leaving it at Martley and going viâ Shelsley Walsh in a futile endeavour to discover Ankerdine Hill.

A Remarkable Climb and a Perilous Descent.

From Worcester we travelled to Malvern, intending to deliver up the machine to its rightful owners, but as we still had an hour or so to spare we resolved to attempt a bold thing. We planned to climb to the very summit of the Worcestershire Beacon, which rears its head to a height of nearly 1,400 ft. above sea level. We decided to make the ascent viâ Red Lion bank, which ascends suddenly and steeply from the centre of Malvern, the average gradient for the first 300 yds. being something like 1 in 5. Before taking the sharp right-angle bend I dropped into low gear—clutch out and gear in in half a second—and then the long climb began. Remember that we had never stopped the engine all the way from Ludlow, and realize the severity of the task before the Morgan. Pumping up pressure and oiling the engine occupied us during the first stretch of the climb as we wound our way up past the donkey sheds, up and up, being met here and there by astonished spectators, who looked on at the little three-wheeled marvel with gaping eyes. Up and up, round a hair-pin bend, now up the other flank of the hill we ground our way. Higher and higher, with the view below us ever widening to our gaze. Now on one side a·sheer drop for hundreds of feet and on the other the grassy slope of the mountain still stretching upwards. The road sadly degenerated, and we travelled on a narrow grass track round and round to the summit. Narrower and more rocky became the track until at last the Beacon itself came into sight a hundred feet above us. We pumped up pressure, and in a few moments were at the summit, the feat accomplished non-stop with two passengers and a hot engine ; a magnificent tribute to the three-wheeled Morgan. After inspecting the stone on which is placed a map of the surrounding country with a " key " to the places that can be observed, together with their correct line of direction, we decided to

descend. Putting the low speed dog in gear and raising the exhaust lifter, we commenced the long drop. I noticed that my photographic friend had one leg over the side of the car, and from his occasional remarks about the precipices on his side of the road I judged that he was in considerable trepidation as to our safety. Especially was this the case when we began to slide bodily sideways towards the yawning abyss. So acute were some of the hairpin bends that twice we had to get out and lift the car round the corners. We might have steered the machine round, but it would have meant going so near to the precipices that the risk was not worth taking, and the passenger insisted, in consequence, on getting out. However, we straightened up, and using first one brake, then the other, and then both together, eventually arrived back in the town in safety. We then delivered the machine over to its makers, and, needless to relate, were most reluctant to part with it

I feel convinced that when a few more side-carists get to know of the existence of this little three-wheeler, and when they have had time to give the machine a trial, they will fall in love with it as much as I have done. Its lightness makes it extremely easy on the very heavy tyres with which it is fitted ; the shaft and chain drive, in conjunction with the double dog clutch system of change-speed gear, the ideal position of the engine for purposes of cooling, the wheel steering and comfortable side-by-side positions of the passengers, are all points that appeal greatly to the motorcyclist. During my 300-mile trial my only involuntary stop was due to an exhaust pipe union shaking loose and causing an otherwise exceedingly silent machine to become noisy. In the garage at Worcester I cleaned a plug ; otherwise I never touched any part of the machine with a tool, which is all the more creditable in view of the bucketing about which the machine received at my hands. My latest notion is to have a single-seater with wheel steering, built to my own special ideas, with wind-cutting body and disc wheels à la Brooklands model. With such a mount, I think that I could " whack " fully 70 per cent. of the solo machines on the road, as well as all the side-cars. At any rate, the show is near now, and " nous verrons."

PLATINUM.

1911 - H.S.F. Morgan bringing his Runabout round the steep rough corner on Arkengarthdale Hill. A.C.U. Six days trial.

MONOCAR OR MOTORCYCLE?

Instructive Comparisons Inspired by a Three-Hundred-and-Fifty Miles Winter Trial on an 8 h.p. Morgan Runabout.

THE telephone bell rang. "Is that Platinum?" said a voice. I replied that it was.

"I'm Harold Patteson, of Cyril Patteson, Wilberforce and Co., Ltd., and I hear that you're going down by road to the race ball at Cheltenham to-morrow. May I come with you?"

"Rather. Only too glad to have a companion. Meet Skindle's, Maidenhead, at 1 p.m.," was my prompt rejoinder.

"Right-o." And the receiver was clicked home again.

As a matter of fact I had not intended to go down to this dance by road, because it would have meant taking a large suit case on the machine, with the probability of the wet and dirt ruining the contents. The 3.15 p.m. express from Paddington seemed more comfortable to me, but then there was the coal strike and the possibility of the service being late. However, as I was to have a companion on the journey, I thought I might as well motor. After some thought I decided that to ride my T.T. Triumph "Puffing Billy" was out of the question. A monocar would be more suitable. Then I remembered that

Harrod's had a Morgan runabout fitted with one of their own design of bodies, and that this concern had invited me to test the machine and recount my experiences. The very thing. And so it came to pass that about 12 o'clock on the next day I might have been seen ensconced in a comfortable 8 h.p. Morgan runabout with a big suit case and a pile of coats beside me.

The machine had a hood and screen. The former was not required, but the latter was certainly a blessing. Having lowered it so as to slope considerably, it was possible to see the road over the screen and yet not feel any draught whatever. As the day was cold, the screen and high side-entrance doors fitted to each side rendered the machine most cosy, the heat of the engine helping to make everything snug. The tramlines in London hindered me not a bit, and the Bath road at Hounslow was reached in half an hour. Through Colnbrook and Slough the roads were heavy, but after leaving the latter place they improved slightly. On ahead I spied another three-wheeler, the single driving wheel being in front and the other wheels behind. The engine was fitted directly over

THE MORGAN RUNABOUT AT THE BALL.

Owing to the miscarriage of certain arrangements the Morgan Runabout provided the only means by which our contributor "Platinum" could reach the ballroom in time. Accordingly the three-wheeler was commandeered for the purpose and driven successfully to the scene of the festivities. Here it was left outside in the street till 5 o'clock in the morning. When the dance was over our contributor returned home not one bit the worse for his unusual experiences.

Monocar or Motorcycle? (contd.).

the front wheel, so that the machine was probably a Cyclone or Phanomobile.

The driver could not be tempted to open out and try the powers of the machine against the Morgan, though further on a covered-in Vauxhall car came to the rescue and provided some incident for copy by entering into a friendly speed trial. Unluckily for me the road was a mass of slime, but so great is my confidence in the stability of the Morgan that I did not hesitate to open out. In spite of severe tail-wagging, the runabout proved more than a match for the car, and arrived at Skindle's a few minutes before its rival.

My friend was waiting for me, having ridden over on a T.T. Triumph. His luggage had been sent by train several days before. Lunch over, we set out together. Our zeal almost ended in disaster, as a constable warned my friend to stop in the centre of Maidenhead, with the result that the Morgan, which was hard on his track, very nearly skidded into him through a too sudden application of the brakes.

The ride via Henley to Oxford

"The only incident on the journey worth noting was an encounter with two wild horses which lashed out at the monocar just as it drew alongside them. A sudden swerve avoided the horses heels by fractions of an inch."

was uneventful, though it gave me an opportunity of comparing the relative merits of the monocar and the motor-bicycle. The two-wheeler was naturally faster than the Morgan, though the latter can average 20 m.p.h. even on winter roads. The three-wheeler had the advantage of greater luggage-carrying capacity, whilst I am sure that I was far more comfortable and at home on grease than my companion. There is no need for the monocarist to deck himself in unsightly overalls, nor is he appalled by the prospect of miles of greasy tramlines or a shower or two of rain. On the other hand there is more vibration on a high-speed monocar than on a motor-bicycle, with the result that unless everything is fixed securely it is apt to fall off or rattle abominably. Spring washers and split pins should be used on every bolt.

A Road in the Making.

In Nuneham we met a G.W.K., but could not spare the time to stop and inspect the machine. Near Iffley the road was under repair, great blocks of stone being piled high on one side, whilst the very foundations of the road were exposed to view for a quarter of a mile or so. The repairs were of the most extensive character, and ordinary traffic had to go round another way. Patteson took to the side track. Not to be outdone, I did the same, overtaking the Triumph rider on the slime. It struck me then that on a road which is bad all over the monocarist, though he has three tracks, possesses an advantage over the motorcyclist, though on ordinary roads the latter scores, as he only require 6 in. good surface, whereas the three-wheeler is bound to strike ruts and potholes with one of its wheels. We stayed a few minutes in Morris's garage, the rendezvous of 'Varsity motorcyclists, as it is called, and then departed on the next stage of the journey.

A glorious skid took place on the tramlines near Oxford station as the rear wheel stuck in the metal, but although going fast the machine never exhibited the slightest tendency to capsize. Here it may be well to impress on my readers that I was driving alone and the extra weight of a passenger would probably have steadied the machine still further. The Triumph man rode

The 8 h.p. Morgan runabout causes some amusement and a good deal of interest amongst the spectators on Aston Hill, near Tring, where the Essex M.C. recently held an open hill-climb.

The Charm of the Three-Wheeler

Features of the Construction and Running of the Latest Morgan, Fitted with a 10 h.p. M.A.G. Engine.

IT has been known for some time past that the Morgan Motor Co., Ltd., have been fitting M.A.G. engines to certain of their productions, and we have recently had the opportunity of carrying out an extended trial of one of the Morgan runabouts so fitted. At the outset we must say that the engine is remarkably powerful, and as fitted to a Morgan it provides one of the most lively and fast hill-climbers that it has been our pleasure to try.

The keynote of the Morgan is undoubtedly economy, but in combination with this M.A.G. engine the power at the driver's disposal is one above the average. The top gear fitted has a ratio of 4 to 1, but it can truly be said to be a top-gear car. It will throttle down to a mere crawl on this gear, and will attain a speed on the level closely approximating to the fifties. A surprising thing is that maximum speed on the level is very little more than the maximum speed on quite considerable hills.

Top Gear Running

To deal specifically with the hill-climbing powers of this popular three-wheeler, we might mention that the run from Malvern to London was accomplished with only one change of gear. This occurred at Fish Hill, Broadway, which has a maximum gradient of 1 in 7, the latter occurring at a very sharp right-angle bend. Owing to the presence of other traffic and the consequent necessary reduction of speed, bottom gear had to be used round this corner, but after a few yards top could be once more engaged, and the climb was finished well over the legal limit without a sign of knock from the engine. London to Brighton and Worthing to London are two of the top-gear runs of this Morgan. From Brighton to London only one change was necessary, on Reigate Hill, and even then the air-cooled Morgan climbed most of the way up the steepest part before a change was necessary, more from considerations of speed than for lack of hill-climbing power.

It is not so much the fact that the Morgan will climb hills on top as that it always gives evidence of a very great reserve of power, a fact which contributes considerably to the fascination of this little car. Should it be desired, hills can be taken at top speed, and in the course of our trial there were very few other vehicles, from high-powered motor-bicycles to racing cars, that could hold the Morgan, much less beat it on an ordinary hill. But should the owner's desires not run in the direction of speed, the same hills can be gently and smoothly taken at a low speed with the certain knowledge that, should a spurt be desired, in spite of the gradient, a slight motion of the throttle lever will at once produce the desired result.

Extreme Economy

Having dealt with the liveliness and general power of the cyclecar, we next come to a very important point, viz., that of economy. In the ordinary course of events a car which will give one very high speed on hills, a violent acceleration and unparalleled hill-climbing properties would naturally be expected to be wasteful of petrol. The very reverse obtains in the case of the Morgan. On no occasion did we obtain less than 40 miles to the gallon, and in most cases the consumption was in the neighbourhood of 50 m.p.g. This economy of fuel is, of course, due to the reserve of power possessed by the engine and to the ingenious carburetter fitted. The latter is one of the new B. and B. with pilot jet. This fitting serves for slow running and starting, crossing over to the main jet for all ordinary work. This carburetter has a tapered needle attached to the throttle slide, and as the throttle is opened this needle is drawn further out of the jet, thus permitting more fuel to pass. With the carburetter as tuned for the Morgan, we found that the air could be set about a quarter open, and then it was unnecessary to move the air lever in spite of very great variations of speed. The attribute of automaticity seems to be very strongly possessed by this carburetter, and all driving can be done on the throttle. The simplification of the control thus entailed will be obvious.

The general construction of the Morgan is well known to most of our readers, but as the design is so striking and so distinctly unconventional, it is well worth a further description.

The frame of the Morgan, if one can use the term, consists principally of a large-diameter tube, which connects the back wheel with a rectangular

CHARM OF THE THREE-WHEELER (contd,).

arrangement of tubes, which takes the place of the front axle. Subsidiary tubes are provided so as to lend the necessary rigidity to the frame, but the large tube, one of the simplest and strongest of engineering components, does practically the whole work. The engine is mounted right on the front of the frame, and behind it is the combined oil and petrol tank. Keyed to the engine shaft is the outer member of a leather cone clutch, from which the power passes down a propeller shaft running in the large tube previously mentioned. At the rear end of this tube is a neat bevel casing, which simply encloses the driving and driven bevels. On the squared ends of the bevel shaft are carried two dog clutches, which can be locked alternately to either of two sprockets connected by chains to the rear wheel. These sprockets are of different diameters, and it is in this way that the change of speed is effected. It will be seen that each gear is equally direct; thus there is no greater friction on low than on top. On the back axle, of course, are mounted the two sprocket wheels, one on each side, and also two brake drums, on which band brakes operate, controlled by lever and by pedal. These brakes are extremely efficient in their action, and when wear takes place adjustment can be easily carried out.

Distinctive Springing.

Reverting to the front end of the frame, which, as previously stated, consists of a rectangle of tubes, the front wheels are mounted on independent pivots, which slide on the vertical members of this rectangle. Coil springs are fitted both above and below the pivots, and in this manner is the suspension at the front obtained. Steering is direct, and so carefully are the angles proportioned that on the roughest road and at the highest speed it is quite possible to drive with both hands off. At the rear, cantilever quarter elliptics are employed with subsidiary coil springs at their forward ends.

In the construction of the three-wheeler it is obvious that special efforts must be made to maintain the back wheel permanently vertical. On the Morgan a very rigid fork encloses the wheel, being hinged by a wide bearing at the rear of the bevel casing. As a result, the back wheel is held very rigid laterally, a fact which, no doubt, contributes to the remarkable steadiness of this three-wheeler on corners.

The M.A.G. engine fitted has a beautiful finish, and considerable thought and care have obviously been devoted to every point of its construction. The inlet valves are enclosed, and are mounted directly over the exhaust valves, being operated by a well-made rocker gear, which, in its turn, is entirely enclosed. Noise is thus remarkably reduced, and lubrication of the valve gear can be automatically carried out by the oil spray which is drawn up from the crank chamber. The engine dimensions are 82½ mm. by 104 mm., which, it will be seen, correspond to a capacity of 1112 c.c. The engine is air-cooled and is semi-enclosed in a neat bonnet. It is but natural that the engine gets hot to a certain extent, but in the course of some very hard driving we have never succeeded in raising the temperature to such a point that any deterioration in running was introduced. Air cooling on this particular model we have definitely proved to give every satisfaction, and there is not the slightest necessity for the extra complications of water cooling. In fact, the latter would be far more trouble than would be counterbalanced by any theoretical advantages which might be obtained.

The ratios of the two gears fitted are 4 to 1 on top and 7¾ to 1 on bottom. This sounds rather high for a low gear, but in the course of our wandering among some of the steepest hills in the Kent district there was never the slightest doubt that the gear was quite low enough for the successful negotiation in comfort of long hills up to 1 in 4.

To sum up, we would express the opinion that the Morgan is one of the most roadworthy cyclecars we have driven. For power, economy, acceleration and hill-climbing it is practically unequalled, and its ease of control is another strong point. The Morgan forms a valuable stepping stone between the motorcycle combination and the car, but, once the fascination of the Morgan has really taken hold of one, it is more than probable that one will remain a Morgan enthusiast to the end of one's days. The price of the 10 h.p. Morgan with sporting body, hood, screen, lamps, hand Klaxon, hood cover, mats, tools and an 80 mm. combination non-skid tyre on the rear wheel is £106 15s. Full details of this and other models may be obtained from the makers, the Morgan Motor Co., Ltd., Worcester Road, Malvern.

The Cyclecar

THE CAR THAT T

Drawn

ED A POLICEMAN

Bateman

39

OCTOBER 31, 1924

For Work
or Play on
the Great
Highway.

M-1925

Morgan Runabout

Stand No. 53

Prices from
£95 to **£147**

40

A TALE OF WOE.

Troubles in the Days Before the War, Related by a Wounded Officer.

CYCLECARRING was a most fascinating hobby in peace time, but to realize its full fascination it is necessary to be compelled to lie on your back in bed, in a military hospital, many thousands of miles away from the scenes of your exploits. Then, when your eyes are weary with frivolous magazines, and you are feeling fed up with things in general, you can lie back and call up long-forgotten scenes—the hills, and the heather, and the open road. You open volume after volume of stored-up memories stored up unconsciously so long ago ; it is wonderful how fresh they are now.

Thus I am minded to tell you of the most peculiar chapter of accidents that I ever experienced in my many adventures with many machines.

on the clutch. So we managed through Borough-bridge and Scotch Corner, amid many showers of watery snow. Hereabouts my hands got a bit cold and my arms stiff, but I had been thinking hard. The chains must be out of line and must be actually pulling out the dog clutch. Rot, of course, but I spent about three-quarters of an hour in the muddy road with numbed fingers and barked knuckles, and cursing split pins freely and often.

" Right now? Of course it is. The wheel is now perfectly true, but I am in a mess ! "

So we started again full of confidence, and, of course, within half a mile the dog clutch popped out again, and the engine raced. We both of us looked at each other. I forget what we said—something

"I spent three-quarters of an hour in the muddy road with numbed fingers and barked knuckles."

'Twas one Easter time when I was the proud possessor of a Morgan. It had been abused generally during the winter. It had ploughed its way through weeks and weeks of mud, and it had lain out o' nights when I was extra busy, and thus was generally neglected, so that these troubles must be laid against the owner and not the poor machine.

My wife had decided to go home to bonny Scotland ; so we agreed to take the Morgan to Edinburgh. That was my share of the holiday.

Five o'clock of a cold and sleety morning when we set off from somewhere in the Midlands. Mad we were, of course—all cyclecarists were more or less mad then, so they said. Anyway it was all serene for a good many miles, through Doncaster and Ferrybridge and the long, straight miles beyond Aberford on to Weatherley.

Hereabouts I began to feel uneasy. The top gear would keep slipping out. I tightened up the lever several times till it jammed, but that did not hold it in.

I held the lever in my right hand and when I felt it moving I slipped it home with a touch of my foot

short and sharp, anyhow. I fell back on the old plan of holding the lever and slipping it home on occasion, but this was irritating and tiring.

Nearing Newcastle, I had been thinking again, so we stopped and I crawled out and under the machine, and removed a mudshield which I had fixed up with much trouble a day or two previously, a beautiful elaborate thing of patent leather, intended to shield the very dog clutch which was giving us all the trouble. This I ruthlessly tore off under the impression that the chain in its passage swayed against the leather and that this reacted on the dog clutch. Anyway things were no better without it. But, nothing daunted, we kept on. We would find some remedy for it some time.

Past Newcastle we came on the little village of Morton, whose further acquaintance we were to make. About six miles beyond that we paused for lunch. Getting going again from the right-hand side of the road the back wheel slipped on the camber, and, simultaneously, the machine sat down—just sank gracefully on its tail with a decided list to port. We hoisted ourselves out and found the back wheel

A TALE OF WOE (contd.).

had collapsed—an absolute wreck. The rim was all shapes, and yet the tyre stuck firmly on.

I could write volumes on the subsequent journey back to Morton, behind a little cart to which the tail of the machine was slung. I ran the whole five miles, steering the machine, and was somewhat done up.

In Morton there was a fine-looking garage, most impressive from the outside. One of those whited sepulchres. You know them. They raised their hands in horror at the hopelessness of the job. We took trains different ways, and I returned in about a week to find that Morgans, like the sporting crowd they are, had sent me a new wheel immediately, and, furthermore, they never charged for it. After some hours work I got going again, and, of course, had no end of trouble with my lamps when it came to lighting-up time.

Then the speedometer drive came adrift, and this was no end of a nuisance to remove. And all the time the dog clutch was continually troubling.

The Result of a Song.

I forged along anyhow and made fairly good progress considering. In fact, I remember, descending a little hill, I burst forth into melody. That did it. Br-r-r-r went the engine—just like a machine gun. I smacked the gear home in the usual manner, but to my horror the engine still br-r-ed, and the machine moved no faster So, what was this? The chains proved to be whole. Then it must be something worse. Nothing to be done here in the dark. I pushed the machine along.

Two fishermen came to my aid. "Ye're in Dunbar. Yes, there's a grand mechanic's shop just on by a wee bittie."

This mechanic I can recommend. He is a real decent sort. His garage is just on the left after you turn that sharp corner in the middle of Dunbar, going towards Edinburgh. But I suppose he's in Flanders just now. A broken shaft it was. I met my wife in Waverley Station as per arrangement, and —we changed platforms.

A week after that we both came off the train at Dunbar, and our hearts were entranced at the fine job the Scotsman had made of it. The machine shone spick and span ; he had fitted a new shaft and had generally overhauled the car. There was a new back tyre, and the dog clutch trouble was all right now, while the bill was quite modest, for all that.

We set off quite gaily after I had looked over a few old friends with the grease pot, for the roads were still wet. Not a mile out of Dunbar and the dog clutch was slipping again, slipping worse than ever it was. Back we went. We had been deceived. We had leant on a broken reed. Scots mechanics fell much below par. All he said was "Why did you let the grease get on those faces" and he took a petrol squirt and washed it. And, believe me, it was quite all right. It never came out all the way home. I replaced it, as it was worn somewhat, soon after.

Our troubles were not yet at an end, though. We were sailing along beautifully and singing—first act of "Faust," I think it was—when "bang" went the back tyre, just like a "75," without any warning. Of course we were all over the road, but we stopped without much trouble. The inner tube was in little tangled bits, much chewed. The tyre had suffered considerably, being cut by the rim. It was not a good make ; anyhow I never bought any more of them.

The Uneasy Wobble.

Fortunately, I had retained the old one, and I had a front wheel spare tube, 2½ ins. The wheel came out, and after prodigious labours the old tyre went on with the tube. I pumped for about half an hour, and then mended two punctures. Back it went again, and seemed "good." The wheel went in and the split pins were again cursed. Half a mile we travelled, and that uneasy wobble announced that the back tyre was softening. Out came the wheel again, and the tube was mended in four minute places.

We eventually reached our old friend Morton by vigorous use of the pump between T.T. spurts. Two new tubes were then purchased. One inserted, and the opportunity seized to bag a supply of new split pins. Even after all this the new tube let us down by giving at the joint within a mile and a half of home.

By the way, Morton is not its real name, but as I hate the place I do not see why I should advertise it.

THE CLAIMS OF THE DYNAMOTOR.

In our issue of 18th October we drew attention to the claims of the combined lighting dynamo and starting motor, pointing out that this form of single-unit machine is very popular in the States, but up to the present there is only one British-made instrument. The makers of this dynamotor, the Scott, have sent us a most interesting letter, pointing out the advantages as they find them on their system. There is a great saving of weight and absolute silence, chiefly owing to the fact that no gears are employed. There is no pedal to push nor switch to be engaged at the same time. All that is necessary is merely to switch on. There is only one machine to attend to, and the accessibility of the instrument is usually greater, because it is fitted direct to the engine and not below the floor boards. As regards reliability, there is only one machine to fail. Owing to the fact that the Scott is slightly larger than the average small dynamo, the parts are consequently more robust. There are no free wheels, and the drive is positive by spur wheel or chain ; thus there is no belt which is apt to stretch and break. The wiring is much more simple, as there is only one set of wires instead of two distinct circuits.

In our editorial we stated the opinion that the combined system would be cheaper than two separate instruments. The makers of the Scott write that with their system the initial cost is not very great,

and in a highly technical system such as a lighting and starting set, with which the public are not absolutely familiar, the question of first cost should not be one of importance. Later on, when the public has got fully used to this system, it will be time enough to reduce the price.

The second point with which they disagree is with reference to our statement that a switch on the dash and an indicator showing whether the batteries are charging or discharging is all that is necessary. In all dynamos for light cars there is an arrangement regulating the output of the machine ; in other words, when the machine is doing several thousand revolutions a minute, it tends to give a greater output than that which it is desirable to use. The makers of the Scott say that with an indicator such as we suggested there is nothing to show the owner of the car whether this regulating system is correct whereas an ammeter having a graduated scale would immediately show such a fault. We quite agree with this criticism, but we would point out that the average owner is not much further when he has ascertained that there is a fault, as the dynamo is probably the last instrument that the average light car owner would dare to take to pieces. If anything goes wrong he invariably takes it to a repairer to have it put right. Thus the reading of the ammeter would not enlighten him much.

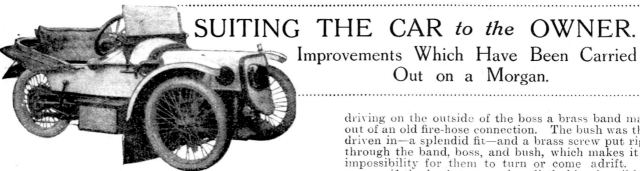

SUITING THE CAR to the OWNER.
Improvements Which Have Been Carried Out on a Morgan.

MY machine left the makers in January, 1914, and was bought second-hand by me through a friend in March, 1915. It was apparently in fair condition, and ran well on a trial run, while my friend drove it home to me, 60 or 70 miles, with only one or two minor troubles.

I immediately had the engine off to examine it, and found the under-mentioned defects, which I proceeded to remedy. At various times I have also added several improvements as time permitted, and just lately I had a complete overhaul, scraping every bit of paint off the body and mudguards, and altering the colour to light grey, lined in with black (three coats flatting and one of varnish, each coat being rubbed down with pumice powder and water). All bright parts were blacked over after polishing.

The body was fitted with a special spring seat and an upholstered back, both of which were in very shabby condition. I therefore made a new back cushion, and re-covered the seat in green pegamoid, which adds greatly to the general appearance of the machine when on the road.

Engine Defects.

The defects in the engine and the consequent remedies were as follow :—

The nut on the crankpin end stripped, the flywheels were all loose and wobbly, and both main bushes were very slack and revolving with shaft. I fitted a new nut, which tightened the flywheels, and turned and fitted two new bushes out of the best phosphor-bronze.

The outside boss on the crankcase (clutch side) which carries the bush was cracked in four places, and prevented the bush being made a good fit without bursting the boss. This was effectually remedied by driving on the outside of the boss a brass band made out of an old fire-hose connection. The bush was then driven in—a splendid fit—and a brass screw put right through the band, boss, and bush, which makes it an impossibility for them to turn or come adrift. Of course, if the bush turns only a little bit, the oil-hole is cut off, and troubles may take place. (After 2000 miles, this bearing was without the slightest shake.)

Improvements to the Engine.

1. To prevent any possibility of a broken valve head entering the cylinder and causing a smash up, a steel pin was fitted midway in the space between the valve chamber and the cylinder.

2. Both compression taps were worn and leaky. I made two new ones to my own design. The more they are used the better and tighter they become.

3. I filed the engine plates to allow room for a spanner to remove the cylinder nuts without shifting the engine.

When overhauling, I found the small bevel wheel much worn in the gearbox, and I think this was the only thing that really required renewal (engine excepted). The large wheel was perfect, but it was slack on its key, so I made a new key. I also found the same as some of your correspondents—that the solid end of shaft which carries the bevel wheel had a little shake in it, owing to the three pins holding it in the tubular shaft having worn. I turned up three new silver steel pins a tight fit to the holes, and squeezed them into place in a big vice (hammering them in bent them). I think if these shafts were examined more often by owners, and the ends kept tight, the pins would not shear off.

4. I made and fitted a switch to the magneto, operated from the steering wheel.

1. I shortened the starting handle and fixed it permanently in its proper place—an invaluable improvement for starting from the seat.

2. I altered the outside change-gear lever to inside (latest style).

Three of the improvements which " CO925 " has carried out on his Morgan. On the right is a device for preventing broken valve heads falling into the combustion chamber; in the centre is a variable ventilator on the dashboard : and on the left is a non-leaking compression tap

SUITING THE CAR TO THE OWNER (contd.).

3. I altered and raised the luggage carrier, to prevent it bouncing down on to the back wheel.

4. I fitted a large leather mudguard from the body down and underneath and forward under the exhaust pipes. This has slots for the chains to pass through and protects the dogs and clutches, etc., from mud. It was fitted before the body was put on. I also fitted large leather mud flaps to the front mudguards, all the leather being obtained from an old portmanteau.

5. The holes and bolts on the steering rods, being unadjustable for wear and somewhat worn, were scrapped, and ball-jointed adjustable rods were made out of two sizes of gas pipe and steel parts. These are a great improvement, as they can be adjusted for wear, and effectually do away with all back-lash of the steering wheel. The connecting rod is also adjustable for re-setting the wheels in alignment.

6. I fitted balance weights on the wheels opposite valves, which undoubtedly prevents uneven wear of tyres and steadies the steering.

7. The steering at first was very wobbly and tiring. I cured this entirely by making a shorter arm at the bottom of the steering column. The arm is about 1 in. shorter than the old one, and just allows the wheels to touch the body when turned to their full extent. The effect of this alteration was wonderful.

8. I fitted a new large toolbox to the right side of the car, scrapped the old left-hand step box, and made one much longer (with a top lid), for carrying parcels, etc. I covered it with smart, green lino, bound round the edge with brass strips.

9. I removed the old fixed screen and fitted a new one. Up-to-date brass adjustable fittings were "discovered" among the scrap at a garage and the glass was obtained and cut at a local glazier's. The total cost of this alteration was 12s.

10. I bought a shop-soiled hood, altered it to my requirements, making it much lower in front, and fitted permanent side curtains.

11. To prevent unpleasant draughts blowing round one's legs when going against a head wind, I made a sheet-iron slot ventilator, and fitted it over the vacant space under the petrol tank. It has a handle for operating it, projecting inside the car, and a hole was also left (covered with a leather flap) through which the hand can be put to turn off the petrol.

12. The old strap across the bonnet was cut off and spring side catches fitted.

13. The ugly piece of wood holding up the tank was used for firewood, and a $\frac{3}{16}$ in. flat steel bracket was substituted.

14. To obtain slow running in neutral with a Senspray carburetter is almost impossible, and after many experiments, I finally obtained very fair results by fitting an ordinary flap valve in the induction pipe. It is only required occasionally, and has a separate lever near the steering wheel. The valve is not quite gas-tight, and, when closed, just allows a "whisper" of gas through, enough to keep the engine turning over very slowly.

For running, I use two-thirds Crown or Taxibus petrol and one-third paraffin, and find no difference to using petrol alone, except that what cost 7s. now costs 4s. 11d. But I always inject neat petrol into the cylinders before starting from cold.

I am always much interested in your Morgan correspondents' letters, and hope that yet more suggestions and improvements may be forthcoming. I might say that I would not part with my old machine in exchange for a brand-new model.   "CO925."

A military motorist starting up his Morgan.

THE 1917 MORGAN.

10 h.p. M.A.G. Engine and Greatly Improved Lines.

WE are able to publish to-day the first illustrations of the 1917 Morgan, the improved appearance of which will be readily discernible. The most striking alteration is in the tapering bonnet, the lines of which now coincide with the body, which also is more streamline in appearance, while the chassis is lengthened. In fact, it is an air-cooled machine with a body and chassis of practically the Grand Prix type. The side valances are carried back further than before, while a short running board is also provided on which is mounted the acetylene generator. The body is raised a little higher, and neater types of hood and screen are fitted. As will be seen from the photographs the Morgan now presents a really handsome appearance, in singular contrast to the various adaptations of the sidecar which are continually being put forward in certain quarters as the ideal type of cyclecar, regardless of their ugly appearance.

All machines are now fitted with 10 h.p. M.A.G. engines, a few of which have been provided during

out in the chassis, notably in one or two points that have been criticised in our columns by correspondents from time to time, thus removing all grounds for further criticism.

We notice that balance weights are now fitted to the front wheels opposite the valves, to add to the steadiness of the steering. Stronger rear springs have been adopted. The starting handle has a revolving metal grip. The front steering has been altered in some slight respect. Formerly the steering arm had to be heated and bent if the wheels were out of alignment, but now an adjustable rod is provided. The tail is neater in appearance. Probably there are a number of other minor details that have received attention of which we have not particulars at the moment.

Popular as the Morgan has been in the past, we predict that it will be in still greater demand. We cannot imagine how any motorcyclist would prefer a sidecar of the side-by-side seating type as is being suggested, to a machine like the Morgan, in which the engine is

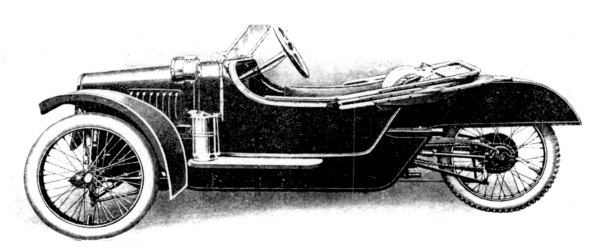

Front and side views of the 1917 Morgan with 10 h.p. M.A.G. engine.

1916. It will now be the standard engine for 1917. A full description of this engine appeared in our issue of the 13th December, 1915, when it was pointed out that it is an exquisite piece of work, various mechanical details being very highly finished. It develops 13 h.p. at 2000 revs. per minute and 14¼ h.p. at 2700 r.p.m. An extremely complete lubricating system is employed, and a notable feature is the fact that the sump carries three-quarters of a gallon of oil. The bore and stroke are 59 mm. by 100 mm., giving a capacity of 1096 c.c. It is, therefore, just within the cyclecar limit of the A.-C.U.

Several detailed improvements have been carried

placed in the most rational position, where it can be most effectively cooled, while ample comfort and protection are afforded to both driver and passenger.

———◇———

G.N. OR MORGAN.

"C.R.A." asks us to distinguish between a G.P. Morgan and a G.N., and he wants a water-cooled model. REPLY :— The Morgan is rather faster than the G.N., but the latter holds the road rather better than the other. Neither cyclecar is made with a water-cooled engine at the present time. They are both satisfactory machines with air-cooled engines.

A REJUVENATED

AN ENTHUSIASTIC
NUMEROUS CLI

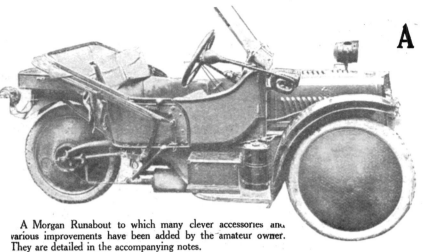

A Morgan Runabout to which many clever accessories and various improvements have been added by the amateur owner. They are detailed in the accompanying notes.

THERE is no production of the motor world which may be considered to have reached absolute finality. Makers of light cars and motor cycles often realise this, and, incidentally, profit at times from the fitments or suggestions of practical riders. There are, moreover, few things which interest the rider of a particular make of machine more deeply than reading about the improvements and additions made by a clever enthusiast of the same make. Each of the special fitments adapted to the Morgan Runabout here described is well carried out, and might almost be taken for standard work by the makers.

Bonnet and Fan.

The machine was, originally, a standard Morgan Runabout, carrying all usual Morgan arrangements. Its date is not certain, but it is several years old, although its excellent condition leads one to suppose it to be of recent origin.

The first noticeable innovation is the bonnet. This is provided with a large number of louvres on the top and sides, and the usual space in front has a series of neatly made louvre bars fitted across it. All this work is well

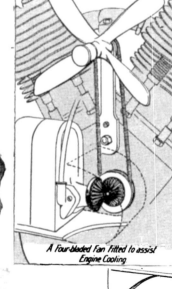

done and smartly finished. On lifting the bonnet a four-bladed aluminium fan stands out prominently, driven by a spring belt from a pulley behind the magneto bevel driving gear. This addition has proved extremely beneficial in the matter of engine cooling. The drive absorbs practically no power.

The silencers are usually just below the engine, but these have been removed and pipes taken to the back to separate exhaust boxes on either side, this alteration resulting in a very quiet running engine; the lubricating oil tank has been arranged on the dashboard with a sight feed and plunger pump, the former oil

The front of the Bonnet is fitted with Louvre Bars

A Four-bladed Fan fitted to assist Engine Cooling.

The four-bladed fan (modelled on the lines of an aeroplane propeller) is driven by a spring belt from a pulley behind the magneto driving bevel. It is found very efficient in practice.

Showing One Silencer & Spring Gaiter.

The Light Car

EXPERIENCES OF A MORGAN.

A Pioneer Motor Cyclist's Opinions and Comparisons of Light Cars and Runabouts.

A G.P. Morgan Runabout travelling well up to legal limit.

I SUPPOSE the career of every motorist of several years' experience is one of evolution. A present Rolls-Royce owner may not have begun with a Ford, but he has most probably had his period of vicissitude before his present home in the lap of luxury. I am not a Rolls owner, nor did I start with a Ford, but I began motoring with a pedal cycle that had the engine tied on to some portion of its base anatomy. The engine had accumulator ignition, too. From a Singer with an engine in the back wheel, I gradually achieved possession of an 8 h.p. Chater-Lea combination. For fine weather I can think of, and certainly desire, nothing better than a sidecar combination. Several times I have with absolute comfort done 250 miles in the day, and this with a lady passenger. But when it rained the picture lost something of its glamour; a little blot over which there is perhaps not much need to dwell.

I drove this combination for the most part over Lancashire roads; consequently my greatest trouble—namely, broken chassis and springs—is to a large extent easily explained. It was, however, mainly on account of weather considerations that I turned my attention to cars, and after experiments with a Crossley and a Ford, I found myself in possession of a German light car. One or two points on this car might well be copied by English designers, such as the staggered seating, enabling three passengers, each facing forward and in a seat of his own, to find comfort under the hood when this had to be erected. There was a mechanical starter, by which one could start the engine from the inside, and this was worth quite a lot. It was something like that in the Horstmann light car, except that you pulled a handle like a gear lever, instead of pushing a pedal like a clutch lever. The adjustable steering column was another valuable asset. After getting comfortably seated you could raise or lower the rake of the column to suit your convenience and favourite driving position. This alteration could be carried out while the car was in motion if necessary, and you could have the column at an angle like that of a three-ton lorry or to resemble a T.T. racer. The engine was splendidly balanced, but otherwise I had perhaps best draw a veil over the mechanical features.

A Distinct Improvement.

After this car with its eternal gear trouble, I decided to have something that might give me peace in this respect at least, and so I bought a Morgan, a 1914 Grand Prix model. Now the staff of the technical press deal with far too many cars to be easily led into enthusiasm over a particular model. Consequently, I am no wild Morgan enthusiast, but I certainly do think that the Morgan *could* be made into one of the best little motor vehicles on the road. I have had no actual experience with the 1917 model, but if all those details in the 1914 model that, according to my ideas, required attention have had it, I should think this year's Morgan is a very satisfactory mount indeed.

I have many little criticisms to offer against the Morgan. However, no single one of them is a really serious matter, with the possible exception of the insulating tape, or similar material, they are contributing towards the maintenance of a higher temperature in the pipe than would naturally be the case. This, of course, is not so because the temperature of an unheated induction pipe is always less than that of the surrounding atmosphere on account of the cooling effect of the evaporating petrol. Consequently, by protecting the pipe from contact with the atmosphere, the rider is lowering its temperature still further instead of raising it. In the air-cooled model these remarks are perhaps subject to a little modification, because the engine gets hot enough to warm the induction pipe considerably by conducted heat.

On the Road.

As for the Morgan on the road, there are really very few things that can show it a clean pair of heels, whether it be for hill-climbing or speed on the level. At speed it is often liable to set up a disconcerting tail-wagging, but I soon found that this was nothing like so dangerous as at first it appeared to be. In bad weather I consider that the Morgan is seen to its very best advantage, and indeed I really believe that the weather protection offered by this body is more efficient than that provided in the ordinary touring car. In the G.P. model one is sitting naturally with one's face only just above the level of the dash and so well below that of the top of the screen. The hood makes a very good joint with the screen at the front, and the hood side curtains, which are fitted as standard, are extremely effective, and I have driven long distances in very heavy rain without getting one spot inside.

As regards general accessibility of the machine, this is a point to which I consider the makers could profitably devote considerable attention. For instance, I recently wanted to take down my cylinders, and from a casual glance at the machine I had formed the opinion that this job would be rather simpler than a similar job in the case of a motor cycle. I rather changed my views, however, when I found that the first thing to be done was to get the engine out of the frame entirely and then remove the crank case plates. The fact that the cylinders have to be removed before the valves can be ground in is a question of the design of the particular engine fitted rather than of the design of the machine as a whole; it is, however, none the less disconcerting when first discovered.

The clutch operation is always a surprise to anyone who drives a Morgan immediately after driving a large car, and I have heard several unkind things said about the clutch; personally I think that anyone who has cause to grumble about the Morgan clutch has only himself to blame. I have found it most efficient and generally quite smooth in action.

Electric Lighting.

As for extra gadgets on the car, I always fight shy of such things, but must confess to a weakness for electric lighting. Now fitting a dynamo to a Morgan is no joke, but in my opinion a dynamo is not always an essential to a small lighting set, and I have for some years used electric lights with a Fuller Block accumulator as the sole source of supply, and am doing this on my Morgan. I carry the accumulator in the body, so that when I am seated it comes comfortably under my legs. I never interfere with the accumulator, and it only interferes with me about once in every four months, when it needs recharging. It is a 40 amp. 4 volt type, and from it I light F.R.S. head lamps (by the way, these are really large side lamps, but they give a splendid light), a tail lamp, and a dashboard lamp, and I find that the accumulator can be left for months and can be relied upon to retain its charge to the full. I have the two side lamps mounted on the mudguards, and find they give good illumination in this position. It is my usual plan to carry the acetylene side lamps without any intention of lighting them, but simply because their backs act as a useful road mirror.

As for comfort, the Morgan is one of the best things to be had. But in the 1914 model it can be improved somewhat by lowering the seat. One can do this quite simply by scrapping the "extra padded seat" that helps to increase the price of a de luxe model, and substituting for it an ordinary cushion. This will be found to be a treble gain: (1) more protection from the screen, (2) more support from the back, and (3) there is some room for one's legs under the steering wheel.

A promising start. His first birthday present, a Grand Prix Morgan.

A Handicapped Driver and his Morgan

In our last issue Mr. R. G. Paine described the alterations necessary to enable a man with two artificial legs to drive, and he also showed how to make the greatest use of the mechanical limbs in a very practical article. The photographs show Mr. Paine and his Morgan. In spite of an amputation of both legs he manages to look after his car without difficulty, as the illustrations will indicate.

Business lines in pleasant places. A Morgan, used for work of National importance, over Newby Moor.

Mountaineering on a MORGAN

Descending from Buttermere Hause on the way to Honister Crag.

THE FIRST CYCLE CAR TO CLIMB HONISTER PASS FROM BUTTERMERE.

BY GEORGE D. ABRAHAM.

(Author of "The Complete Mountaineer," "Motor Ways in Lakeland," "Mountain Adventures at Home and Abroad," etc., etc.)

NOT long ago the story in *The Light Car* of a remarkable record ascent of Honister Pass from both sides by a little Swift coupé, standard in every respect, roused considerable attention. Several attempted the same performance, but with scanty success. Gruff old Honister handled all very roughly, until at last a David arose in the form of a little Morgan. In the writer's opinion, this seemed scarcely a likely conqueror, for friends who in pre-war days owned these mounts had never seemed keen on trying their machines on real motor-mountaineering. Thus an invitation to join in an attack on Honister from Buttermere was accepted gladly.

A young Danish enthusiast, Mr. Neils Svanso, was the owner of the Morgan. His stories of hill conquests in other districts made one almost apologise for having nothing better than Honister Pass close at hand. The quiet air of the lower dales echoed with the names of Litton Slack, Cowdale, and innumerable other "pimples" as we sped westward from Keswick, bound for Buttermere by the Vale of Newlands and Buttermere Hause. There was no mistaking the extreme efficiency of the Grand Prix model. With three lusty passengers and a very important member of the party in the form of a heavy camera

outfit aboard, it was no light undertaking to tackle at the outset one of the toughest mountain roads in Cumberland.

The Charms of a Bob-sleigh.

The little machine carried us up to the heights and slid us down to the depths of the dales with fascinating ease and smoothness. Those wonderful downhill glides on the low-seated outfit recalled the charms of a bob-sleigh or toboggan run, and instinctively one swung to the balance on the curves.

The hardened "Morganites" were amused at the tendency, and with the crush aboard their places on the machine were sometimes in jeopardy. Apparently there was no need to "swing" with the Morgan, even on the sharpest curves taken swiftly. But as we sped down from the sunny heights into the larchy shades under the huge towering mass of Causey Pike, the sight of the Devil's Elbow recalled memories of a certain rashly-driven Morgan which capsized recently on the notorious hairpin. The writer warily suggested that an interesting photograph should be taken, and from the solid mountain side it was a revelation to see the present machine and driver rush the tricky hill so splendidly. With the two standard gears fitted

Mountaineering on a Morgan.

—4½ to 1 and 7¾ to 1—this was no mean performance. The writer's want of confidence totally disappeared.

In the Vale of Buttermere.

Then with all aboard there came the delightful dash skywards 'midst the brackened heights, until the forbidding scarp of Newlands Hause rose ahead. There was now no photographic excuse. The little machine fairly sprang at the opposing slope, leaping, bumping, and skidding on the treacherous shale, but always under a sure and skilful hold.

Surely never has the pass been so speedily climbed; the summit seemed no sooner in view than it was attained. After another photographic halt, we were soon sliding carefully down into the Vale of Buttermere, 'midst all the grandeur of rugged mountains and beauty of blue lakes set in an emerald underworld. It was good to have companions who realised the unique and varied beauty of this corner of Lakeland, so unlike an unappreciative Lancashire tourist at Windermere, who said bluntly, "When tha's seen half a mile on't tha's seen t'lot."

On Honister Pass.

Then came the engrossing run along the lake shore, with Honister Crag looming ahead just as grandly as in the peaceful times when throngs of enthusiasts now crowding far distant trenches came to try their luck and pluck on the most famous of English hills. Unlike those days, there now arose no strident note from behind to hurry us to speedier travel mountainwards. Yet once the actual climbing began there was no holding back the machine. The lower part of the pass was tackled with remarkable ease, and the writer, now alone and afoot, walked up the slope rather doubting whether Honister would retain its reputation in the face of the dashing Morgan. They were out of sight, but far overhead the noise of the lusty engine echoed persistently in the huge crags. Surely the fearsome gradient of Hill Step—the crux of the climb—could not be ascended at the first attempt.

The noise continued until the view of the upper part of the pass was revealed, and there was a certain satisfaction in seeing far above the midway bridge a tiny black speck almost hidden in blue smoke roaring furiously but absolutely still. The Morgan had stuck on a steep, stony, 1 in 3½ gradient about fifty yards below Hill Step. Even this was a very astonishing climb considering the fact that no rope or chain had been used on the driving wheel. The special, sturdy, Stepney road-grip tyre had behaved excellently, and now its grip was augmented by a rope bound round the driving wheel. An excellent restart was made despite the extreme steepness, but unfortunately the unsuitability of the Morgan driving wheel for any non-skid attachment was quickly revealed. There was a crash from below, and a "dash" from the driver —the low gear driving chain had broken on account of its entanglement with the rope. Luckily a spare chain was carried.

(Top) The first cycle car over the crest of Hill Top, above the most difficult bit of the pass. The road is seen winding valleywards over 500 feet below.
(Bottom) A tough struggle up the 1 in 3½ gradient below Hill Step, the crux of the climb. Observe the rough sliding rock-strewn surface.

"Over the Top."

Despite an annoying surfeit of links, as well as a lack of proper tools, the new part was made the correct length to be eventually fitted, and the grimy

Mountaineering on a Morgan.—

operators restored to the semblance of white men once more. Then ensued the final struggle which made the driver forget all other hills. Honister upheld its reputation. Machine and driver stuck to their work

By the shore of Buttermere, with Honister Crag looming grandly in the distance on the left.

bravely, and despite the wildly whirling driving wheel, which even the weight of two extra passengers failed to stay from slipping perpetually, the rugged slope was gradually overcome. Loose stones were flung all round, and it was positively dangerous to approach the tail of the machine.

There was an ominous smell of burning rubber, and when the crest of Hill Step was topped we found the corrugations of the driving tyre had disappeared. Still, the driver was delighted; in his opinion the success was worth many new tyres. On the upper part there was much jubilation and photography, but the photographer of the party discovered a serious trouble. A valuable lens had been left behind somewhere earlier in the day. Thus instead of finishing the day's run on the eastward side of the pass to Borrowdale, the backward journey was made by the morning's route.

The return to the hotel gave momentary satisfaction to those who had previously prophesied our failure on

Honister, but there were no sceptics, and had there been, the camera held proof of the successful achievement. That wonderful homeward bound rush up Buttermere Hause was certainly well worth the *détour,* the more so as the lost property was safely recovered from the top of a wall where it had lain all day. The Morgan had proved its powers and efficiency in astonishing fashion, but those who repeat the adventure would do well to use the lowest gear available, viz., $11\frac{1}{2}$ to 1. With the capital independent chain system for each gear, this could be easily done without spoiling the fast long-distance running of the

In the shadow of Honister Crag. The Morgan swinging round the first corner below Hill Step.

machine. On gradients approaching 1 in 3 the carburetter was so placed that it failed to provide full power to the excellent engine, but with a good supply of petrol in the tank this drawback would scarcely occur. There was no overheating, and the writer looks forward with pleasure to further exciting hill conquests on the Grand Prix Morgan when normal times return.

PETROL FOR MINERS.

A NUMBER of applicants for assistance in obtaining petrol licences have been received by the Auto Cycle Union from miners and other workers at coal mines. They were originally referred to the Ministry of Munitions for the necessary recommendation, but no sympathy could be obtained from that department. The Union, therefore, approached the Controller of Coal Mines at the Board of Trade,

who promptly recognised the advisability of helping those colliers who, although owning motor cycles, are now compelled, owing to their being unable to secure supplies of petrol, to walk long distances to the coal mines. The necessary particulars of each individual case have to be furnished on a form which can be had on application to the Secretary, Auto Cycle Union, 83, Pall Mall, S.W.1.

The Light Car

Leaves from a Lady's Log

" Evelyn's Experiences."

HER choice had fallen on a Morgan. She had long hankered for a car, and probably the final vote had been influenced by the smaller strain on her banking account than by any preference for a three over a four-wheeler; that and the satisfactory exhibition that this gallant little runabout had put up in pre-war trials and competitions. The results of these were tabulated in her memory, and a recital of them, in and out of season, she was apt to launch on all her friends and acquaintances. She was a fair motoring enthusiast, born with a taste for mechanics, and bred amid an atmosphere of " the open road." After many perusals of the columns containing second-hand bargains, Evelyn had early in 1914 proudly owned and driven a gaily-painted canary-coloured Morgan.

The Penalties of a Slender Purse.

Speaking to me of the joys and otherwise of her possession, in the days before petrol restrictions were a nightmare to such as she, she would volunteer that, to one with a slender purse, motoring was not all jam; the engine would run admirably for many miles, but just when one's confidence had reached its happiest point, the driving chain would break, a cover would need replacing, or some little thing happen which called for dipping more or less deeply into " the all-too-modest allowance."

A common trait of the more early type of feminine driver was inability to grasp the fact that, with use, wear is naturally always " telling up." She would expect the parts that have responded

cheerfully so often, while miles have been running into thousands, to continue to serve for ever, and when at last a climax is reached and a much-used part does eventually snap or cease to function owing to fair wear and tear, she is apt to feel peevish instead of remembering the miles that have been covered, and the generous service that has been rendered.

War-time Experience.

The W.A.A.C. will open the eyes and educate the mechanical side of many a woman who previously motored as a pastime. The arduous service required from one whose experience has previously been of the soft variety will mean that on the return of normal times the lady driver will resort less often to the assistance of the garage hands; changing tyres, decarbonising, and replacing worn parts will never again present insurmountable difficulties. The women who have fulfilled their part in the great campaign will in the future need greater things to deter them. Intricacies of the past will be intricacies no longer. Evelyn, the Morgan enthusiast, has long since turned the key in the door of her miniature shed, and has gone to drive a War Office lorry, a vehicle that in size must dwarf her own little car like St. Paul's would a Highland kirk. Some day she will return, and then, with all petrol bans removed, the faded little Morgan will once again haunt the roads in her district, unless by that time Evelyn has saved enough shillings and pence from her Army pay to buy a newer model, which is not very likely! MAY WALKER.

Evelyn takes the open road with her Morgan and soldier friend.

The FIRST *and* LATEST MORGANS *to be* RUN ON GAS

SPECIAL interest attaches to the two photographs on this page. The first depicts a 1914 sporting Morgan converted to run on coal-gas by Mr. Charles Potter, a Leeds motor agent. . He had it running on the 13th November, and claims it to be the first Morgan to be equipped with a gas bag. The second illustration shows a 1915 Grand Prix Morgan fitted with an overhead gas container by Messrs. Edwards and Parry, 89, Wigmore Street, London, W.

A comparison of the two outfits will interest all owners of Morgans who are thinking of converting

from Mr. Potter's design. The following is a brief description. The tray is made of wooden slats, supported by four ¾ in. solid round iron stanchions. The sides and bottom of the tray are covered with canvas. The gas bag measures 7 ft. 10 ins. in length, 4 ft. in width, and 3 ft. in height, and the whole outfit is so compact that any means of lowering the bag and tray was considered unnecessary. No alteration was made to the carburetter—an Amac, the connection between the gas bag and induction pipe being effected by a ½ in. metallic flexible gas pipe. The flow is checked in the first place by a handcock easily accessible from the driver's seat, and in the second place by a butterfly valve controlled by an accelerator pedal. Finally the metallic flexible gas pipe is connected to the induction pipe at the junction of the leads to each cylinder by means of an ordinary union.

When fully charged the container holds about 96 cubic feet of gas, sufficient to run the car about 30 miles, the operation of charging occupying less than ten minutes.

The first Morgan to be fitted with a gas bag, by Mr. C. Potter, of Leeds.

Size of Gas Container.

Now that owners and the public are becoming accustomed to the sight of a gas bag, designers are turning their attention to the problem of designing containers of more generous proportions. The cubic capacity is limited to 180 to 200 cubic feet owing to the length of chassis, etc., but no designer seems to have considered the practicability of extending the container in a downward direction over the tool-locker. Such a design was illustrated in the pages of this journal a few months ago. There is, without doubt, a good deal to be said in its favour, but we do not think it has yet been tried. A capacity of 250 cubic ft. might then be possible.

their machines, and good points in design and construction can be gleaned from each.

Mr. Potter has designed an overhead tray for the bag supported by four iron uprights. The tray has lattice sides, 12 ins. high, hinged so as to fall down to allow the car to enter the garage. The length of the bag is 8 ft. 6 ins.; width and height 4 ft., and when filled registers 170 cubic feet. The carburetter fitted for petrol was an Amac. To the air intake of this was fitted the spraying chamber (only) of a B. and B. carburetter with controls to the steering wheel, the gas being fed into the jet opening by a ¾ in. pipe. When using coal-gas, the Amac control levers are left full open and the engine is driven on the B. and B.; when using petrol the opposite arrangement comes into operation. No difficulty is experienced in starting up on gas, one charge (costing ninepence) being sufficient fuel for 22 miles.

The equipment fitted to the 1915 Grand Prix Morgan by Messrs. Edwards and Parry differs in a great many respects

The latest Morgan fitted with a gas bag, by Messrs. Edwards and Parry.

TRAINING FOR INVASION.
Middlesex Volunteers in Action.

REMINISCENT of the pre-war days of reliability trials, the Middlesex Motor Volunteers carried out a successful one-day enterprise last week in the form of a despatch carrying test. The competitors, of whom there were eleven, had to carry messages from point to point over some of the most difficult roads in the Kent-Surrey borderland, and it speaks well for the efficiency of the unit when it is stated that every rider succeeded in getting through. The feature of the event was the performance of Pte. Sharp on a Morgan cycle car. Sharp weighed sixteen stone, and had a twelve stone passenger up, but, despite this, he more nearly conformed to the difficult time schedule than any other rider, and won the contest with a total time loss of two minutes, one minute being lost on each of two despatches. Every other rider competed on a Harley-Davidson sidecar, and this called forth the suggestion that the unit should be called the Milwaukee Volunteers. The itinerary embraced Limpsfield (the start), Sevenoaks, Penshurst, Hever, Lingfield, Hartfield, L a n g t o n, and Sundridge, and included some steep hills and a very winding course. As a result it was no easy task to keep to the difficult time schedule framed. Nevertheless, the first three men only lost sixteen minutes between them, the other riders suffering very largely from tyre troubles.

Sharp, on the Morgan, had a trouble-free run, and, thanks to a remarkably fine turn of speed, was enabled to keep to time on one of his most difficult despatches despite having gone four miles out of his way on a wrong road. The course was arranged with a view rather to testing the map reading abilities of the competitors than to anything else, and there were remarkably few instances of the men going wrong.

The return journey was made *en masse* and with such decorum as to provide an object lesson in good manners on the road. The first six men were as follows: 1, Pte. Sharp, Morgan Runabout (2m. late); 2, Pte. Willshear, Harley-Davidson (6m. late); 3, Pte. Horne, Harley-Davidson (8m. late); 4, Pte. Wilson, Harley-Davidson (15m. late); 5, Pte. Clark, Harley-Davidson (31m. late); 6, Pte. Pike, Harley-Davidson (48m. late).

It is interesting to note that the first two men—Sharp and Willshear—are both members of the H.Q.C.D. (A.A. Section) of the Special Constabulary, and have had experience of active service riding on air raid nights.

(1) The winner of the trial, R. Sharp (on right), receiving a despatch. (2) Major Valentine Smith reviewing the D.R.s. (3) The Morgan, which came through the trial so successfully, and the Harley-Davidson, which ran second.

In view of enquiries we receive from time to time, we again state that no priority certificate is required for repairs to motor cycles at a charge not exceeding £10, provided a declaration as to the use to which the machine is put accompanies the order, thus saving considerable delay. In cases where the costs of the repairs exceed this amount, application for priority certificates may be made to Ministry of Munitions, Priority Branch, Caxton House, Westminster, S.W.1.

The Tyseley—a good-looking three-wheeler shown at Olympia in 1911.

THE three-wheeler may be regarded as the pioneer of the English automobile. If the history of the type were traced back to its source it would be found that most of the brains of the automotive world, at one time

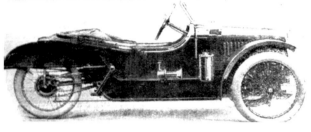

The Morgan—the vehicle which has done more to popularise the three-wheeler than any other machine.

or another, have been devoted to the solution of the problems which still confront the designer of the modern runabout.

Then why is the Morgan practically the only representative of the type to-day? Since emancipation day scarcely a year has gone by without at least one three-wheeler being introduced to the public. They have come, left their record, if not a mark, in the history of motor mechanics, and have disappeared. Some are forgotten, a few reappear in an improved form and again disappear. Without fear of giving offence to makers of three-wheelers, I can say that only two or three have, in Yankee parlance, "cut any

ice." Two of these are the Morgan and A.C. Sociable. Another I have in mind is the P.M.C. Motorette, but in mentioning the latter perhaps I should also mention a few others which were made in about the same quantities. These include the Girling, Wall, Crouch, and Enfield.

Most of the three-wheelers that have been made have been introduced by small firms to whom the slightest reverse in the opening of their campaign has meant defeat, but a large company with almost unlimited capital could not have made a success of most of them.

Disappointed designers often remark that to attempt to please the buying public with something new is a gamble at the best of times. They cannot understand why the Morgan and the A.C. should be successful selling propositions, while their own, which they claim to be superior to both, is a rank failure.

The Morgan and the A.C. Sociable are totally different propositions with separate markets, but each was proved efficient in the reliability trials. No other three-wheeler has won award after award in competition with motor cycles. From this it is clear that to launch a commercial proposition, first it is necessary to prove that it will accomplish all that is claimed for it.

THREE CYC

SOME NOTES ON THR AND THE POSSIBILIT

The A.C. Sociable—on picture a

There are se wheelers. In divided by the c

if we do this types:
(1.) With-th A.C. with the

2

BRITISH AND CONTINENTAL DESIGNS.

(1) The Wall tricycle, with shaft transmission and differential. (2) The Matchless three-wheeler. (3) The Cyclone—a continental p (5) Another front wheel-driven machine—the Stanhope (6) The Eric—a three-wheel car pure and simple. (7) The la

HEELED
CAR

RS, PAST AND PRESENT,
HE FUTURE TYPES.

types of three-
, they may be
heir wheels, and

three-wheelers. In this
is shown.

ve three general

the Morgan and
hind.

(2.) With three tracks, as the Wall, with the single wheel in front.

(3.) With two tracks, as the Scott, which follows sidecar practice in this respect.

We can subdivide each class by separately classifying them according to the location of the engine and seating accommodation. In the first class the Morgan type has the engine before the passengers. In the A.C. the positions are reversed.

The second class, too, can be similarly subdivided by the position of the engine—(a) in the front end of the chassis and driving the rear wheels; (b) at the front of the chassis and driving the front wheel, as the Stanhope and Phanomobile, etc.; (c) with the engine at the side as in the Unicar and the Condor, which were made just before the war.

In the third mentioned class, the Scott represents the latest development of the sidecar type of two-track vehicle, in which group come all motor cycle sidecars built integral and double-seated sidecars with the driving controls within the body, as the A.J.S., U. and I., Seal, H.S.M., etc.

Disregarding for a moment all questions of efficiency, theoretical and practical, one has only to glance at the photograph of the Morgan to see where it has scored over its competitors. It is good looking. Some of its contemporaries may embody theoretically perfect principles and the finest workmanship, but not one of

The Jackson three-wheeler, which embodied many interesting features.

them appeals so strongly to the buying public. Comparisons are odious, but this is a case where comparisons can be of real service to would-be designers of three-wheelers.

It may be said that it is too "sporty" for certain classes of potential buyers of three-wheelers. If a more "sedate," more docile-looking machine is found among the repre-

A French tandem-seated three-wheeler—the Torpelle.

sentative collection of pictures, it will be found that it has certain points tending to produce the very things that offend that class requiring something "sedate."

Take, for example, an all-chain driven machine with the engine in the front. We will assume that it is not the kind of vehicle appealing to the sporting buyer, and that in appearance it has those characteristics of "dignity" the potterer generally likes. Probably, however, when such a buyer came to try this type of machine he would find it too noisy, for no machine with long chains—especially a long chain for the primary drive from engine to gear box—can be quiet.

3.

7.

igine connected to front wheel.   (4) The Crouch three-wheeler—the predecessor of the present-day light car of the same nam
o be marketed—the Williamson.   (8) The Enfield Autorette—the predecessor of the Enfield light car.

The Three-wheeler.—

The Eric, Enfield, and Crouch were not intended as sporting machines. They were designed as three-wheeled cars, and I do not think there are a hundred buyers in this country to-day who want three-wheeled

The Scott Sociable—probably the most remarkable vehicle among three-wheelers at present extant.

cars. When such a vehicle assumes the size and shape of the orthodox car, the absence of the fourth wheel gives it a " freakish " appearance, and the very people for whom it was designed are the first to notice this. They do not want anything tending to freakishness, they really want a Rolls-Royce for about £100, but, failing that, a Ford for £50 will satisfy their requirements.

In other words, no one has succeeded in meeting the demand which exists for an economical low-priced motor vehicle among those who so far have not motored, and designers should not overlook this vast potential market for a runabout of the right design. I am fully convinced that next to the question of mechanical reliability, appearance is the most important point to be considered.

The designer who tries to cover all classes of buyers of three-wheelers probably will fail to interest any one

class. There are vast possibilities in catering for the motor cyclist who wants something as fast, as sporty, and as reliable as the best sidecar outfits. There is just as immense scope in providing for the potterer who wants something cheaper and more economical than the cheapest car. But the man who has never motored in any form of vehicle will be interested in three-wheelers only when their numbers on the road render them more " orthodox " than they are at present.

The success of the Morgan can be attributed to four points. It is smart in appearance. It in no way resembles the car, and therefore is not mistaken for an imitation or a substitute. It has been proved efficient, and it has fewer transmission noises than the majority of runabouts. This latter point is of paramount importance, and in the case of the Morgan this reasonable degree of silence is due to the primary drive being by shaft instead of by chain, as in the majority of machines designed for the same purpose.

To be a success as a commercial proposition, the three-wheeler of the immediate future must have all the good points of the Morgan plus others of its own, but nothing will be gained by the designer who over-

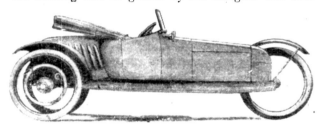

The Duryea three-wheeler, designed and marketed by one of the best known American motor engineers.

develops the type, because a three-wheeler must cost very little more than the sidecar combination of the same power. There will be some cheap light cars after the war, and the designer of the ultra-refined three-wheeler may find that for another five pounds he can make his proposition a four-wheeler, which will bring him in competition with small cars of the orthodox type. VEDETTE.

Lubricating the Gear Box.

A DETAIL which will require thoughtful attention after the war is the lubrication of counter-shaft gear boxes. Whereas the average car gear box contains a bulk of lubricant equivalent to at least twenty times the bulk of the moving parts inside the gear box, a motor cycle gear box is so cramped for space that there is remarkably little clear space to hold lubricant. The owner can hardly ever tell how much lubricant the box contains, since the sole orifice for inspection is a hole about ¼in. in diameter, which is inconveniently situated and blocked up by a gear wheel within ⅛in. of its base. In practically every case the lubricant is awkward to insert. If oil is used the help of a funnel is desirable, and cold oil flows so sluggishly down a tiny funnel that the owner gets sick of the job before the case is full, and at best it does not hold enough for a long

distance. If grease is used it exudes round the plug hole quite early in the proceedings, and gives the illusive effect that the box is full. Oil and grease guns are filthy things to handle, and are generally left at home when the machine goes on tour. A large percentage of the lubricant inserted by the trustworthy minority of owners leaks out along the countershaft bearings, where a leak is more perilous than it would be along the joints of the casing, as the user is less certain to detect it. We want walloping big inspection holes through which we can plug lubricant in lumps. Till we get them the only safe plan is to heat the oil till it runs like water, and then pour it in through a funnel till it obviously wells out at the top. After that the next precaution is to relubricate after half the mileage recommended in the makers' maintenance book. IXION.

THE MOTOR CYCLE

A FOUR-SEATER MORGAN.

Solving the Problem of Carrying Addit'onal Passengers on a Three-wheeler.

An 8 h.p. Morgan constructed with a special body to carry four passengers. The owner, Mr. E. B. Ware, who is head of the J.A.P. experimental department, is shown aboard with Mrs. Ware and family.

IT is a common sight to observe side-cars carrying three or four passengers. This year especially sidecar owners seem to have schemed their utmost to accommodate all the family on their pleasure outings, and they have succeeded

Overhead view of the four-seater Morgan.

better than the majority of owners of runabouts could hope to do. The owner of the Special Morgan which is illustrated on this page has, however, solved the extra passenger accommodation

problem in a most satisfactory manner. Ample room is provided for two adult passengers in the extra rear seat, the addition of which has not detracted from the appearance to any great degree. Messrs. Morgan do not list this type of body, but, as it has created a deal of interest wherever it has been seen, possibly such an additional model would be welcomed.

Mr. E. B. Ware, the owner of the Morgan—incidentally he is an old Morgan enthusiast—says that the additional two seats make less difference than might be

imagined; neither is the steering affected by the additional weight on the rear wheel.

Mr. Ware is associated with the J.A.P. engine firm, which accounts for the particular type of J.A.P. engine employed. This is an experimental model, of which more may be heard anon. It will be noted that the oil sump has been enlarged, and a cleaner crank case obtained by die instead of sand casting. Another innovation is the jacket on the induction pipe connected with the water-cooling system, thus securing better vaporisation.

The new 8 h.p. J.A.P. water-cooled engine. An alteration immediately noticeable is the fitting of a large oil sump.

THE MOTOR CYCLE

THREE & FOUR WHEELERS

The M.B. cycle car, fitted with water-cooled engine and final chain drive.

THE MERRALL-BROWN THREE-WHEELER.

Made by the Premier Motor Co. of Bolton, the Merrall-Brown runabout is a most distinctive machine, embodying many refinements in finish and equipment. The engine fitted is a water-cooled 10 h.p. four-cylinder, driving a two-speed and reverse gear box by shaft, the final transmission being by a single chain. The rear wheel is of the twin type, sprung by underslung quarter-elliptic springs, while semi-elliptic springs are used at the front axle. Chain tension is adjusted by radius rods controlling the movement of the back wheel. Wheels of the standard Dunlop detachable variety are fitted with discs. On each side of the back wheel are hand and foot brake drums, but the detachability of the wheel in no way interferes with the adjustment of these. Quite a pleasing design of body has been adopted, a streamline effect being obtained with approximately upright sides. In addition to the bonnet, the wings and wheel discs are of polished aluminium. A door is fitted in each side.

THE PREMIER RUNABOUT.

This three-wheeler, introduced by the Coventry Premier Co., who, before the war, made Premier motor cycles, was fully described in *The Motor Cycle* of October 30th. Its features include a three-speed and reverse gear box; shaft and chain drive, the latter by a duplex chain enclosed in a quickly detachable case; quickly detachable rear wheel, with spare wheel carried on the tail of the body; quarter-elliptic springing front and rear, the latter being in an inclined position;

rack and pinion steering; foot acceleration; and a mechanically lubricated water-cooled V twin engine, with a bore and stroke of 80 × 105 mm. respectively (1,055 c.c. capacity). Fitted with hood, screen, and lamps, the provisional price of the Super Runabout, as it is called, is £210, at which price it is a most attractive proposition.

MORGAN.

Up to the present date, no three-track machine has earned such popularity as the Morgan, and it is not without good reason that one sees so many of these handy little runabouts on the road, for they have thoroughly proved their reliability. Only is made, and this is so straightforward that it would be difficult to suggest any part which could reasonably be lightened or rendered more perfectly simple. The engine, which may be either a water or air-cooled J.A.P. or M.A.G. or air-cooled Precision, is carried at the front of the chassis, and drives through a clutch to a propeller-shaft enclosed in one of the three main frame tubes. To the rear of this tube is attached a box containing a pair of bevels. The cross-shaft carries a sprocket on either side, each of which is connected by chains to the rear wheel. By sim-

A rear view of the new Premier "Super" runabout.

ply "dogging up" one or other of these sprockets, two different gear ratios are obtained.

The bodywork for air and water-cooled models forms units with or without the radiator, according to the type of engine used. Three main models are provided, the Grand Prix—a sporting water-cooled vehicle with racy lines—the standard touring model with air or water-cooled engine, and the family machine, which is provided with accommodation for children behind the usual seats. In the latest models a ball thrust has been added to the clutch withdrawal mechanism, longer bearings are fitted to the front wheel steering heads, and much stronger bevels with a different tooth formation are employed.

THE 1920 TAMPLIN.

The well known Carden runabout will in future be known as the Tamplin, and a tandem-seated model has been introduced for 1920. The power is provided by an 8 h.p. twin air-cooled engine, the final transmission being by a long belt on either side of the body. It has a very sporting appearance, and should appeal to many.

THE A.V. RUNABOUT.

Closely resembling the pre-war Carden monocar, the A.V. two-seater models come into the category of passenger machines. The engine is located at the rear of the seating accommodation, and the design is probably the simplest form

De Luxe air-cooled model Morgan

is fitted with an 8 h.p. water-cooled twin engine, the other being equipped with an air-cooled engine of a similar size.

A NORTH OF ENGLAND THREE-WHEELER.

A new three-wheel proposition will make its *début* to the public at Olympia. This is the L.S.D. cycle car, produced by Messrs. Sykes and Sugden, Ltd., engineers and ironfounders, of Huddersfield—another of those established engineering firms at last turning their attention to the automobile industry.

The engine fitted is an 85.5 × 85 mm. J.A.P. air-cooled twin, placed in front of the axle member and driven by shaft, through a leather-faced cone clutch, to

The L. S. D. three-wheeler, the production of a Huddersfield engineering firm.

a two-speed and reverse gear box located at the rear of the frame.

Quarter-elliptic springs are used at the rear wheel, and a patented system of enclosed coil springs at the front. Dunlop 700 × 80 mm. tyres are fitted on Sankey pressed steel wheels, the rear wheel being readily detachable without disturbing the single chain final drive.

Direct steering by a large diameter wheel, brakes of the external contracting type, and a roomy two-seater body with doors on both sides, are included in the specification. The dimensions are : wheelbase 6ft. 6in., track 4ft., overall length 9ft., width 4ft. 7in., and the price, complete with hood and screen, is 185 guineas.

A NEW THREE-WHEELER—THE T.B.

Several large munition firms have devoted their peace time energies to the motor manufacturing field, and one of these—Messrs. Thompson Bros. (Bilston), Ltd.—is producing a very pleasing little three-wheeler with all-shaft transmission. The T.B., as it is called, has an 8 h.p. engine integral with a two-speed and reverse gear box.

THE BLERIOT WHIPPET.

A light and low-priced runabout, produced by a large firm of aircraft engineers, the Blériot Whippet is another small four-wheeler which is in direct competition with the sidecar outfit. The power unit is a Blackburne 8 h.p. twin with outside flywheel and detachable heads. A Ferodo-lined clutch is fitted

on the left-hand extension of the crankshaft, and a mechanical starter, by which the driver may start the engine from the seat, is included in the specification. The transmission is by chain to a countershaft, thence by belt to the live axle. Variation in gear ratio is obtained by means of a large variable pulley on the countershaft—an ingenious device which permits the tension of

A newcomer in the runabout world, the T.B., which has shaft drive.

the belt to be kept constant. 700 × 80 mm. tyres and hammock seats form part of the equipment.

THE SPEEDY CYCLE CAR.

One of the few new cycle cars embodying final drive by twin belts is the Speedy —a little vehicle made by the Pullinger Engineering Co., New Cross—which it

is proposed to market at a price considerably below that of the average sidecar outfit. It has a simple specification, direct steering being employed, and provision made for an adjustable rake of the steering column. The gear box provides two forward speeds and reverse, the gear change lever being situated in the centre of the floor. The countershaft, driven by chain from the gear box, consists of two separate shafts, one sliding within the other. The outer one, to which is attached the inner flanges of the belt pulleys, rotates on two plain bearings bolted to the longitudinal chassis members. The inner one, however, which carries the outer flanges of the pulleys, is allowed to slide within the outer shaft by means of a longitudinal slot, on which a key on the outer sleeve is fitted. By these means a differential action is obtained automatically on the countershaft by the different speeds of the road wheels on turning a corner. The engine is an 8 h.p. Chater-Lea, having a bore and stroke of 85 mm. = 964 c.c.

The Speedy, which has an 8 h.p. engine, two speeds, and final drive by twin belts.

THE L.J. FOUR-WHEELER.

The L.J. cycle car, which was illustrated and described in last week's issue of *The Motor Cycle*, is another of the several little four-wheelers which embody motor cycle practice at several points and sell at a figure approximating to that of the sidecar outfit. The engine is an 8 h.p. J.A.P., which will be offered both in the water-cooled and air-cooled types. The specification includes a pressed steel frame, quarter-elliptic springs, duplex chain transmission, friction disc change-speed, Lynton steel disc wheels, internal expanding brakes, and 700 × 80 mm. tyres. The body is somewhat higher than is usual with cycle cars, and the passengers are thus well protected. The whole car is particularly handsome and will be sold at a figure in the neighbourhood of £200.

A racy little runabout—the Bleriot Whippet.

WITH A MORGAN IN FRANCE AND BELGIUM.

A Useful Article to Those Who Wish to Tour the Battlefields by Car.

Snapped in Bourbon village, showing how the baggage was taken.

SUCH varied reports have been circulated about the state of the roads in France and Belgium that the following notes may be of use to those who are thinking of visiting the battlefields this summer. Although the roads in many places could hardly be distinguished from the surrounding country, they were covered by a 1919 model sporting air-cooled Morgan, the only troubles met with being one puncture and the fracturing of the hinges holding the "tail," due to overloading with souvenirs.

Preliminary Arrangements.

The following luggage was taken:—One gladstone bag and one kit-bag, containing clothes and emergency food, two sleeping-bags, (one to sit on, and one to lean against), two waterproof sheets, two spare tins of petrol, and an old Army pack containing cameras, maps, etc. The less luggage taken the better.

The A.A. and M.U. will arrange everything—procure Triptyques, International Passes, tickets, and transport, and the only thing one has to do is to obtain passports and have them viséd within a fortnight of leaving England. The boat leaves Dover at 10.30 a.m., and if the car is handed over to the A.A. representative there he will do everything and see one through. On reaching Boulogne, hand all papers to the A.A. representative there, and the car should be clear of the Customs by two o'clock.

The first night we stopped at Dunkirk (Hotel des Arcades, in Square). The road via Calais is bumpy,

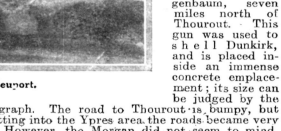

The Bridge of Sighs, Nieuport.

The ugly snout of "Lange Max," a 15 in. German gun at Langenbaum.

but improves slightly further on. The next day we went up the coast as far as Zeebrugge and spent the night at Bruges (Grand Hotel du Commerce, Rue St. Jaques). This is well worth "doing," for the German defences along the coast are interesting, the "Vindictive" can be seen at Ostend, the Mole at Zeebrugge, and the front line at Nieuport. The roads on the whole were pretty good, although the pavé near Bruges makes travelling uncomfortable at any speed. The Customs were at Ghyvelde and Adinkerke, but presented no difficulties.

Poperinghe was our next objective, and we went via Thourout and Ypres. A detour well worth making is to go and visit the German 15 in. gun at Langenbaum, seven miles north of Thourout. This gun was used to shell Dunkirk, and is placed inside an immense concrete emplacement; its size can be judged by the photograph. The road to Thourout is bumpy, but on getting into the Ypres area the roads became very bad. However, the Morgan did not seem to mind, and plugged along on low gear without showing any signs of distress.

West Roosebeek, Langemark, St. Julien, and St. Jean were all visited, although our pace was necessarily very slow. At Poperinghe Skindles Hotel provides good accommodation, but it is advisable to reserve rooms beforehand as they are usually full up. Next morning we returned to Ypres via Kemmel and Dickebush, the roads being only fair, and then went out through the Menin Gate, along the Menin road, which was in good condition as far as Gheluvelt.

Messines and Ploogsteert.

From here we retraced our steps and visited Messines and Ploogsteert, the roads again becoming very bad. The French and Belgian Custom houses are situated about a mile south of Neuve Eglise, these being the only ones within 10 miles, so it is advisable to cross the frontier there. Lille was our stopping place that night, the Hotel Royal, Rue Carnot, being excellent. The town has suffered little, although only about 10 miles behind the lines, but the pavé roads, which mostly date back to Napoleon's time, are

WITH A MORGAN IN FRANCE (contd.).

execrable, in fact the worst we came across anywhere.

The next day we went to Arras (Hotel du Commerce, near the station). Here, also, it is advisable to book rooms as accommodation is limited. Our route took us through La Bassee, Neuve Chapelle, Bethune, Loos, Lens, and the Vimy Ridge, the view from the latter being extraordinarily fine, and the roads slightly better. At Cambrai, where we went next day, the Hotel du Mouton Blanc is comfortable, and the Arras battlefield is well worth seeing, especially Queant and Moeuvres. We also visited Bourlon Wood, which saw such hard fighting in November, 1917. On our ninth day out we went to Gouzeaucourt, and on to Peronne, the road, although bumpy in places, being better than usual. At Peronne we turned north and ran along a beautiful road to Bapaume. Here we could find no accommodation, but luckily got put up by some friendly British troops in the vicinity. Starting early next morning, we went down the Albert road, which is still quite good, and turned off at Courcelette to Miraument, from there working up the Ancre valley, and finally arriving at Douilens in the evening. (Hotel des 4 Fils d'Aymon). Boulogne was reached next day, and catching the boat the day after, we arrived back at Folkestone at 4 p.m., getting clear of the Customs an hour later.

The total cost of the trip was £19 each for two for 10 days, which compares favourably with 38 guineas charged by some touring companies for a trip of only five days. Anyone wanting an extremely interesting holiday "on the cheap" is well advised to go to France, and need have no fear of doing any damage to his car, provided he drives slowly and carefully over the bad places.

Petrol can be procured in all the large towns at from 10 fr. to 12.50 fr. per gallon, but it should be well strained, as it is poor stuff, and full of dirt and water. Rooms averaged 12 fr. per night, dinner

Canadian memorial and traffic policeman's shelter at Vimy Ridge.

15 fr., and breakfast 8 fr. We bought biscuits and cheese for lunch and tea, which we ate en route.

Anyone possessing old war maps should take them, and in any case Messrs. Philip's two miles to the inch map of the British Front (6s.) should be obtained. Camera refills are almost unobtainable, so supplies should be taken out in tins, as otherwise they are apt to get wet.   W.H.S.C.

THE LIGHT CAR AND CYCLECAR

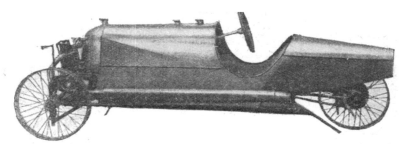

The Grand Prix Morgan. which will be driven by Mr. E. B. Ware.

THE LATEST GRAND PRIX NEWS. .. .. ..

Details of the Morgan— The French Favourites.

IT will be remembered that in the famous Grand Prix Cyclecar Race, held on the Amiens Circuit in 1913, a Morgan, piloted by Mr. W. G. McMinnies, gained first place. This year, when the race will be held over the Le Mans Circuit, another Morgan will compete. This time the machine will be driven by Mr. E. B. Ware, whose Morgan at Brooklands has proved so successful. However, Mr. Ware will not drive this machine in the French race, but a specially constructed three-wheeler, which we are able to illustrate this week. This Morgan has been made under his supervision at the works of J. A. Prestwich and Co., Northumberland Park, Tottenham, London, N., and is, of course, fitted with a J.A.P. engine.

The latter is of the water-cooled, overhead valve type, the bore and stroke being 90 mm. by 85 mm. respectively.

Behind the engine is fixed the radiator, which is a standard one cut down. The body has very pleasing lines, and should reduce wind resistance to a minimum, although there does not appear to be much room for two people side by side, but Mr. Ware informed us that he and his mechanic could sit in it comfortably. A very low sitting position is obtained, the floor boards being some inches below the central propeller tube.

The tail is constructed so that the sides can be lifted up, thereby giving access to the rear wheel and the driving chains. Mr. Ware hopes to have the machine shortly on the road, and it will not be very long, therefore, before we are able to give a photograph of the completed car.

The makers of the Bignan-Sport have entered three cars—at present under test. It has a four-cylinder engine with a bore and stroke of 61 mm. by 119 mm.

Front view of Mr. E. B. Ware's special Morgan.

A SPORTING MONOCAR.

A Single-seated Morgan, built to the Owner's Special Design.

The racy appearance of this light sporting single-seater will be appreciated by the speed man.

IT is the ambition of many motor cyclists to have a fleet of machines in order to have one for every purpose. One of our readers owns two Morgans and a solo motor cycle, but all are on sporting lines.

On this page his two G. P. Morgans are shown, of which the single-seater is perhaps of greatest interest. The body is 21in. wide, and the scuttle is of exceptional depth and height, a specially narrow and high radiator being fitted to follow out the streamline effect.

The owner wishing to eliminate the windscreen had the dash made several inches higher than standard, and so successful was the innovation that the owner found it quite possible to smoke comfortably at 50 m.p.h. The seating

The single-seater Morgan alongside the Grand Prix Model. The various differences of design will readily be observed

position is such that the driver is given a clear view of the road ahead through the "slit" between the rim of the steering wheel and the top of the dash.

With regard to the engine, this also is special, and consists of an overhead-valved 90 × 85 mm. J.A.P. (1,082 c.c.). This engine is not very well known, as we believe only a few were manufactured. It is excellently balanced and splendidly made, and gives nearly 20 b.h.p. at 2,500 revs. Although the valve springs have

very high tension, the valve gear is unusually quiet for this type of engine. Originally the compression was 100 lb. p.s.in., but this proved extremely destructive to plugs and rendered starting difficult. Washers, ⅛in. in thickness, were accordingly fitted, with excellent results, and, even with this reduced compression, the speed and acceleration are considered ample. The oil consumption is phenomenally low, and the petrol consumption varies from 40 to 60 m.p.g., according to the make of carburetter fitted. A pilot jet, B. and B., suits the engine extremely well; it gives high speed and exceptionally slow "tick-over" in neutral.

The standard two-speed gear box gives ratios of 3½ and 6 to 1. On the dashboard are two eight-day clocks, speedometer, and revolution counter, the latter being a very useful and interesting fitment.

In designing the outfit, it was feared that the machine would be unstable owing to the absence of weight in the rear portion, but experience has shown that it is extremely steady on grease, tramlines, etc. The steering, in fact, is excellent, and this we attribute to the exceptionally heavy engine fitted. Although the frame has not been reinforced, no distortion has occurred during 6,000 miles running over the war-worn roads of this country.

THE MORGAN.

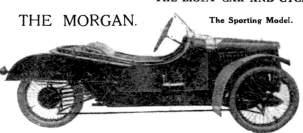

The Sporting Model.

Six Models to be Shown, a Number of Improvements. Including More Readily Detachable Rear Wheel.

wheel, the advance and retard lever protruding through the dash.

Various models of the Morgan are familiar to the majority of our readers, but for the information of those who are making their first acquaintance with this well-known make of three-wheeler, we might mention that the De Luxe model is, as its name implies, an elaborate example, fitted with a door and those little refinements which are dear to the heart of many cyclecarists.

The new type fork for the rear wheel which is now easily detached.

IN our last issue we dealt with certain improvements which have been effected in the design of the 1921 Morgan, chief amongst which is the more readily detachable rear wheel, by means of which it is not necessary to unfasten the chains. The stand of the Morgan Motor Co. is sure to create considerable interest, for no fewer than six models will be shown, excluding the plated chassis which shows the Morgan lay-out at a glance.

The following are the actual exhibits:—Two de luxe models, standard Grand Prix, new aero model, family car, and sporting model. Space does not permit of a detail description of each individual model, but the general specification of the chassis includes a J.A.P. or M.A.G. engine, B. and B. or Amac carburetter and an M.L. magneto.

The clutch is of the cone variety, transmitting the drive through an enclosed propeller shaft, to a bevel box at the rear, wherein is contained the bevel reducing gear. The countershaft passes through the bevel box at right angles to the propeller shaft, and upon this are mounted the dogs, by means of which the two speeds are obtained.

The gear shift mechanism consists merely of a couple of arms connected up by rods to a gear lever placed on the driver's right, and the control is thus as simple as possible. The final drive, as outlined above, is by chains to the single driving wheel at the rear. The gear ratios are 4½-1 and 8-1, but different gears can be obtained if specially ordered. The engine is not controlled by accelerator, but ordinary two lever carburetter controls are secured to the steering

The Grand Prix model is distinct owing to what might be called the gap underneath the oil and petrol tanks and immediately behind the radiator. The engine itself is placed in front of the radiator, where it obtains the full benefit of the cooling air. The new Aero model has a tapering fish tail and a V-fronted air deflector behind the radiator, the object of which is to form an easy means of exit for the cooling draught of air which has passed through the radiator.

The family car will appeal to many cyclecarists for, by adding very little extra weight to the ordinary standard body, an extra seat is arranged which is quite roomy enough to accommodate two children. The sporting model has an air-cooled engine enclosed within the bonnet.

OUTSTANDING DETAILS OF THE 1921 MORGAN.

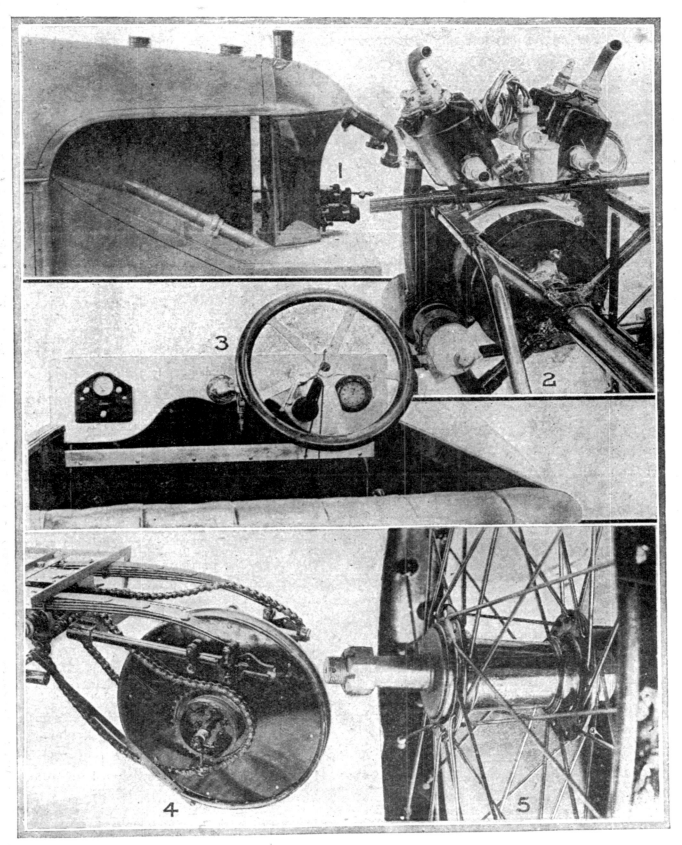

KEEPING A MORGAN IN TUNE.

How the Best Results Can be Obtained from this Popular Machine

THE Morgan has been improved considerably in many details for the year 1921. I was fortunate in obtaining delivery of one of the new machines shortly after the Motor Show, 1920, and, since that date, have covered many hundreds of miles by its aid.

At the outset, I would say that many men are disappointed with the Morgan, because they do not treat it fairly and do not understand what it is—a cyclecar.

A glance at the Morgan chassis reveals the fact that it is astonishingly simple and light, but, nevertheless, very sound in its design and construction.

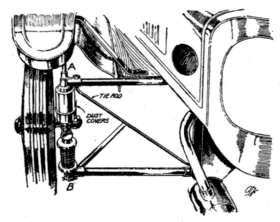

Fig. 1.—The swivel arms should be kept well greased to prevent undue wear.

There are not many points in the chassis which can give trouble. The first important point to keep an eye on is the tension rod bracing the two points of the upper frame tube, via the tubes used to convey the exhaust gases away. This rod should be watched, to see that the small friction pieces used where it rubs against the exhaust tubes have not slipped out.

Preventing Rapid Wear.

The front swivel arms require a little attention in the form of grease, and plenty of it. The construction here is very simple, but, unless watched, rapid wear will take place. The swivel arm itself is a brass casting, sliding on a steel tube, through which passes the mudguard stay, being secured by a nut (B, Fig. 1) at the bottom.

The steel tube fits into two recesses situated at the top and bottom of the frame tubes respectively, the nut at the bottom of the mudguard stay drawing the whole assembly tight.

This nut must not be unduly tightened, otherwise the steel tube may bend slightly and thereby cause much wear to take place in the bearing surface of the swivel arm.

The bevel box is now fitted with much stronger bevels, and it is a very nice job. I find that the grease supplied by the manufacturers is apt to harden, and the crown wheel and bevel cut a track in it, so causing an unpleasant note to come from this region. This I have now entirely cured by emptying the box and mixing a handful of flake graphite and about a gill of heavy gear oil with about three-quarters of the grease. This makes an excellent preparation. The lid (Fig. 2) of this box is, I find, still secured by small screws, as of old. An improvement is needed here; two wing-nuts would be a better fitting, and make it much less awkward for the owner to inspect this vital part. The improvement in the manner in which the rear forks are secured to the bevel box is very good indeed. So far, my machine, with the many hundreds of miles to its credit, has shown no wear at this point.

Rear Wheel Removal.

The fork ends have also been altered, with a view to facilitating the removal of the rear wheel. The first time I tackled this job I confess I thought the "easy removal" something of a myth. However, once the knack is acquired, it is quite a simple operation. The great thing to do is to jack the car up high —quite 5 ins. or 6 ins. off the ground. The lower brake band pins must be removed, and the axle nuts slacked off to allow the chain adjusters to swing clear; then the wheel is slid forward and down; the chains can then be lifted off quite easily. The bottom of the bevel box, through which a frame tube passes, forms the best position for the jack (Fig. 3).

It will be found a difficult business to obtain a jack that will just slide under when it is in its screwed-down position. To overcome this, I carry with me a small block of wood cut to size.

I give the chains quite a fair amount of attention. I have read the recent correspondence in the motor journals about running chains dry, but must say it will not do on the Morgan. An important point is to keep the small nut which secures the chain fastening pin in its place and held tight by a split pin. This is quite a small point, but means a lot when the day comes that the chain has to be removed. Periodically I remove the chains, give them a bath in paraffin, and replace. I lubricate them with the special preparation supplied by the County Chemical Co., which actually does what the manufacturers claim—viz., clings to the chains. All oil that is drained from the engine crankcase I keep, and every now and again put plenty on the chains and "dogs."

Probably I went farther than most when I obtained delivery of the machine. I have a deep

Fig. 2.—Wing nuts as suggested in the sketch would form an improved method of securing the bevel box cover.

respect for wheels and their bearings. Accordingly, I took the rear wheel out to look at the bearings, to ascertain that everything was in order, also an adequate supply of lubricant was given. The nuts holding the brake drums and sprockets must be removed. Much patience has to be used in getting the brake drums off. Care must be exercised in this operation, and the use of a hammer strictly avoided, because these drums crack easily. I filled the rear hub and the front hubs with Prices' hub lubricant. This is as much as anyone can do, and is a fine guarantee of no trouble.

To obtain the maximum comfort from the Morgan

the rear springs, which are of the flat leaf type, must be lubricated. As yet I have not gone to the expense of fitting spring gaiters, although I certainly consider them an excellent fitting.

Spring Lubrication.

My advice, in connection with spring lubrication, is " a little and often." Plain yellow grease inserted between the leaves is better than squirting oil on the surface, but I find graphite grease better than either. It holds to the surface better and in wet weather tends to keep out the water and mud.

The radiator and tanks have been much improved, and are a very much better job than in previous years. However, there is a fault here which the manufacturer could easily remedy, as it is a nuisance and an awkward job for the owner to perform. I refer to the manner in which the oil pipe from the Best and Lloyd automatic pump is secured to the tank.

The pipe simply leaves the pump and passes through the top of the cylindrical oil tank (as shown in Fig. 4); its only security is a blob of solder! On my machine this did not last long, as it was loose

Fig. 3.—The best position in which to place the jack is immediately below the bevel box housing.

and waving about when I took it away from the agent. Through the courtesy of Best and Lloyd, Ltd., I have obtained suitable unions, etc., and, with much soldering and cutting of the oil pipe, I have now made a satisfactory job of it. I think that the manufacturers could rise to the occasion a little more and provide a sounder fitting.

The petrol tank calls for its fair share of criticism. It is well made and does not " drum " when the machine is in motion, but the trouble is the filler cap. It is of the plain brass screw-down type, with a small hole drilled in the top to act as an air vent: it does—and also as a petrol vent! With the tank well filled, it will "vent" petrol in an alarming manner.

This I have cured by fitting a trap on the inside similar to the stoppers used in motorcycle tanks. The radiator (touch wood!) has not yet commenced to leak. I would even venture the remark that it will not leak for quite a time yet, as its construction is very sound.

The engine I deal with very quickly. It is a water-cooled M.A.G., and, if only left alone and given a good supply of oil, will pull away day and night, without complaint, and in that silent, silky manner peculiar to these machines.

I have dealt with most of the mechanical features of the chassis, and I will now pass on to the body-work. The finish is quite good, and the lining well

Fig. 4.—The lubricating system, showing that the only security for the oil pipe is a blob of solder.

done. Another coat of varnish before the machine left the works would have improved matters. The bonnet fits moderately well, and when clipped by the four holders provided, does not rattle. I think the manufacturer could devise some means of providing a support for it when it is raised, because, unless one is careful, it falls back on to the windscreen, and in time the screen cuts a line in the paintwork on the top of the bonnet. With the windscreen and hood I have no fault to find. The hood is cut well, fits properly, and in pouring rain one can keep practically dry. The tail of the machine is hinged, so that it can be lifted up and the rear wheel conveniently inspected.

This is quite satisfactory and much appreciated, but it should be secured in a better manner. At present two spring clips hold it, and, when travelling fast over a bumpy road, it occasionally lifts.

Details Which Might be Improved.

In general, I should like to see the tie-rod pins enclosed in grease-retaining covers. The shackle pins at present fitted at the rear of the leaf springs would be well replaced with greaser bolts. A more accurately machined clutch thrust bearing would be an advantage.

The present one gives no trouble. It receives plenty of oil, but grinds quite a lot. The starting handle could be improved. My handle has already become distorted. On the whole, I am very pleased with the machine. I have never been let down on the road with this model or my last. For comfort, one must keep the rear springs lubricated and the rear tyre inflated to 35 lb. air pressure; front tyres 25 lb. air pressure. One must never forget it is a cyclecar and that it requires a little attention from time to time. If one gives it plenty of grease and oil, petrol and water, and one keeps the bolts tight, no trouble will ensue, and the little vehicle will serve one in a wonderful manner. M.

— A — "WIRELESS" MORGAN.

Striking Example of Radio Equipment Fitted to Popular Cyclecar.

THOSE of our readers who are resident in London will probably have seen the vehicle illustrated and described herewith, for wherever it stops it commands a great deal of attention, both among those who are interested in radio as well as those who are mainly concerned with motoring matters. Owned by the Stratford Wireless Co., this cyclecar is equipped with two enormous Magnavox loud speakers, which face forward near the front axle, and running fore and aft over the heads of the occupants is a conspicuous sausage-type aerial that gives the vehicle the appearance almost of one that has been rigged for participation in a carnival.

Showing the general arrangement of the cage type aerial and valve panels.

Efficient in Operation.

In addition to its striking appearance, however, the wireless receiving set fitted to this vehicle is very efficient in operation, and we are informed by its owner that he has heard the Cardiff Broadcasting Station while the Morgan was in the vicinity of Stratford, which those who know anything about radio will recognize as being no mean feat. The news and concerts radiated from 2 L.O., the London

The passenger can operate the tuning circuit while the vehicle is moving.

station of the British Broadcasting Co., are reproduced with great vigour and volume by the two Magnavox loud speakers, and a description of this set, which, comparatively speaking, is small, cannot fail to be of interest.

The aerial consists of several lengths of copper wire spaced on a circular framework, and the "lead in" from it is taken to a two-valve receiving set which is mounted on the tail of the car. There is apparently nothing extraordinary about the circuit, one of the valves working as a high-frequency amplifier and the other as a detector, and from the latter the current is taken to a Burndept two-valve power amplifier which is fitted on the offside running board. From this a couple of leads go forward to the Magnavox loud speakers, which are so prominently observable in the illustrations. The receiving set is under the control of the passenger when the vehicle is moving, and when any small adjustments have to be made to the power amplifier these can be carried out quite

easily by the driver. It is interesting to note that the magneto had to be screened with copper foil and "earthed" to the framework of the car, otherwise the noise of the sparking interfered with the proper functioning of the set; but after a certain amount of experimenting had been carried out the London broadcast was reproduced faithfully and very loudly when the Morgan was travelling at speeds up to 45 m.p.h., the sound being readily distinguishable above the ordinary noise of the engine, etc. There is no earth connection, which is considered to be unusual. The Stratford Wireless Co. have succumbed to an impulse of humour, and, as the result of numerous inquiries regarding the precise location of the earth connection, have provided an obvious answer by mounting a small flowerpot filled with earth on the nearside running board!

The address of this concern is 26, Martin Street, Stratford, London, E. 15, and it is interesting to note that they are now experimenting with a portable set which can be stowed in the toolbox of a light car and which will work satisfactorily off an aerial fitted to the hood. The Magnavox loud speakers, made by

The two Magnavox loud-speakers are very conspicuously mounted.

the Sterling Telephone Co., of Tottenham Court Road, London, W., are in no way deranged by the vibration due to the running of the Morgan, and it would seem that this set represents another highly successful adaptation of an efficient radio receiving set to an automobile.

FOUR SPEEDS FOR MORGANS.

Foolproof Gearbox with Single-chain Drive.

WHILST the Morgan cyclecar with its two-speed gear and twin-chain drive gives the highest degree of reliability and a road performance equalled by few cars, irrespective of type or price, there is always the enthusiast who requires something a little better. Simplicity is the keynote to reliability and, incidentally, low production costs, and whilst the Morgan Motor Co. very wisely refrain from over-elaborating their production in response to a small percentage of owners or prospective owners, there are many concerns who specialize in what might be termed "de luxe" extras. One such is the Caton Machine Tool and Engineering Co., Ltd., Waterloo Street, Leeds, which concern has recently introduced a four-speed-and-reverse gearbox unit for this popular make of three-wheeler.

The complete box is similar in size and shape to the standard bevel box, therefore no alterations to the frame are necessary for its incorporation. · It may be thought that a four-speed component is unnecessary when three speeds suffice on 90 per cent. of light cars. It would, therefore, be as well to mention that in this case four speeds are obtained by using no more pinions than are usually employed with three speeds, so that the advantage of an additional ratio is provided without extra manufacturing costs.

A Wide Range of Gears.

In fixing the ratios the third and second gears in the Caton box represent the standard ratios of the Morgan, the additional speeds providing an emer-

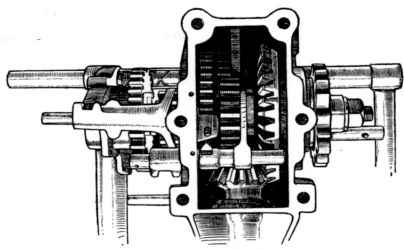

THE COMPLETE BOX.

It will be noted that the box itself is similar in size and shape to the ordinary Morgan bevel box. No alterations to the frame are needed for its incorporation.

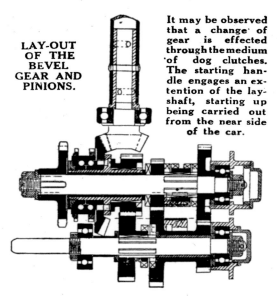

LAY-OUT OF THE BEVEL GEAR AND PINIONS.

It may be observed that a change of gear is effected through the medium of dog clutches. The starting handle engages an extention of the layshaft, starting up being carried out from the near side of the car.

gency low gear and an unusually high gear of 3.7 to 1 for speed work on the level Thus the third gear, which, incidentally, is direct, can be used for general running as though the standard two-speed box were in use.

The top gear ratio of 3.7 to 1, however, is optional, as in another arrangement the top gear is direct and gives a ratio of 4.5 to 1.

Adjustment for Bevel and Crown Wheel.

An important feature, and one which Morgan owners will appreciate, is that means of adjusting the bevel pinion and crown wheel are provided; thus it is possible accurately to mesh the teeth and obtain quiet running.

Owing to the fact that dog clutches form the means of meshing the gears there is no possibility of crashing the gear teeth—an important consideration. Although manœuvrability is a strong feature of the Morgan, the reverse gear incorporated in the Caton box adds more than 50 per cent. to this feature, and Morgan owners will not lose sight of the convenience of being able to reverse under the power of the engine.

There are arguments in favour of the two chains which are at present employed on the Morgan, a very important one being that a broken chain does not mean being stranded, as it is always possible to get home on the other. However, there is this disadvantage that it is by no means easy to maintain correct tension of two chains running over sprockets on common centres. With the Caton gear single-chain drive is employed, and, as we understand that 3,000 miles have been covered with this gear with successful results, it would appear that the single chain is quite satisfactory.

The gear lever on the propeller shaft tube.

Central control of the gears is adopted, the mounting and lever being secured to the propeller shaft tube. We understand that the extra charge for a Morgan fitted with this gear would not be unreasonable—that is to say, the Morgan could be sold at a popular price; but from the point of view of economy it is essential that the component be taken up energetically, as a brisk demand only would justify putting the box into production.

THROUGH SOMERSET AND DEVON IN A FAMILY MORGAN.

Economical Touring De Luxe. The Charm of the West Country.

Our outward route lay through Lichfield, Birmingham, Worcester, Tewkesbury, Gloucester, Bristol, and Weston-super-Mare, where we stayed the night, having covered, between 8.30 in the morning and 7.30 in the evening, approximately 160 miles.

It should be explained that thus far we were familiar with the road, but to anyone contemplating this route for the first time there is much of interest to be seen, notably the beautiful cathedral at Lichfield, and the Clifton Suspension Bridge, which spans the Avon Gorge at a height of 245 ft.

Avoiding the Steepest Hills.

We had previously decided, after a prolonged study of the map, that it would be venturesome to attempt the coast road through Porlock and Lynton without better means of braking than the Morgan possessed, and accordingly the next morning we headed for Bridgwater and Taunton, passing on through Milverton, Bampton, and South Molton to Barnstaple. Soon after leaving Taunton we were able to appreciate the wonderful scenery of South Somerset, but the road was somewhat hilly, and it was necessary to make frequent use of the lower gear.

Speaking generally, however, the hills were long rather than steep, and the Morgan showed her pulling qualities on top gear to the best advantage. The surface of the road between Bampton and South Molton was sufficiently poor to test the springing effects of our little car, and, if the truth is told, we were thankful that we were fairly well laden.

The ancient town of Barnstaple, with its old-time buildings and historical associations, proved a great source of interest, and we called a halt of over an hour before entering upon the last stage of our journey. (Incidentally it may be mentioned that we had our first taste of Devonshire cream.) On leaving Barnstaple we were advised to take the road through Pilton, Muddiford, and Bittadon in preference to going around Braunton. There was a good deal

A S an indication of the capabilities of the Morgan cyclecar under touring conditions, an account of a holiday in the West Country may not be without interest to those readers of *The Light Car and Cyclecar* who, like the writer, aspire to something offering more protection than the motor bicycle and sidecar while costing less than the average car.

South-westward Ho !

Having decided to spend our holidays at Ilfracombe this summer, we left Derby on a Friday morning with the intention of getting to our destination on the afternoon of the following day. Our mount was a 1922 Family Morgan, with 8 h.p. J.A.P. water-cooled engine, geared 5 to 1 on top and 11 to 1 on bottom.

The load comprised myself, wife, son of 12, and as much luggage as could conveniently be stored in the back seat with the boy. The engine had previously been decarbonized (for the first time after about 6,000 miles), and everything promised well.

(Left) Outside the old-world abbey at Glastonbury.
(Right) In the picturesque bay at Combe Martin.

to the front-wheel brakes and the central hand lever to the existing rear-wheel foot brake.

Similarly, at various times, I have toyed with the idea of fitting an accelerator pedal. The closeness of the clutch and brake pedals to each other and to the side of the body and the frame tube respectively indicate, however, that this might not be an easy job.

The road-holding qualities of the machine are quite good, but I have improved them by fitting B. and D. shock absorbers to the rear suspension. These fittings tend, perhaps, to make the springing a little harsh at low speeds, but in the open country, when advantage can be taken of the speediness of the Morgan, the back wheel clings to the road like a leech, and even bad pot-holes can be taken very fast.

I have never had the machine "clocked" for speed, but, according to speedometer, which I have every reason to believe is accurate, I have several times exceeded 70 m.p.h. in top gear, and 48-50 m.p.h. may easily be obtained in second, and these speeds are not accomplished at the sacrifice of a good petrol consumption, because, with the B. and B. carburetter, consumption on long runs is often so low as 50 miles per gallon.

I cannot give oil-consumption figures, because the engine is so economical in this respect that the quantity used is negligible; in fact, before I became thoroughly used to the machine it caused me no small amount of worry, because I could not rid myself of the idea that the engine was being starved of oil. This idea was dispelled, however, by a slight increase in the number of drips per minute passed by the Best and Lloyd lubricator almost immediately cutting out one cylinder, due to an over-oiled plug.

Engine Improvements.

I have very little fault to find with the Blackburne engine, but I must confess that it is a mystery to me why the makers fit inverted cups to the overhead valve rockers and use a ball at the top ends of the push rods. With this arrangement it is impossible to keep the balls and cups lubricated, and the escaping lubricant runs down the tappet rods, where it gathers dust and makes an unsightly mess. By cupping the top ends of the push rods and fitting balls to the rockers this would be entirely overcome and increased silence of operation would result. In fairness to the makers I must remark that this alteration, together with other improvements, is incorporated in their 1926 engines.

I am touching wood as I write it, but I should like

To sit at the wheel of an Aero-Morgan gives the feeling of being in an aeroplane cockpit. The controls and facia-board dials are handily placed.

to place on record that during the entire mileage of the car I have not suffered one single puncture, and it has never been necessary to give attention to the tyres beyond occasional slight inflation.

I took the precaution, however, a little time ago of changing the rear tyre on to one of the front wheels, and it was whilst doing this that I felt myself inclined to side with those readers who have written to me at various times and deplored the fact that the Morgan

is not fitted with detachable wheels. The operation of changing the straight-sided tyres is, of course, simplicity itself.

The chains have given me no trouble whatever and have very seldom required adjustment, whilst, as yet, they show very little signs of wear—a remark which may also be applied to the sprockets.

Being tied down rather closely to town during the week, I take advantage, whenever possible, of indulging in long runs during the week-ends, secure in the knowledge that my machine is as fast as anything I am likely to meet on the road and that it will climb every hill on which the back wheel can obtain a grip. I feel that it would be superfluous to talk about times and speeds on hills, because everyone knows the capabilities of the Aero-Morgan in this direction, and those

To overcome the blanking effect of the hood sides, "Shacklepin" cut holes as shown in this photo. Weatherproofness was not greatly impaired.

who do not have only to imagine a machine weighing only 7 cwt. laden and driven by an engine which will develop 45 b.h.p. Even with a bottom gear of 8 to 1 it would take something in the nature of the side of a house to bring the machine to a standstill.

In connection with long week-end runs, especially at this time of the year, I have a grumble regarding the lighting equipment, which is that the dynamo itself is not large enough to supply the battery with sufficient current. When the headlights are fully on, in the case of my car, and with the dynamo charging, a discharge from the battery is taking place, and it is necessary from time to time to have this charged, a trouble which could be avoided by supplying a dynamo with a larger current output.

Another point which bears on long-distance touring is that of driving comfort. This would be improved considerably on my car by the fitting of a more adequately padded squab to the seats. The present one seems very hard after a few hours at the wheel. Another 2 ins. or so in the width of the body would also be of advantage, especially during the winter months, when heavy overcoats are the order of the day.

Touring Speeds.

Still keeping in mind that we are dealing with long runs, I should say that a cruising speed of 35 to 40 m.p.h. seems very comfortable, and at this speed the road-holding and steering are very good, whilst, of course, the machine takes all main-road hills in its stride.

In spite of the fact that the machine has been used in all weathers and often is parked in open spaces for hours at a time, its appearance has not suffered in any way, which goes to show that the paint, varnish and plating used in its construction are of the very best.

To sum up, I can say, without fear of contradiction, that the Aero-Morgan is a cyclecar which is particularly well adapted to the high-speed touring enthusiast, and at the same time it is a sufficiently all-round vehicle to be suitable also as a hack, but one which, nevertheless, can at all times be relied upon to make drivers of other cars "sit up and take notice."

The Three-Wheeler's Place

Some Interesting Comparisons of the Three-Wheeler and Sidecar for Passenger Work.

BY " THE SENIOR CLUBMA

THE cyclecar, or runabout, having three wheels, and of which the Morgan is the most familiar make, is the mystery vehicle of the motor industry. In almost the same words I began an article that appeared not long ago in a trade journal, but I think the phrase is possibly worth repeating here : if it makes only one private owner bring more seriously the claims of the cyclecar to his attention and patronage, it will have served a useful purpose. And the cyclecar *is* a mystery machine. It came into existence, as a type, and more or less in its present form, somewhere about fifteen years ago. And yet it is represented on the road and in the market to-day by one predominating make, the Morgan, and by some three other makes that have only recently appeared on the scene. Contrasted with the present position of the sidecar combination, the fate of the cyclecar seems difficult to explain.

no special reason why, taking the components of a combination, one should not build up a 3-wheeled vehicle with all the virtues of the motor cycle and sidecar, but without the defects that arise from, and are inherent to, a makeshift and none too mechanical union.

And actually this can be done, and has been done. But the rock on which most cyclecar building enterprises have been wrecked is that of over-elaboration : refinement was piled on refinement, complication followed complication, and gadget was added to gadget. Everybody, or nearly everybody, tried to make the super runabout, forgetting that prices had to be kept to an economic level, and that the type was not one to be developed hurriedly without serious risk of mechanical trouble. Consequently, the public got landed with 3-wheelers that were dear, or bad, or both, and makers, on their side, experienced difficult days. Buyers returned

H. F. S. MORGAN (MORGAN) ON THE SLOW HILL CLIMB IN THE VICTORY CUP TRIAL.

Theoretically, the cyclecar should have beaten the combination in the race for popularity. It would have been by no means a runaway win, and the combination would have come home a very good second, but there seems no doubt, on paper, that the runabout ought to have made the stronger appeal of the two to the man in the street. Only, for various reasons, it didn't.

The sidecar outfit is, as we all know, a remarkably serviceable vehicle of personal transport. It is astonishingly cheap, and it has a better road performance than that normally obtainable from a small car. It has, however, certain rather serious defects—the chief of which is that, while the passenger rides in comfort, the driver has very little protection from the elements.

It is, too, an unsociable machine, conversation among the crew being, as a general rule, difficult, when considered by car standards. Now there seems to be

to sidecars, or went ahead into the car market, and the manufacturers turned their attention to more profitable things.

Only the Morgan people—I believe I am right—weathered the whole period : I doubt if any other firm in the world has been turning out 3-wheelers continuously since about the year 1910. They had the good sense to stick to a very simple design of well-proved merit ; they kept their prices within reason, turned out a range of models to suit the needs of most classes, and built their cars well. Thus they have done what must have been a remarkably steady and quite remunerative business : the history of the firm is, I consider, one of the minor romances of the motor industry.

However, of late there has been evidence of another cyclecar revival. At Olympia in September we had two

THE THREE-WHEELER'S PLACE—*Continued*

newcomers, the Coventry Victor and the Omega, while a French machine, the d'Yrsan, made its second appearance at the Show. And one hears of experiments being made in other quarters; in fact, if the Omega and the Coventry Victor "get away with it" during the coming season, there seems very little doubt that another cyclecar or two may make a bid for public favour by the autumn.

Frankly, I hope that that will be the case. I should like to see the Coventry Victor and the Omega make good : I happen to know that the former is the result of a great amount of very careful experimental work, carried out over a long period of time, and the efforts of the two companies concerned merit a good reward. And the more cyclecars there are the better, provided that their makers do not go astray again in the direction of trying to do too much with a type of machine of which simplicity should be the keynote. Competition is good for all of us : the advent of these new machines is likely to increase Morgan sales, for example, and the more makers there are, the stronger the cyclecar movement will become.

It is arguable at least that the cyclecar is not as fully developed a vehicle as the combination. In a sense, I suppose that is true, though it provides no reason against buying one : the results of open competitions amply prove that the Morgans can meet the best of the combinations, and frequently give them a beating. But if the cyclecar has not been developed,

TWO MORGANS AT SPEED ON BROOKLANDS TRACK.

it is because nobody has taken the trouble to develop it. It is, unfortunately, rather an unwonted child : the Junior Car Club quite obviously does not love it, while the Auto-Cycle Union—to keep up the metaphor—loves it rather as a duty than as an act of genuine and spontaneous enthusiasm. Cyclecars, in my opinion, ought to have been allowed to compete with the sidecars in the Isle of Man. Again, they should have been permitted to enter for the last 200 miles' race organised by the J.C.C. That they were not strikes one as being manifestly unfair. However, should the movement grow as I hope to see it grow, the situation may be altered. Given a greater enthusiasm for the type, which it well merits, its claims will be regarded more sympathetically by those who rule in the competition world.

1926

DERBYSHIRE GRADIENTS. An "Aero" Morgan driven by G. H. Goodall making a good climb of Blacker Mill Hill, the gradient and surface of which caused a large number of failures among those who competed in the International Six Days Trial.

The de luxe model " Omega " three-wheeler. It has a roomy body and quarter elliptic springing front and rear, while the all-weather equipment is particularly effective.

A PLACE FOR THE THREE-WHEELER.

A Few Reasons why every Agent should Handle a Class of Vehicle Offering Car Comfort at Motor Cycle Cost. — Where the Three-wheeler Scores.—Selling Arguments that Influence Sales.

ASK the average motor cycle agent what he thinks of the three-wheeled runabout as a selling proposition, and it is likely he will at once reply, " No good." Press him for reasons as to why he holds this opinion, and he will eventually murmur something about this type of machine being "unsafe," "prone to skid," and "troublesome" when it becomes necessary to change or repair the back tyre. These criticisms are old ones, and in respect of the modern three-wheeler cannot be justified. Further, they are based upon the performances of machines made before the war—machines which cannot be compared to those now upon the market. But even the earliest three-wheelers deserved better treatment than was accorded to them by the trade when they represented the "last word" in the runabout world and were actually in production, since, although they possessed defects which have since been overcome, they were in every sense "roadworthy" and capable of giving reliable service under arduous conditions.

An Essentially Marketable Product.

In the chaotic days subsequent to the signing of the Armistice several new three-wheelers made their appearance on the British market, but, despite the fact that they were both well designed and manufactured with scrupulous care, they enjoyed but fleeting existences, not because of their inefficiency or because they were lacking in other respects, but merely for the reason that they were too expensive. Most of them were produced by firms in a comparatively small way of business—firms not in a position to place large contracts for raw materials and components, and thereby to buy on the most advantageous terms. Price, and nothing else, prevented the makers of these newcomers from consolidating their positions, the cost to the public of their products being very much higher than the expensive sidecar outfits against which they had to compete.

Now, however, all is changed, and to-day the three-wheeler is essentially a marketable proposition—a line upon which the agent can concentrate with every prospect of success. The modern three-wheeler, in addition to being superior in every way to the pre-war and immediate post-war products, is available at a price which compares very favourably with that of an 8 h.p. sidecar outfit. Scientific weight distribution and steering design have made it an essentially safe vehicle, which is controllable in every way and capable of "cornering" at high speeds in either direction without loss of stability. It is, moreover, extremely simple to drive, economical to run, and last, but by no means least, weatherproof for both driver and passenger. Indeed, the protection it affords to both occupants is a feature which commends itself to many people who are hesitating as to whether they shall purchase a combination or a small car.

The tax, too, is low, being but £4, and all other expenses are proportionately low. That there is a market for the three-wheeler, and a place for it in the agent's scheme of things, is proved beyond question by the fact that one concern has manufactured nothing else for a period of no fewer than sixteen years, and also by the recent introduction of two new runabouts of this type, which made their bow to the public at the last Olympia Show and have since established themselves firmly in public favour. And, as must be obvious to every agent, no thinking concern would go to the expense and trouble of introducing new three-wheelers unless they knew that there was every possibility of a demand justifying a steady output of sufficient volume to make the new venture a successful and profitable undertaking.

Where the Three-wheeler Scores.

In the matter of design and, to a degree, in the matter of price the three-wheeler may justly be characterised as the "missing link" between the cheap light car and the sidecar outfit. For two persons the latter is undoubtedly the cheapest possible form of mechanically propelled vehicle, always excepting the solo machine and pillion seat. But it cannot be denied that it lacks something in the direction of weatherproofing. Even though the possession of a hood and screen will adequately protect the passenger, the rider of the motor cycle is invariably exposed to the elements, and it is this fact, coupled with the variable weather conditions for which this country is noted, that frequently influences the sidecar owner in the direction of a small car selling at a moderate figure.

It has been said, and with considerable truth, that "once a motor cyclist, always a motor cyclist." Certainly many a man who has deserted the two- for the four-wheeler regrets the extreme "liveliness" and considerable reserve

For the speedy and economical delivery of light loads—the "Ivy" commercial three-wheeler.

of power which he has lost by the change over. It is here that the three-wheeler scores very strongly, for although it gives complete protection to both driver and passenger, it retains the most attractive characteristics of the combination, and imparts to the driver that feeling which, among

Capable of comfortably accommodating two adults and three children—the Morgan "Family" model. The hood covers all the occupants when it is erected.

car owners, is experienced only by those fortunate enough to possess "sports" models.

That so many sidecar owners, upon deciding that more comfort is essential to their interests, turn to the small car is largely the agents' own fault. They do not make known the advantages of the three-wheeler, and, indeed, themselves are far too often completely ignorant of the undoubted charms of the runabout. Not being aware that the three-wheeler is the ideal vehicle for their requirements, those of the public who insist on better protection facilities than those afforded by the sidecar simply go to the nearest car dealer, and the motor cycle agents lose customers which might well have been retained had they adopted the right policy.

The Rear Tyre "Bogey."

The old idea that trouble with the rear tyre of a three-wheeler spells disaster dies hard, and is a relic of the old days. Certainly it is an idea completely out of place in these times, but, nevertheless, it persists, even in trade circles, and has been responsible for many lost sales. The rear tyre on a modern runabout can be dealt with quite easily, and agents should broadcast this fact on every possible occasion. Many agents, too, also hold the opinion that the rear tyre of a three-wheeler wears out very quickly, whereas the truth is that the modern vehicles of this class are equipped with tyres of such a generous section as will ensure long service. Incidentally, these large tyres, in conjunction with an effective suspension system, make the three-wheeler one of the most comfortable vehicles on the road for all-round touring purposes.

Enough, we think, has been said to indicate to agents that there is a place for the three-wheeler in his sphere of activities. It will enable him to retain customers when otherwise he would lose them, and as it sells at a modest figure sales are not difficult of accomplishment. Not for one moment do we suggest that an agent should neglect motor cycles in favour of the three-wheeler. But we do

feel, and feel strongly, that the motor cycle agent who fails to handle three-wheelers is missing business—a thing nobody can afford to do in these days when money is not over-plentiful. Again, apart from the "pleasure" vehicles, there are commercial three-wheelers available, and these, being non-seasonal lines, are particularly interesting to the discerning agent whose wish it is fully to explore every possible avenue leading towards the further development of his business.

Principal among the touring three-wheelers now on the market are the "Morgan" (first exhibited at Olympia in 1910), the "Omega" (introduced last year), the "Coventry Victor" (also shown at the 1925 Show for the first time), and a more elaborate French product, styled the d'Yrsan, equipped with a four-cylinder engine.

The Morgans are all fitted with V-twin power units, those of J.A.P. manufacture being standardised, although other engines can be supplied to order. Five distinct models are listed:— The "Standard" (short wheelbase) at £95; the "De Luxe" at £115 (water-cooled £125); the "Family" (carrying three children as well as two adults) at £116 (water-cooled £126); the "Aero" (a "sports" model) at £130 with water-cooled J.A.P. or o.h.v. Anzani "Summit" engine, and £142 with new Blackburne racing engine; and the "Grand Prix," a "sports" model at £123 (water-cooled). All models are equipped with Lucas lighting and a complete equipment. The Anzani "Summit" o.h.v. engine can also be fitted to the "Grand Prix," "De Luxe," or "Family" models. The manufacturers of the Morgan range are the Morgan Motor Co., Ltd., Malvern Link.

An Attractive Coventry Product.

Produced by W. J. Green, Ltd., of Omega Works, Swan Lane, Coventry, the "Omega" runabout is manufactured in three models. The "Popular," with 980 c.c. J.A.P. air-cooled engine, sells at £95, or £105 if water-cooled; the "De Luxe" air-cooled costs £110, £10 extra being charged if the engine is water-cooled; while the "Family" model, for the family man, costs £115 and £125 respectively. An illustrated description of the "Omega" appeared recently in these columns.

The "Carette"—an inexpensive and handy little commercial vehicle with a carrying capacity of 4 cwt.

The "Coventry Victor," made by the Coventry Victor Motor Co., Ltd., of Coventry, has a water-cooled flat-twin power unit, of the firm's own manufacture, rated at 7 h.p. The chassis is of ingenious, but substantial, design, and the layout as a whole is excellently arranged with a view to securing maximum strength with minimum weight. With two-three-seater body and very efficient weatherproofing equipment the price is £99 15s.

For commercial work there is the "Carette"—an interesting little vehicle, produced by the Carette Trade Carrier Co., Ltd., of 15, Carlton Vale, Maida Vale, London, N.W.10, with a capacity of about four hundredweight, and propelled by a single-cylinder engine capable of maintaining a speed of some 25 m.p.h. It sells at £85. Then there is the "Melen" carrier, made by F. & H. Melen, Ltd., Sydenham Road, Sparkbrook, Birmingham (and at 314, Gray's Inn Road, London, W.C.1); the "Warrick," produced by Warrick & Co., Caversham Road, Reading; and the "Ivy," emanating from the house of S. A. Newman, Ltd., Lichfield Road, Birmingham, and introduced but a short time ago.

For the "sporting" driver—the Morgan "Aero" model. As supplied it will exceed 70 m.p.h.

It will be appreciated from the foregoing that the agent has a fairly wide choice, both in the direction of pleasure and commercial machines, at his command. None of the vehicles enumerated is an untried product. On the contrary, it has been fully proved under actual service conditions. No trader, therefore, need hesitate to link up his fortunes with the manufacturers of current three-wheelers. Obviously, the motor cycle agent is the man to handle the three-wheeler business, by reason of the fact that the bulk of the users of this type of vehicle are recruited from the ranks of motor cyclists.

A SPECIAL SINGLE-CYLINDER MORGAN RACER.

BUILT for the purpose of attacking records and for use in speed events, both in this country and on the Continent, a single-cylinder-engined Morgan Special belonging to Mr. E. C. Fernihough has many points of interest. The machine has already been used with success in speed events, and this has encouraged Mr. Fernihough to concentrate on it with a view to obtaining a still better performance.

The Morgan frame design lends itself readily to the fitting of a single-cylinder engine. The cradle plates are drilled for lightness.

Beyond the fitting of a single Hartford shock absorber on a bridge-piece over the rear wheel, the chassis is very little altered from standard. A petrol tank holding 2½ gallons is slung under the main frame tube, and an oil tank of 1¼ gallons capacity is fitted under the bonnet. Geared-down steering is used, and the track rod and drag link have ball-jointed connections.

The engine is a 1925 model, 494 c.c. J.A.P., with push-rod-operated overhead valves. It is fitted with an Amac carburetter and an M-L magneto. At present the maximum r.p.m. of the engine is 5,700, but Mr. Fernihough hopes to get 6,000 r.p.m. by further tuning. For the preliminary tests the gear ratios chosen are 5.28 and 10.1 to 1, but it is possible that the low-gear ratio will be raised to 8.57 to 1.

There is no gear control lever proper; instead, a short bell-crank lever is arranged with one arm projecting horizontally from under the side of the body, the other arm being connected to the rod which slides the dog clutches. The "lever" can easily be reached from the driving seat and it has the advantage of being positive in action.

Drip-feed lubrication is arranged for the bevel box and chains, whilst on each side of the aluminium body there is a fabric flap, secured by turn-buttons, through which the dog clutches and so forth may be inspected.

A Dunlop s.s. cord tyre is used on the rear wheel, the front tyres being 26-in. by 3-in. Avons. Front-wheel brakes are, of course, fitted.

In the general view of the machine, which appears in this issue as the heading to "Cyclecar Comments," it will be seen that a large fuel tank is fitted on the tail. This is to supplement the main pressure-fed tank for long-distance work.

Every part of the machine bears evidence of having received careful attention, stays, lock nuts and split pins being used in a lavish manner. This care, of course, is necessary when high speeds are contemplated, as the strains set up by vibration and road shocks are often of considerable magnitude.

Mr. Fernihough has already set up several records with this cyclecar in Class I at Brooklands. This class is for three-wheeled cyclecars having engines not exceeding 500 c.c. A passenger must be carried. Four records were established on March 31st last, the five miles (flying start) being covered in 4 mins. 16.16 secs., equal to an average speed of 73.12 m.p.h., whilst 10 miles from a standing start were covered at a speed of 69.65 m.p.h.

SELLING THE MORGAN THREE-WHEELER.

Hints for Agents Handling the Morgan Runabout—Car Comfort with Sidecar Upkeep Cost.

SPECIFICATION FEATURES.

ENGINE.—10.4 h.p. Blackburne, over-head valves, water-cooled.

TRANSMISSION.—Shaft to counter-shaft, thence, via a two-speed gear, to rear wheel by two large chains (interchangeable).

GEAR RATIOS.—Top, 4.6 to 1; bottom, 7.9 to 1; 5 to 1 and 10 to 1 available as alternative.

GENERAL.—Fabric-lined cone clutch, self-contained and dustproof. Rear wheel easily detachable without removing chains. Two independent brakes operating on rear wheel, foot- and hand-controlled respectively.

700×85 cord tyres, 3-gallon petrol tank. Generous equipment.

ROAD PERFORMANCE.

ACCELERATION.—10 m.p.h. to 30 m.p.h.; top gear, 5½ seconds; bottom gear, 2⅘ seconds.

BRAKING.—40 m.p.h. to rest; foot, 34 yards; foot and hand, 26 yards.

MAXIMUM SPEED.—72 miles per hour.

PROBABLY the greatest difficulty which confronts the trader who is endeavouring to secure a sale for the Morgan three-wheeler, is the apparent prejudice which the average person has against the three-wheeler. That such prejudice exists there can be no doubt; that it is unreasonable all who are familiar with this handy little vehicle will agree. In view of these circumstances, contrary to our usual practice in detailing the more outstanding features to be reviewed in endeavouring to effect sales, we propose to deal with the road performance and advantages of the machine before turning to the technical features embodied in its general lay-out.

When an agent first moots the subject of a Morgan runabout to a potential buyer, he is frequently met with the remark that three-wheelers are unsafe, first, because they are prone to skid on greasy roads or wet tram-lines, and, secondly, that they are unstable, and easily turned over. It is, therefore, of paramount importance that the agent should scotch such ideas at the very outset. Let him take the customer for a run, and demonstrate that stability and road worthiness are pronounced selling features, rather than points to be smoothed over. Our own experience with a Morgan convinces us that any retailer who has similarly had driving experience with a Morgan can quickly combat such prejudice in this way. Naturally, should the back wheel become caught in a wet tramline there is a danger of skidding, but this is certainly no more pronounced than with a four-wheeled car, whilst in the case of the Morgan, the direct steering considerably facilitates the correction of any tendency to skid when an attempt is made to pull the wheel from the tramline. At the same time it can be proved that, under ordinary road conditions such as are met with by "the man in the street," who desires a convenient and comfortable means of travel from one place to another, the three-wheeler of this make is every whit as stable as its light four-wheeled competitor and the sidecar outfit.

Among the principal road performance features which can be utilised as sales levers are, exceptional liveliness, ability to climb hills on top gear, and at the same time to thread a way through the thickest of traffic without recourse to the lower gear ratio, and also reliability which can become positively monotonous.

Before attempting to demonstrate the numerous technical points which can be advanced in favour of the Morgan, it is

A Blackburne-engined Morgan Three-wheeler.

essential that the retailer should make some reference to its innumerable achievements in competitions during the past sixteen years. In this connection it may be mentioned that, since its inception in 1910, samples of this vehicle, both in the hands of its designer and also those of private owners, have time and again proved themselves as severe opponents of both the sidecar outfit and the four-wheeled car, and, time after time, they have secured highest awards for performances of outstanding merit.

To our mind the technical feature which should be first touched upon is that of simplicity, for in the Morgan, from the engine situated at the front, to the very rear of the chassis, there is no complicated mechanism of any description, in fact, nothing which even the most unmechanically minded could fail to understand. Two further items bearing upon the technical side of the proposition are the sturdiness of the whole layout, and the accessibility of every component.

Turning now to the more important items of the chassis specification, the power units utilised, viz., either the J.A.P. or Blackburne engine, are in themselves a recommendation to the machine. In regard to the transmission, although, as we have already indicated, this is simple in the extreme, it is necessary to impress upon prospective customers the importance of the fabric-lined cone clutch, with its self-contained and dust-proof ball thrust bearings, and ease of adjustment.

Another objection which has been raised against the three-wheeler is the question of tyre trouble with the rear wheel. This has received special attention from the manufacturers, who are now fitting rear fork ends which allow the back wheel to be removed with the greatest ease, and without removal of the chains. So one may go through every portion of the Morgan chassis, and find in it details which can be utilised as telling sales levers.

Before concluding, it is necessary to emphasise the commercial aspect of the purchase of a Morgan, for the machine forms, as it were, a connecting link between the sidecar combination and the car, mainly in providing the comfort of the last-named with the low initial cost and up-keep charges of the sidecar. Finally, depreciation has been reduced to a minimum by the manufacturers themselves, who, although improving the machine in detail from year to year, have allowed their original design to remain practically unchanged.

Cyclecar Comments.

THREE - WHEELERS AT OLYMPIA

"SHACKLEPIN" REVIEWS THE MAKES AND MODELS WHICH WILL BE AVAILABLE FOR NEXT SEASON.

The latest Aero-Morgan, showing the new head-lamp supports and the improved mudguards. The engine is a 1,096 c.c J.A.P.

AFTER a period during which no particular changes were made to the design of existing makes of three-wheeler, it would seem that the year 1928 will see many improvements. In addition, a new three-wheeler, the Royal Ruby, will make its début at the Motorcycle and Cycle Show which opens at Olympia on Monday next, October 31st.

The other two makes of three-wheeler which will be on view are the Morgan and the Coventry-Victor. With regard to the Morgan, I understand that a complete range of models and a stripped chassis are being staged. The Popular model has been improved considerably in appearance; a larger bonnet, bringing the windscreen closer to the driver, and a better proportioned tail being responsible largely for this improvement. The standard colour for the Popular model is to be dark red.

Speed merchants will, no doubt, concentrate their attention upon the new super-Aero model, which has a lower chassis and body than the standard Aero type. It will be fitted with the latest J.A.P. engine, and the dynamo will be gear driven from the bevel-box counter-shaft. Incidentally, this method of driving the dynamo has been adopted on all Morgan models for 1928. Although it is not quite ready at the moment, the new steering gear giving a reduction of 2 to 1 will be available very shortly.

A business vehicle during the week and a pleasure

car on Sundays, combined in the same machine, is something which many people desire. They will find their needs met in the new family model Morgan, which is arranged so that a box body can readily be fitted to, or removed from, the rear seating space.

No special alterations have been made to the de luxe models, but from the foregoing it is obvious that the Morgan exhibits will be well worth careful examination.

An addition to the range of three-wheelers manufactured by Coventry-Victor Motors, Ltd., will be available for 1928.

The new car is a sports model with a streamlined

A Royal Ruby chassis, showing the looped rear fork and long springs. Transverse front suspension is used.

body, cellulose finish in two colours, of which a choice is given of blue and grey, strawberry and cream, or two shades of brown.

The engine is of entirely new design with push-rod-operated overhead valves and, of course, horizontally opposed water-cooled cylinders. It has a capacity of 750 c.c., and the price of the car, £110, includes a neat folding hood.

So far as the existing models are concerned, no great alterations to the chassis have been made for the coming season. The clutch operating mechanism, however, has been redesigned to provide a very light control, whilst, in addition, a larger silencer is being fitted. The family model has a four-seater body, the front seats of which are adjustable. The tyres are 27-in. by 4-in., Dunlop reinforced balloons, and the car complete with hood, screen and full tool equipment will be priced at 95 guineas.

Really good weather protection is claimed for this Royal Ruby model. The engine is a single-cylinder air-cooled two-stroke.

CARE and MAINTENANCE of the MORGAN

Some Notes on How to Obtain the Best Results.

By W. A. CARR.

FOR some time I could not understand why Mr. H. F. S. Morgan appeared to be so apathetic to the appeals for such things as reverse gears and detachable wheels, and it was not until, as the result of trial work, I acquired close intimacy with the various working parts of the Morgan that I appreciated the wisdom of his policy. Owing to its simplicity, the average owner can tackle any maintenance work apart, perhaps, from dismantling the bevel gears and driving shaft. My object in this summary on the care of a Morgan is to endeavour to assist in some small way those who, like myself, want the best possible results from their machines.

Keeping the Engine in Tune.

Regarding the power unit, which is a proprietary article, the question of tuning would require too much space to go fully into the subject, and I cannot do better than refer those interested to the manufacturers' instruction booklets.

As expert engine tuning is not within everyone's capabilities, I would suggest that if such points as the valve clearances, the fit of valve stems in their guides, the induction pipe joints, and the compression, are in order, then the engine can safely be relied on to deliver the horses.

As regards carburation, I have found that very little improvement can be effected by altering the makers' setting. Careful attention to the feed and the float chamber is desirable, and in this respect it is surprising the amount of foreign matter which will be found to accumulate.

Fortunately, magnetos are now so reliable that one is apt to forget how essential they are, and even the little excitement one used sometimes to have when the fibre bush of the contact breaker seized up seems to have vanished. An occasional cleaning of the slip ring, and examination of the high-tension cables and brushes are generally all that is needed.

It is a good plan to see if the machine runs freely in neutral by testing it on a hard, flat surface and observing whether there is any undue stiffness of movement. If stiffness is noticeable, the adjustment of the brake bands and driving chains should receive attention; the latter adjustment should, of course, never be attempted when the back wheel is jacked up.

Front Wheel Wobble.

The driving wheel runs on two robust ball races, and, as these are well packed with grease, not much trouble will arise in this quarter if the nuts on the axles are kept dead tight. Any wear in the front wheel bearings can be taken up in the hubs.

Sliding axles do not last for ever, and excessive wear, together with any looseness in the tie rods and steering arms, will probably set up front wheel wobble. This can be eliminated by compensating for wear in the steering system, and employing washers of friction material between the tie rods and wheel arms.

Driving chains are usually patient sufferers, and in the majority of cases they are either coated with thick grease, to which mud and dust adhere, or they are entirely forgotten, with disastrous results. Their lives can be considerably lengthened if, after removal and scrubbing with a wire brush in a paraffin bath, they are allowed to soak in hot graphite grease. Before replacing the chains, allow the superfluous grease to drain off. Badly worn or stretched chains will have a tendency to ride the sprocket teeth, and may cause considerable damage. Chains may be tested for wear by laying them out straight on the ground and then alternately pulling and pushing on their ends

Morgan chassis lay-out.

Care and Maintenance of the Morgan.

It is not wise to run the tyres to destruction if one wishes to avoid the unpleasant delays which are bound to occur. The removal of rust from the inside of the wheel rims will amply repay one's trouble. If standard tyres are used, then from the point of view of comfort it is not advisable to run them board hard, as they then convey shocks which are not appreciated by either the human or the mechanical frame; if, on the

The twin–cylinder water–cooled J.A.P. engine.

other hand, they are run too soft, there is the possibility of the tyres rolling off the rims. Generally, the best compromise results from the use of the maker's recommended pressures. The question of punctures brings one to that of roadside repairs, and even if it is necessary to remove the back wheel the job should present no difficulties. As an essential to this operation, I would advocate a jack which, when placed under the bevel box, is capable of lifting the car sufficiently high to enable the back wheel to be easily removed after the brake bands and chains have been uncoupled. This tool will remove a lot of the difficulties which are associated with the operation of repairing a rear wheel puncture.

The possession of a kit of serviceable spanners is very

Rear of the chassis ready for attention to the bevel box and gear operating mechanism.

desirable, and with the exception of the one big adjustable, I much prefer the spanners to be of the flat type. Apart from the flat set spanners being easy to carry, they do not round off the corners of the nuts. If a flat box holding the spanners is placed in the bottom of the car, it forms a useful footrest for the passenger.

When the owner contemplates either touring or trial work, careful and systematic attention to the details I have mentioned will considerably add to the pleasure and success of the undertaking, and obviate the necessity for carrying a small host of spares.

On the subject of trials, there is no reason for Morgan owners to avoid the big events on account of their magnitude, as it has been my experience, especially in the open trials, that much of the pleasure derived from this particular kind of sport is due to the able management and good feeling which exist all round, together with the assurance that a sporting chance is guaranteed.

But I would mention, as a personal experience, that it is wise to discriminate in the choice of both your passenger and your gears, as each means much towards the success of your efforts, and on each depends, to a large extent, your enjoyment.

Care and Maintenance of Popular Machines

The 1,096 c.c. o.h.v. J.A.P.=engined "Aero" Morgan.

By "UBIQUE."

THERE are some who seem to think that the coach-built body of the Morgan conceals a mass of inaccessible complications, and that in consequence they would be unable to maintain or overhaul such a vehicle without expert assistance.

Far from this being the case, the modern Morgan is almost the simplest possible form of mechanical conveyance for two (or, in the case of certain models, more than two).

Early Attention Pays.

Though this article deals specifically with the water-cooled, overhead-valve J.A.P.-engined Aero model, the remarks which concern the components other than engine parts are applicable to practically all comparatively recent Morgan models.

A good machine is worthy of a little extra attention in the early stages of its life, and well repays such trouble. The treatment needed by the Morgan is very similar to that of a motor cycle. Never drive hard for the first five hundred miles, add a little oil to the fuel during this period, check the tappet adjustment frequently, do not forget to grease and oil all parts regularly, and use a liberal oil setting for "running-in." These are the golden rules, and they need but little amplification.

Tappet adjustment is important. The instruction book recommends a clearance of 2/1000in., but if the adjustment is set so that there is no per-

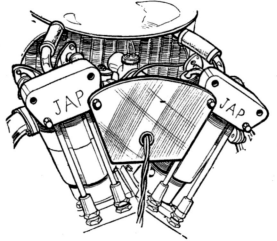

A shield attached to the rocker covers will protect the carburetter and inlet pipe from cold air.

ceptible play between the rocker and valve stem cap, though the hardened valve stem cap can be rotated freely, all will be well. This setting must be carried out with the engine cold.

Engine oil, frequently applied, forms the best lubrication for the rocker ball-end cups, though a light grease is moderately satisfactory and lasts longer.

A Push=rod Hint.

If a ball-end cup should become quite loose on the push-rod tube, the tube may be tinned and the cup pushed *right home* while the solder is still soft. The cups are only a good push fit when new, so there is no need for tinning unless the fit becomes really "sloppy." The rocker bearings are fitted with grease nipples, which should be kept well filled.

The magneto should be timed in such a way that the contact breaker points begin to separate on the appropriate cam when the piston of one cylinder is 7/16in. before the top of the compression stroke, with the control fully advanced. This advance may be increased to 9/16in., though such a setting will involve an intelligent use of the spark control lever.

The engine is remarkably free from "pinking," and any normal plug will stand up to road conditions; in fact, a moderately priced plug with comparatively light electrodes may prove more satisfactory than a "hot-stuff" plug, as it is less likely to oil up.

This raises the question of lubrication, and it is amazing

Care and Maintenance of Popular Machines.—how little oil is required by the big engine.

After the process of running-in has been completed, the sight-feed may be adjusted to give about fifteen drops per minute, and this will prove ample for road work unless very high speeds are being indulged in. If the feed is very much in excess of this there will be a tendency for the off-side cylinder (corresponding to the rear cylinder in the case of a motor cycle) to oil its plug when the engine is running slowly.

If there is a tendency for the sight-feed to fill, the trouble may be cured in a very simple manner. Screw up the ring which retains the glass until it is just nicely tight, and then unscrew it a quarter-turn. In this position drill a small hole (not larger than 1/16in.) right through the rim of the cap and the body of the sight feed; then carefully remove burrs and retighten the cap. Any tendency to choke can then be cured by turning the cap till the holes register, though no oil will flow from the tank until the cap is again tightened.

A careful owner will decarbonise his engine for the first time after about 1,000 miles of gentle work. Thereafter the heads may be inspected as a precaution at 3,000 - mile intervals, though much greater mileages are possible owing to the cool running of the engine and the small amount of oil required.

Decarbonising.

Before starting the process of decarbonisation the owner should decide whether or not he wishes to inspect the pistons. If he decides to do so, he will probably find that it is most convenient to remove the whole engine from the frame. This process is not absolutely necessary, as all the cylinder nuts can be reached with the spanners supplied, after the removal of the carburetter and oil pipes, but it is so simple that it may prove to be the most convenient method. It is only necessary to disconnect the petrol, oil and water connections, remove the pivot pin of the clutch-withdrawal fork, and undo the four set bolts which hold the engine to the

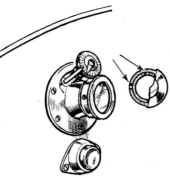

A simple method of overcoming flooding of the sight feed glass.

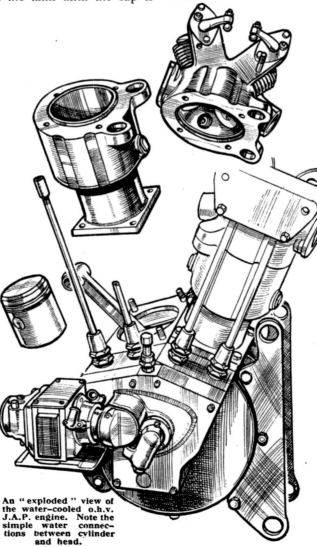

An "exploded" view of the water-cooled o.h.v. J.A.P. engine. Note the simple water connections between cylinder and head.

frame. The whole engine and clutch unit may then be withdrawn forward and placed on the bench. There are no "snags" about either removal or replacement, except that the unit is heavy and four hands are, therefore, better than two. The square on the propeller-shaft must, of course, be set to register with the square hole in the clutch.

Before removing the cylinder heads obtain spare gaskets, but if these are not to hand they are easily cut from thin fabric packing material; there are only two water connections, and these are well away from the bore of the cylinder. It is wise to use gold-size or other good jointing medium on both sides of the gasket.

Cylinder Head Removal.

Four bolts hold each cylinder head in position; in the latest models the two front bolts are extended upwards for greater accessibility; if the earlier short type are fitted they can be replaced by the new type, obtainable from the makers of the engine. To start the short bolts it is advisable to remove the lower bolts holding the rocker bearing side plates, as this will leave more room for the spanner.

Having removed all four bolts, obtain a flat steel strip tapered to form a wedge (an old flat file ground down is admirable) and drive it gently into the gasket; this will loosen the head joint so that the head can be lifted off. Carefully plug the holes which receive the head holding-down bolts, as dirt in these holes will cause the bolts to bottom and thus preclude a sound joint.

Decarbonisation follows normal practice, and needs no detailed description. The valves can be removed easily with the special tool supplied if they are held on their seats by a block of wood placed in the hemispherical head. The cylinders may be removed and the pistons examined for high spots. Any such spots may be eased by a touch with a very smooth file; never use emery or any abrasive cloth or powder. The correct piston ring gap is 10/1,000in. to 12/1,000in. with the ring in the cylinder.

Care and Maintenance of Popular Machines.—

When reassembling the engine make certain that all parts are scrupulously clean and have a film of clean oil over the working surfaces. The inlet pipe must be erected with care, and the nuts pulled well home on the taper metal gland packings. If these packings have been damaged they should be replaced, otherwise air leaks will occur, which will result in poor slow running. Any tendency for the carburetter to "freeze" in cold weather may be cured by fitting a metal shield in front of the instrument.

Morgan clutch springs seldom, if ever, require adjustment; in fact, if they should become weak it is better to replace them with new ones. The clutch, however, is apt to become fierce unless it receives proper attention. A grease nipple is fitted in the flywheel rim for lubrication of the fabric cone, but by far the best and most lasting method of ensuring smooth engagement is to squirt a liberal dose of oil into the clutch cover. This may sound rather drastic, but if all is in order the oil will not cause slip, and, if a good dose is applied, the metal clutch cover will retain it for a long time.

Removing the Body.

If any major operation on the gear box becomes necessary (a most unlikely event) the body must be removed—a tiresome performance, but not a difficult one. The procedure is as follows: First remove the two securing bolts, one on each side of the gear box (under the tail) and the two U-clips on the front cross tube. Then remove the fabric floor cover under the propeller-shaft tube; it is held down by tacks. Take off the head lamps, mudguards, silencers, starting handle bracket, and change-speed rod. Disconnect the steering arm from the squared end of the column, the pedal connections (top end), speedometer cable, and dynamo leads.

When replacing these dynamo leads remember that the red lead goes to the terminal marked "1" or " +," the green lead to "2," and the black to "4."

The body can then be slid forward to clear the brake lever bracket, and lifted clear. The assistance of at least three persons is desirable for this operation in order to avoid damage to the paintwork. The very simple chassis is now revealed, and the most drastic overhaul can be carried out with ease.

The gear box contains nothing but a pair of spiral bevels, the mesh of which is adjusted at the works and cannot be altered by an amateur. If, however, an owner should desire to remove " the insides," he should proceed as follows Remove the striking forks and outer dog clutches; this will expose a spring circlip on each side, which retains the sprocket through a short distance

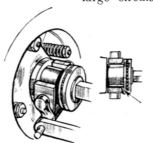

If the clutch withdrawal fork is dismantled, the radiused edge of the fibre blocks must be assembled next to the withdrawal thrust race.

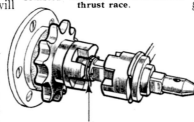

To remove a sprocket it is necessary to detach the outer dog and striking fork and to prise off a spring circlip.

The rear fork pivot pins are held in the gear box by a long central bolt and are tapered into their sockets.

piece. Extract these clips, and the sprockets can be slid off the shaft. The shaft may now be driven out towards the off side of the machine.

If the body is removed, the opportunity should be seized for an inspection of the rear fork pivot pins These pins fit in long, tapered holes on either side of the gear box casting, and are held in position by a long bolt passing right through the centre of both pins. In order to take the compression strain of this bolt there is spigoted into the back of the gear box casing a large circular steel inspection cover, the diameter of which bridges the inner ends of the pin bosses. Grease nipples are fitted to the fork-end to lubricate these pins, but if wear takes place there is no adjustment. It is, however, quite an easy matter to fit over-size pins (which can be supplied), since, after the central fixing bolt has been removed, the old pins can be knocked out and new ones substituted.

The standard gear ratios are $4\frac{1}{2}$ to 1 and $8\frac{1}{8}$ to 1, and with these in use the two driving chains have exactly the same number of links. Therefore, if the high gear chain shows signs of stretch owing to constant use, it should be exchanged with the low gear one until the wear has evened up. By this means and by the chain adjusters it is possible to keep both chains properly tensioned at all times.

Adjustment of Dampers.

If friction shock dampers are fitted to the rear forks, they should not be over-tightened, or undue stress will be thrown on the front of the gear box.

Both rear springs are carried on angle-steel cross-members attached to the gear box, and the attachment bolts must be kept tightened well home.

The front wheels are, of course independently sprung. The steering tie-rod is adjustable for length and the wheels should " toe in " a the front from 1/8in. to 1/4in.

At each end the tie-rod is attache to the steering arms by special bolt with spring-loaded conical seatings These must not be lubricated, as they form steering dampers without which wheel wobble is liable to occur

After prolonged use the bronze slides to which the wheels are attached may develop play. They slide on tubular supports, and either or both are easily replaced. First remove the wheel spindle and steering arm by undoing one large nut, then slacken the front diagonal frame tie-bar and castellated nut below the steering head. Take off the front mudguard and pull the front stay right out in an upward direction. Now spring the front axle tubes slightly apart, and the springs, supporting tubes, and slide can all be removed.

The replacement of these parts is quite simple, though it is advisable to make sure that the support tubes fit

Care and Maintenance of Popular Machines.

into the recesses in the axle ends, and that the front brake stop meshes with its squared boss.

Keep all exposed working parts well lubricated; to reach the countershaft, dogs, and striking forks, a force-feed oil gun that will throw a good jet of oil is almost essential, and it is a good plan to keep such a gun held to the dashboard in spring clips. Put a drop of oil on the rear spring shackles where they lie alongside the fork-ends, and

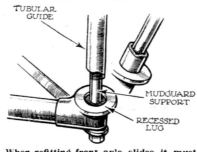

When refitting front axle slides it must be ascertained that the tubular guide is seating in the recessed lugs at both top and bottom.

do not forget to grease the front spring slides and rear fork pivots frequently. The geared steering should be greased at the same time, and a few drops of oil fed to the lower steering column bearing through the hole in the front aluminium apron.

On very cold nights do not be content with opening the radiator drain tap, but take out the plugs at the base of each cylinder jacket, or, better still, fit good taps in each plug, and so obviate all possibility of trouble.

The MotorCycle

THE CHARM of the THREE-WHEELER

MANY people have expressed the opinion that the possibilities of the three-wheeler have not been anything like fully exploited, and as a thorough-going three-wheeler enthusiast, I agree. There also seems to be a slight prejudice against the three-wheeler—a prejudice based on ignorance as to the characteristics of the modern cyclecar of this type.

Curiously enough, whenever I have championed the cause of the three-wheeler in the presence of car drivers and keen motor cyclists, somebody has always managed to say, "Yes, but three-wheeled cars are liable to overturn." It generally transpired that the statement was either the result of lack of knowledge or was founded on some experience before the War. During the past five years, four different types of three-wheeled cars have adorned my garage. My mileage in them has been considerable, and sometimes my driving has been hectic, but not one of them has shown the slightest inclination to misbehave itself on the road.

Only recently I concluded a thousand-mile trip with an "Aero" Morgan, and although the roads were often greasy, the little car did not skid. Front wheel brakes have, of course, made three-wheelers much more stable in this respect.

Adequate Weather Protection.

When I drag out these facts, I find myself confronted with the argument, "Exactly; but then you have the happy knack of handling three-wheelers." However flattering this sort of remark may sound, it simply is not true. There is nothing extraordinary about driving a three-wheeler.

Many motor cyclists, for various reasons, long for really adequate protection from the weather, but are not prepared to give up the thrill of motor cycling in order to achieve their end. That was exactly my position when I bought an old "Grand Prix" Morgan. After all, the average man with the average sort of job does not get a particularly large amount of leisure time. On several occasions after a tedious day's work I have longed to burn up a few miles, but the prospect of an entire change of clothing before wheeling the bus out

Cycle cars with the Performance and "Life" of a Motor Cycle.
By "NORSEMAN."

of the garage has proved too much. One of the outstanding advantages of the three-wheeler is that it is not necessary to don special clothing. One can enjoy a couple of hours on the road and then go straight to the office or to the theatre. The argument is often forward that a car is a valuable adjunct to sports such as tennis, cricket or golf. Here, again, the three-wheeler is particularly useful.

I must confess that for me the charm of the three-wheeler lies in its "sportiness." Even the ordinary tourer with, say, a 980 c.c. side-valve J.A.P. engine is fast enough to hold its own on the road, but a low-built sports model with an overhead-valve engine can put up a most exhilarating performance. Some criticism is often levelled against the low-built three-wheeler simply on account of its lowness, but in actual practice one soon gets used to "being near the ground." The "Aero" Morgan, for example, is delightful to handle at all speeds and quite good when the going is rough.

However, it is not my intention to put forward the claims of three-wheelers simply on account of their sporting possibilities, but as thoroughly good vehicles for touring. A soundly designed three-wheeler does definitely give car comfort, and it is a really "sociable" vehicle. Another advantage is that a young child can be properly accommodated during a tour. Also, quite a reasonable amount of luggage can be carried even on the sports type if a little ingenuity is used.

Need for Reverse Gears.

On each one of the three-wheelers I have owned I have undertaken journeys of nearly three hundred miles, and never have I felt any undue fatigue. In the case of two of them I fitted a foot accelerator, which was of great assistance in this direction.

The general handiness of these cars is an important factor, although it must be admitted that, to be ideal, a three-wheeler should have a reverse gear. However, it is certainly not worth any sacrifice of simplicity just to be able to reverse.

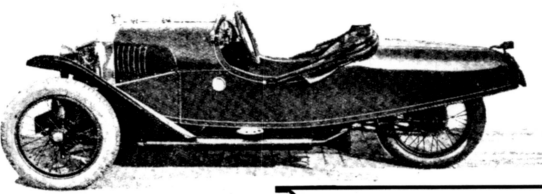

Two Thousand Miles with a Speedy Three = wheeler — the 1,100 c.c. "Aero" Morgan.

By "UBIQUE."

WHEN first I announced my intention of purchasing a three-wheeler I was the recipient of much good-natured chaff. Motor cycling friends began to speculate (aloud) upon my increasing and to make unkind remarks about th eed of a third wheel to keep me up in greasy weather.

In spite of this, I persisted, and when a racy dark blue "Aero" Morgan was at last revealed to their eyes these friends began to wonder if, after all, there was not something to be said in favour of my third wheel. It was not a family model, as they had pretended to expect, for excellent as these true utility machines are, I wanted something with rather more sporting lines, and, above all, a vehicle that would give me speed and acceleration comparable with that of a sports motor cycle. In this I have not been disappointed, and, as a matter of fact, my latest acquisition is faster than the majority of two-wheelers which I have possessed.

Luck was with me, for the manufacturers had managed to spare me a super-sports 1,100 c.c. overhead-valve J.A.P. engine with polished ports, high compression, and high-lift valves, and in its test stages the machine lapped Brooklands at well over the seventy mark.

A Perfect Little Lady.

I was not accustomed to three-wheelers and had been crammed with horrible tales relating to the ease with which they were upset. Therefore, for some hundreds of miles during the running-in period, I treated *Mabel* (the heroine of this story) with the utmost respect. Fortunately, she proved to be a perfect little lady, and would behave as such in traffic or at modest road speeds. A snatchless twelve miles an hour on top gear (4.5 to 1) is a simple task for the big engine, and from this speed *Mabel* will shoot away without any fuss or pinking; indeed, if the clutch be kept in proper order and used with discretion the Morgan is, to all intents and purposes, a one-gear machine.

An "Aero" in Action

Now, about this clutch, which first of all gave me some worry. It has a fabric-faced conical driving surface, and if it is allowed to get dry it becomes most unpleasantly fierce. On the outside of the flywheel is a nipple through which grease can be injected on to the clutch surface, though only if the clutch pedal is depressed at the time. As this involved the calling-in of a helper, who was not always available, I shaped a piece of wood so that it could be wedged between the pedal and the front of the seat to fix the clutch in the "out" position for the duration of the greasing period. This system worked well, but the grease smelt horribly when the clutch was slipped, and the effect of each application did not last long. I therefore consulted the manufacturers, who supplied a far more simple and effective hint. All that is required is a force-feed oil gun with which to inject a good healthy dose of engine oil into the clutch. The oil is retained by the flywheel back-plate and the clutch will remain delightfully smooth in action for long periods. So much for the clutch; now let us get back to the road.

I very soon found that these tales of upsets were either founded on some myth or on the sins of some type of three-wheeler other than the modern Morgan Aero model. I daresay that it *is* possible to turn one

104

over; but I have seen more than one four-wheeled car upside down. It may even be possible that an Aero will turn over more easily than a car. I don't know; I have never tried. But this I do know—if only a reasonable amount of care is exercised the Aero can be cornered at really high speeds without so much as a wheel lifting an inch. If the rear brake is jammed on when traversing greasy tram lines the machine will skid; so will a motor cycle, so will a car. But the cure is simple: use the front brakes, which are excellent. Here I would solemnly advise purchasers of Aero Morgans to make a habit of using the front wheel brakes; the lever is conveniently placed, the habit is easily acquired, and there is far less liability to skid the machine. These brakes will just stop the bus on a gradient of 1 in 7. and the foot brake will lock the rear wheel if applied with sufficient force. At a fairly

"... this most exciting three - wheeler."

The "Aero" Morgan toying with the gradient of Sunrising.

early stage in *Mabel's* career, my son, who is at the age when speed counts most, expressed a desire to travel fast. He came for a run with me, and even *his* speed lust was temporarily satisfied. I will not attempt to state the figure registered by the speedometer needle, which was still curving pleasantly round the dial when road conditions entailed deceleration, but one of the charms of the Morgan Aero is that it feels even faster than it is. This is brought about by the seating position, which is so low that it is possible to touch the ground by holding one's hand over the side of the body; the result is that speeds over the sixty mark provide a delightful sensation of record-breaking velocity; and 60 m.p.h. is child's play to *Mabel's* engine, and can be attained amazingly quickly.

Mabel on "Edge."

On that same run I thought it would be interesting to see how the machine behaved on a gradient, so as Edge Hill was handy we turned in that direction. We reached the hill, opened out, the result was astounding—Edge, with its 1 in 7 gradient, simply disappeared. The matter of changing down never entered my mind, which was only occupied with slowing down sufficiently to take the bends in safety. Having taken the last bend at a modest touring speed, I opened throttle rather further, but not fully, and *Mabel* accelerated rapidly on the last and steepest slope, the speedometer registering 38 m.p.h. and still

An " Aero " in Action.—
rising. I have never had cause to try the machine on freak hills, but I am convinced that nothing would stop her provided that wheel grip is obtainable; I have yet to be brought to the low gear by gradient alone.

When *Mabel* was delivered she managed to pick up a nail from the road, with the result that the rear tyre was flat next morning. As it happened, I had an idle Saturday afternoon, and this gave me the opportunity of tackling the job in a leisurely fashion. An inspection of the tread did not reveal the cause of the puncture, so I decided to remove the wheel just to see how it was done. A jack under the front end of the rear fork raised the wheel in a jiffy, and the rear brake band was disconnected from its operating lever and the anchor pin removed. All was then plane-sailing, and the wheel was removed in a few minutes without the necessity for disconnecting either chain. As straight-sided tyres are fitted to my machine the tube was easily removed and repaired. Then started the job of wheel replacement. The chains were slipped on to the sprockets and the pair of rather long arms which I possess enabled me to lift the wheel into its forks from above, but when next I tackle the job I rather fancy that it will be easier to sit down and lift from below.

The cockpit of " Ubique's " Morgan.

Attention to the Chains.

Being a careless person, I gave no attention to the chains other than an occasional dose of oil from the outside. This probably accounts for the fact that at the end of 2,000 miles the high-gear chain showed a considerable extension from the normal, owing to wear in the rivets Both chains have the same number of links, so they may be interchanged, and wear, therefore, equalised; if it becomes necessary to fit a new chain it is desirable, though not essential, to replace both, otherwise it may prove difficult to keep them in approximately correct adjustment.

During the 2 000 miles I have covered with *Mabel* our only involuntary road stops have been due to sooted plugs; it took me some time to realise that the engine runs so coolly that racing type plugs are unnecessary and that the oil supply can be cut down to a rate of only about fifteen drops per minute, which seems ridiculously inadequate for such a big engine. Plug trouble has now vanished, yet the engine is lubricated quite satisfactorily.

Starting has always been an easy matter, even in cold weather, but in winter the carburetter is apt to freeze up, causing poor and uneconomical slow running and sometimes a rather disconcerting freezing-open of the throttle valve. A shield between the cylinders, fixed to the nuts which secure the rocker covers, has overcome the trouble in *Mabel's* case, and is well worth the slight expense entailed.

I don't grudge a little time spent on tappet adjustment. The correct clearance is a rather tight " two thou.," all round, and if this is maintained the engine will tick over nicely and hold its tune well.

When this super-sports engine was first fitted to the Aero model (I believe I have the first) it was in the nature of experiment, and the balance was not quite perfect. The effect of this was to bring about an unpleasant vibratory period between 50 and 60 m.p.h. The fault was corrected on later engines, but though the manufacturers offered to rectify matters in my engine I. put up with things as they were for a long time; it is only recently that *Iabel* returned to her home for re-balancing. The result has been satisfactory, though there is still a vibration period between the figures mentioned: it resembles propeller-shaft whirl.

Endless Power in Reserve.

In normal circumstances I do not drive very fast, but it is pleasant to be able to maintain or even to exceed a good round touring speed on any hill with a reasonable surface, and the sensation of endless power in reserve has a charm which must be experienced before it can be realised

I have owned more than one modern sports motor cycle, but I have no hesitation in claiming that the all-round performance of the Aero Morgan compares favourably with that of the majority of two-wheelers. *Mabel* has, then, the performance of a good motor cycle with—well, no, not quite—the comfort of a car; though the wheels are independently sprung a three-tracker is bound to get some of the bumps which could be avoided with two tracks.

As regards comfort, I have fitted B. & D. shock absorbers to the rear forks with most satisfactory results, and more recently Newton dampers have been added to the front springing. These have made a wonderful difference to the comfort and road-holding.

I have never regretted my choice of machine. The joy of a high power-weight ratio and the instant surge of power when the throttle is opened, even when one is travelling at 45 or 50 m.p.h., provide a fascination which never fails.

Cyclecar Comments

BY SHACKLEPIN

CHECKING WEAR IN MORGAN SLIDING AXLES — REMOVING AND REFITTING THE AXLES — SPECIAL POINTS RELATING TO GEARED STEERING.

LAST week I dealt fully with the universal joints and track-rod pins of the Morgan steering. We can now turn our attention to the methods of checking play in the front wheels and sliding axles.

Jack up each front wheel in turn, and, holding the wheels at the top, pull and push sideways. A little movement here may be ignored, but if the amount seems at all excessive, attention is called for at some point in the locality. Having made certain that it is not the wheel bearings themselves which are in need of adjustment, see to it that the front spindle is not loose in the sliding axle. The special tongued or "star" washer—the three tongues of which should embrace the flats of the nut holding the spindle in the sliding axle—serves the very useful purpose of keeping this nut tight, but if it should have been left off, or if the tongues are not doing their job, the nut will almost certainly work loose in time, and this may lead to unpleasant results.

* * *

Having passed this point, the remaining possible source of trouble lies in the phosphor-bronze sliding axles themselves being worn. These are renewable at a cost of 10s. each, and while the job is in hand it is as well to fit new sliding-axle tubes, which are quite cheap. I have known cases where sliding axles have been bored out for a short distance each end and steel bushes inserted, with fairly satisfactory results, in spite of the fact that, in theory, steel running on steel is not to be recommended.

* * *

The top ends of the sliding axles seldom wear quite so rapidly as at the bottom, and if the axle tube is a fairly good fit here, there will be no need to bush the sliding portion at the top.

In order to remove a sliding axle, raise the front wheel from the ground with the jack (or a box), preferably under one of the middle lugs on the lower chassis cross-tube,

just behind the crankcase bottom. Disconnect the front-brake cable, if any, remove the front-spindle nut and, with a hide-faced or lead hammer, give the threaded end of the spindle a few heavy blows, when, complete with the front wheel, it should leave the sliding axle. Slack off, but do not remove, both nuts holding the chassis tie-rod, remove the wing, then the split-pin and nut at the bottom of the wing stay, when the latter may be withdrawn. Now, by lightly pressing the lower chassis tube downwards the sliding axle may be removed complete with its tube and springs.

* * *

As these springs usually have a tendency to fly in undesired directions it is a good tip to secure the bottom one to the sliding axle with a piece of stout wire passed through one of the coils and up to the hole where the wheel spindle normally fits. If the sliding axle is then pulled away bottom first the top spring will have no tendency to fly.

Reassembly calls for no special instruction, being merely a reversal of the foregoing proceedings in the main, but it will be found that wrestling to get the complete sliding axle back into position between the upper and lower chassis cross-tubes is made easier if the bottom end is put in first, making sure the sliding axle tube is properly located in the recess in the chassis lug.

* * *

Broadly speaking, there are only two types of geared steering found on Morgans. First, there is the maker's set, which gives a reduction of 2 to 1 between the steering and road wheels. The reduction gearbox is located a foot or so below the steering wheel, and beyond occasional greasing—a grease-gun nipple is fitted—calls for little attention. Any undue backlash in the gears may be felt on the steering wheel, and if it is desired to take this up all that is necessary is to remove the three 3/16-in. hexagon-headed setscrews

which hold the upper portion of the steering column to the box.

This upper portion may then be turned by hand when, as the driving and driven wheels are eccentrically mounted in relation to one another, the teeth may be more deeply engaged. As a rough guide, it is safe to turn round the column by hand until it feels somewhat stiff. It is impossible absolutely to take up all steering-wheel play where geared steering is fitted, and in any event a little backlash in the steering box will not be responsible for wobble at the road wheels.

* * *

No difficulty will be experienced in starting the three setscrews in their threads, as there will be found a number of suitable holes drilled round the flange of the steering-column boss, and it is always possible to find three of these registering with the three threaded holes in the reduction box itself.

This system of steering, it may here be pointed out, gives either a "high" or "low" steering-wheel position. That is to say, the column does not run into the centre of the steering-box cover but meets it at one end. Therefore, assuming the wheel is now in the high position and it is desired to lower it, all that is necessary is to remove the four bolts which hold on the cover, and replace it with the erstwhile top edge, now at the bottom of the reduction box. In doing this job it is not necessary to undo any other fittings.

* * *

The other form of reduced steering, which, incidentally, is not fitted by the manufacturers of the Morgan, is usually an adaptation from a well-known American car. The ratio between the steering and road wheels is 4 to 1, and, owing to the comparatively large amount of travel which the steering wheel has to pass through with this gearing, it is almost essential to have a foot accelerator fitted, because the Bowden wires of the normal controls are apt to be "wound up."

CYCLECAR COMMENTS

By "SHACKLEPIN."

Mrs. Stewart and Mr. Douglas Hawkes with their record-breaking Morgan at Montlhery.

Full Account of Mrs. Stewart's Record-breaking Successes in a Morgan— 101.55 Miles in the Hour.

THE remarkable series of record-breaking runs which have been made recently at the Montlhéry track by Mrs. Stewart in her Morgan have created considerable interest in the cyclecar world. It occurred to me, therefore, that a description of the machine and some remarks about the record-breaking attempts would be well received by my readers; accordingly I got into touch with Mr. W. Douglas Hawkes, who has been responsible for the preparation of the machine and for the general supervision of the attempts, asking him to let me have a few details. His remarks are as follow:—

* * *

"At the beginning of this season I was asked by Mrs. Stewart, who has done a large amount of racing in three-wheeled and four-wheeled vehicles, if I would prepare a three-wheeler with which it would be possible to cover a hundred miles in one hour. As I could not see any good reason why this should not be done, I promised to undertake the task and to set about finding a suitable machine.

I chose a sports model Morgan, fitted with a 998 c.c. air-cooled sports-type J.A.P. engine, and started preparing both machine and engine with extreme care, as reliability was my first consideration.

As Mrs. Stewart had not had very much experience of really high speeds in three-wheelers, although she had lapped the Montlhéry track at over 120 m.p.h. in a Miller car, I thought that perhaps a little preliminary training might not come amiss. I, therefore, entered her for an attempt on the 5-kilometre and 5-mile records then held by a supercharged four-cylinder Sandford. She succeeded in lowering these records at over 103 m.p.h. Next I suggested that she should attack the existing hour record.

which stood at 91 m.p.h., as a preliminary canter for both driver and machine. The record was lowered at a speed of 95 m.p.h.

Having thus satisfied myself that both Mrs. Stewart and the Morgan were capable of the performance which we were about to attempt, I set to work in real earnest with the preparations. Knowing that I had more than the necessary speed available, I concentrated upon reliability. Both engine and chassis were completely stripped and every part was examined, renewals being made where necessary.

* * *

I decided to use a compression ratio of 7.25 to 1, and as high a gear ratio as the engine would pull, bearing in mind that it had to run at 4,500 r.p.m., for a lapping speed of 103 m.p.h. The fuel used was ordinary commercial alcohol, Castrol R. being used as the engine lubricant. Other accessories were Dunlop tyres, Lissen plugs, M.L. magneto, Coventry chains and Amal carburetter. The tyres, incidentally, were the 27 in. by 4.20 in. track-racing variety.

A very careful schedule of running speed was then prepared according to which the 100 miles were not due to be completed until the end of the last lap necessary to make up the one hour's run; this was done so that the machine should never have to go faster than was necessary. However, racing managers propose and drivers dispose. In this case, Mrs. Stewart lapped consistently at 2/5ths to 3/5ths of a second faster than my elaborately worked out schedule, with the result that 101.55 miles were covered in the hour.

Apart from this, everything may be said to have worked according to plan; almost too exactly as it turned out, because as Mrs. Stewart crossed the line for the last time,

and was flagged off, the engine cut out. We, in the depot, thought that she had switched off voluntarily on receiving the "stop" signal, but we discovered afterwards that the fuel tank was bone dry. I certainly had not intended to work to limits as close as that!

* * *

When the engine was examined afterwards it was found to be in perfect condition, and so also was the rest of the machine. As a practical demonstration of this the same engine and machine four days later captured eight world's records, ranging from seven hours to twelve hours, at speeds varying from 66 m.p.h. to 68 m.p.h., thus proving conclusively that the Morgan was by no means a freak; in fact, the only secret of the tune was the hard work and attention to detail which had been given. Incidentally, when these records were lowered, a higher gear had been substituted together with smaller carburetters and a lower compression, whilst a small quantity of benzole was added to the alcohol.

The following details are interesting for purposes of comparison: for the 100 miles in the hour record the fuel consumption worked out at 15 m.p.g., whereas on the 12-hour run it was 36 m.p.g. This very great difference in consumption is accounted for by the use of large carburetters and undiluted alcohol in the 100-mile record.

* * *

The difference in tyre wear also was instructive. For the 100-mile record, as I have already stated, Dunlop 27 in. by 4.20 in. track-racing tyres were used, whilst in the long-distance records the same make and size of tyre was used but with road racing treads. In the former case there was very little rubber left on the back tyre, whilst the two front tyres were worn on one side, whereas in the long-distance records, although the machine had covered 800 miles as compared with 100, neither the rear nor the front tyres showed any signs of wear.

In conclusion, I should like to pay a special compliment to Mrs. Stewart and to the makers of the machine which allowed her with a 998 c.c. unsupercharged motorcycle-type engine to attain a speed only 1.69 m.p.h. slower than the 1,100 c.c. car hour-record, which was obtained with a supercharged four-cylinder engine of 1,099.5 c.c."

THE 10-40 H.P. AERO MORGAN

Impressions of the Latest Model With the "M" Type Chassis Over a Distance of 1,000 Miles —Fine Performance A Prominent Characteristic

AT A GLANCE.

ENGINE: *Two-cylinder V; bore, 85.7 mm.; stroke, 95 mm. (1,096 c.c.); Treasury rating, 10 h.p.; tax £4; mechanical lubrication with sight-feed; magneto ignition; motorcycle-type carburetter.*

TRANSMISSION: *Cone clutch, 2-speeds forward (countershaft) (ratios 4.5 and 8 to 1), right-hand control, enclosed propeller shaft to bevel box, final transmission by ¾-in. pitch interchangeable chains.*

SUSPENSION: *Front, independent vertical helical springs; rear, underslung quarter-elliptics; wire wheels; 27-in. × 4-in. tyres.*

DIMENSIONS: *Overall length, 10 ft. 3 ins.; overall width, 4 ft. 9 ins.*

PRICE: *£128 10s.*

MANUFACTURERS: *Morgan Motor Co., Ltd., Pickersleigh Road, Malvern Link, Worcester.*

THERE is and always has been something altogether delightful about a Morgan which defies definition, and when one sets out to put on paper impressions gained during a road test of 1,000 odd miles, difficulties arise immediately. There is, in the opinion of the writer, no independent standard with which the performance can be compared; a Morgan is a Morgan, and it can be compared with nothing else but another Morgan.

The model tested was an Aero with a racing o.h.v. J.A.P. engine fitted in the latest "M"-type chassis. For the benefit of those not acquainted with the new chassis it should be pointed out that the rear suspension is now underslung and a knock-out spindle allows for easy removal of the back wheel. The foot brake is of the internal-expanding type arranged inside the low-gear sprocket and operated by a flexible cable from the pedal. A further improvement is the re-designed bevel box with its two forged-steel wheel-supporting beams arranged co-axially with the countershaft.

With the new design it is possible to remove the whole of the rear mechanism, for the bevel box is now bolted to a flange at the end of the propeller shaft tube—the smaller bevel wheel shaft being mounted on ball bearings and coupled to the end of the propeller shaft. This improvement means that the wheelbase is shortened by some three inches, although the body dimensions remain unchanged. Furthermore, the propeller shaft is also shortened, and any tendency to whip at speed is minimized. In other respects the chassis is unaltered. Geared steering with a ratio of 2-1 has, of course, been a feature for some time now.

The racing J.A.P. engine is of improved design,

the valve gear having been altered considerably. The rockers and push-rods are totally enclosed, neat aluminium boxes being mounted on standards screwed into the cylinder heads. The rockers run on roller bearings and the rocker boxes have quickly detachable covers to facilitate tappet adjustment. Another engine modification is the simplification of the oil pump which is now much easier to dismantle.

As regards bodywork, the Aero body, with its squat bonnet, streamlined tail and flared wings, remains unchanged except that a very neat and efficient two-panel V-screen replaces the aeroplane-type adjustable shields used formerly.

So much for the refinements. As to performance—it is perhaps easier to say that it is typically "Morgan." Readers who have themselves driven these cyclecars will understand what is meant; those who have never sampled a Morgan have missed an interesting and instructive experience quite apart from the fun and thrills which only motoring in something "live" can give.

The Aero is built essentially for the sportsman. Family men, potterers and the really genuine he-speed-coveters are catered for with suitable Morgan models, but the Aero appeals to that vast crowd of young, moderately well-off people who have become tired of motorcycles and yet require a vehicle with that comforting feeling of a big reserve of power which only motorcycles, very high-priced sports cars and three-wheeled cyclecars can give.

The most noticeable characteristic of the new Morgan —after the driver has recovered from the shock of the tremendous acceleration available—is the greatly improved stability and springing. There was a time when the charges of top-heaviness and a tendency to overturn on corners were levelled against these three-wheelers. In the early days there was perhaps some small justification, for the first Morgans were much higher and narrower of track. Driver and passenger used to sit over the bevel box and, furthermore, high-pressure tyres did not make things any steadier.

During the past few years, however, the chassis has been lowered, the track widened, and the seating accommodation re-arranged; these alterations, together with the fitting of low-pressure tyres, have made the Morgan one of the steadiest high-speed vehicles on the roads.

The ease and safety with which fast cornering can be indulged in has to be experienced to be believed, whilst the machine's stability at speed over bad roads is almost uncanny.

Really shock-free suspension is not expected of a sports car, and Morgan springing is certainly not what is usual on a touring car, but nevertheless the new chassis reveals a great improvement and quite long journeys can be accomplished at high average speeds without either driver or passenger suffering any more fatigue than is natural when concentration and a constant alertness are necessary.

Ample Leg-room.

The pneumatic cushions and a well-padded squab are most comfortable, and there is ample leg-room for tall people—in fact, a driver of 5 ft. 9 ins. found it advantageous to put an extra cushion behind his back to enable him to reach the brake and clutch pedals more easily.

The V-screen gave quite adequate protection, whilst the hood can be very quickly erected and forms a good roof with plenty of head-room. No sidescreens are supplied, but it was found that little rain blew in.

The 2-1 geared steering, whilst being a little on the heavy side at slow speeds, was just right for the job when travelling fast. It would be interesting to try, however, a 3-1 reduction in order to learn if the high-speed-handling qualities would be marred by a ratio which would give greater ease of manœuvrability in traffic and at low speeds.

The adoption of such a ratio would, of course, necessitate the use of an accelerator pedal—a fitting, incidentally, which it is thought would really be more useful and greatly appreciated. With the lever controls now used it was found somewhat confusing when the wheels were on full lock and the location of the levers changed either to top or bottom dead centre of the steering wheel. Furthermore, a foot accelerator would enable drivers to make much neater gear changes.

Another small point which would also help towards quicker and more accurate changes would be the arrangement of the gear lever in a central position.

These are, however, the only criticisms which need be made. In other respects the Morgan tested was in every way a wonderfully pleasant vehicle, and it says much for its appeal that not only was it used on every possible occasion—even on wet days, when a saloon car was available—but also that the number of interested and sometimes sceptical acquaintances who openly "cadged" for joy rides was most surprising.

Sceptics Convinced.

The sceptics were without exception convinced when the capabilities of the machine had been demonstrated to them. Few enthusiastic motorists can find it in their hearts to withhold praise for a machine which merits it, and if ever a 10 h.p. 1,100 c.c. two-seater car possessed a meritorious performance it is the Morgan. The manner in which the model whisked its way up hills, always with an ample reserve of power for sudden acceleration, was most impressive, whilst suitable "straights" on which the throttle could be opened wide were few and far between.

On the other hand, from a vital pulsing "75" the J.A.P. can be throttled down to a sedate, sweet-running tick-over, the 8-1 bottom gear ratio being ideal for traffic. The slow-running capabilities are most creditable—few fast engines will revolve as slowly and steadily as a well-balanced "twin." The foot-brake was sufficiently powerful at moderate speeds to bring about good retardation, and at high speeds the front-wheel brakes could be relied upon.

The equipment includes the customary electric control panel—with ammeter—horn switch, oil sight-feed, a magnetic speedometer on the stippled aluminium facia-board and coco-nut mats on the floorboards. The six-volt electrical system incorporates a dynamo positively driven from the countershaft, three lamps, and a battery which is stored in a locker behind the seat squab. The chassis of the model tested is black, and the body dark red cellulose with white lines—a most attractive vehicle.

FOR SPEED WITH ECONOMY.

Externally, the 1930 Aero Morgan differs little from its immediate predecessors, an improved screen and hood being the only important alteration. The model tested had the latest "M" type chassis which represents a considerable advance.

Acceleration—and an Aero— give-and-take roads. Of course, if you're going to thrash the model up the Great North Road from London in time for lunch at Newark, then the vehicle with a cruising maximum of 65 to 70 m.p.h. is going to score heavily. But how often, under modern road conditions, is it possible to get really clear stretches

"The tricycle (as the licensing authorities so vilely dub it) . . ."

where such speeds can be held? I am not one of those who hold that these speeds are impossible anywhere, but they are mostly impracticable unless you have such a crashing acceleration that you get up to them quickly.

Apropos this maximum speed question, I was told an interesting thing the other day. In America, since the roads have been nicely saturated with the new Ford (American brand—with a large engine), the speed of traffic has gone up ten miles an hour simply and solely because the new Fords cruise at a speed just about ten miles per hour faster than the flivvers used to do. That, however, does not affect the general trend of argument.

Finally, in the course of, I suppose, as little as seven years' riding, I have discovered that acceleration will get you out of at least 35 per cent. of your narrow scrapes on the roads. So many people, when things do not go as they had planned, stamp hard on the brake, while a spot of judicious acceleration would have got them through nicely.

But you must have *confidence* in the acceleration when you really want it; perhaps you're overtaking something gently and you find things are crowding

up, then it is only safe to accelerate if you *know* you can beat the car even if the driver happens, at the same time, to put his foot down. Once or twice I have known perfectly well that I couldn't stop in time with any degree of certainty, but that I could accelerate through the gap with plenty of time to spare.

Returning to the Aero, I must confess that to some extent it has spoilt me for anything else. I have become, in fact, something of a Morgan fanatic, and I am selling it before the symptoms are any worse.

It is hard to explain its charm. It is less comfortable than a car, a little more comfortable than a motor cycle, it has some degree of weather protection (though it is difficult to look through the screen in rain, and when it's heavy it comes through the odd spaces), it handles very easily when you have become accustomed to the rather heavy steering, it shoots away at a touch of the throttle like one of Mr. Brock's super-sports rockets. . But none of that seems to explain it.

". . . sitting low down . . . you feel as if you are handling something rather Brooklands."

Perhaps it is because, sitting low down, with the wheel in your lap and with everything handily placed, you feel as if you are handling something rather Brooklands. Cornering is a real thrill, and the regular use of the hand-brake savours rather of the good old motor racing days.

I don't know. Certainly, at a little over a hundred pounds you get the sort of thrill that is only obtainable at the wheel of a thoroughbred sports four-wheeler costing quite a lot more money.

SARTOR.

COMPETITORS in the Motor Cycling Club's classic 24-hour trials—the London-Exeter, the London-Land's End and the London-Edinburgh—if they are fortunate enough to qualify for a gold medal in the three events in one season, can compound their three gold medals and instead receive a "Triple Award." This, naturally, is a coveted trophy amongst members of the club.

How I should value such an award, the writer thought at the time of the last Show, if it could be captured on the three classes of vehicle, a solo motor-cycle in the London-Exeter, a three-wheeler in the London-Land's End, and a four-wheeler in the London-Edinburgh.

Stage 1 happily was successful, but stage 2 at the time of writing is still in doubt. Whatever award may result from it, however, and no matter what stage 3 may bring forth, this year's London-Land's End trial will never be forgotten.

As the illustrations show, No. 117's chosen mount for the three-wheeler attempt was one of the very latest Morgan Super-sports models, a romantic racy low-built little beauty in battleship grey and scarlet. The dearest of the Morgan models, it costs, with full equipment, including an electric starter, £153. The refinement of an electric starter—which works extremely well, by the way—puts £8 on to the price of the cyclecar.

New Mechanical Features.

When the model was first taken over its various new features were viewed with great approval. Notable amongst them, of course, is the detachable rear portion of the frame, which is exceedingly robust, convenient and accessible. It provides easy chain adjustment, a much-improved method of supporting the back wheel, a silent adjustable bevel drive, a two-piece propeller shaft entirely free from whip and very easy access to the dog clutches and other parts needing lubrication. Further, it ensures definitely that the chain tension is always constant and unaffected by the action of the springs.

We made our way 45 miles to Virginia Water, the starting point of this year's London-Land's End trial, in torrents of rain, but in the best of spirits. The little machine behaved perfectly on the greasy roads, giving no anxiety concerning skidding and the great nobbly tyre on the back wheel paying no heed to tramlines. The hood was kept down as it restricted headroom and visibility, but the useful screen and the tall scuttle kept out almost all the rain whilst the car was under way.

With Virginia Water dropping astern, the powerful headlights throwing a splendid beam and the lusty

o.h.v. engine taking us over the ground at about 45 m.p.h. on quarter throttle, the world seemed indeed a very pleasant place. Inside all was snug. The rain had almost stopped and the driver's vision was not interrupted by the wet screen because, although it gives excellent protection, his line of vision is over the top of it.

The light of an electric torch showed that the dashboard drip-feed lubricator was taking care of the engine's needs, that the dynamo was charging with one amp. to spare over and above the requirements of the headlamps and that our maps and route cards were safely stowed beside the passenger's seat. Behind

EEL OF 117

rgan Figured in the Second
iple Award Attempt

There is no finer way to test the power, brakes and stamina of a car than to run it in the London to Land's End Trial. The photographs depict the ascents of (left to right): Ruses Mill, Hustyn, Beggars' Roost, and Bluehills Mine. A "broadside" of the car, showing its very low build and workmanlike lines, is given below.

the squab, sharing the space occupied somewhat extravagantly by the powerful starter battery, were two bulky haversacks, spare gauntlets and a heap of paraphernalia, whilst under the seats in two roomy compartments was a lavish tool kit and space for plenty more.

These under-the-seat toolboxes, incidentally, could be abolished and the seat lowered two or three inches if one wished. With the standard arrangement, however, the seats are so low that if the driver drops his arm over the side his finger-tips are on the road!

With this wonderfully low build the twists and turns on the way to Taunton were thoroughly enjoyed. The Morgan round any bend or curve was definitely faster than most four-wheelers, with no rolling at all and with the most admirable feeling of stability and security.

On the Hills.

It was not until the strenuous part of the trial began, however, that the cyclecar started really to unfold its charms. Grabhurst's gradient it devoured on a whiff of gas. On the two-mile pull up Dunkery Beacon, which set nearly all the cars boiling as they toiled their way up, it chafed at the 30 m.p.h. limit which was set and probably, if pressed, could have averaged 45 m.p.h. over the whole section.

Wellshead hair-pin was rounded with a triumphant swirl and a pound or two of its surface flung into the air as the back wheel bit the road and hurtled the little machine over the summit. Really it is a wonderful sensation to have some 40 b.h.p. at call and nothing to restrain it save 7½ cwt. of rigid little motorcar!

Down Countisbury we trickled, not bothering to change down as the rear brake alone was more than sufficient for the 1 in 4½ descent without the aid of the powerful f.w.b.

Lynmouth proved to be a repetition of Wellshead—just a matter of not turning on too much throttle in case the spectators should be alarmed. On Beggars' Roost, however, no such qualms for the onlookers' peace of mind was felt. The starting signal was given at the bottom, the clutch was let in and the throttle gradually opened until it reached its limit. With a bound, it seemed, this once-dreaded terror of the West was flattened and the f.w.b. hand lever was being grasped to check the speed for the right-hand turn on to the main road at the summit. Beggars' Roost to a super-sports Morgan is no more of an obstacle than is a mole hill to a greyhound.

They are splendid miles those 60-odd which the M.C.C. selects to include between Beggars' Roost and Launceston. The little Devon lanes wind and twist in all directions, dipping steeply, rising sharply, and giving a good car every opportunity to show the best that is in it. They left the writer's passenger a disillusioned man. He had started the run with the belief that three-wheelers are not stable—and arrived at Launceston declaring that with their £4 tax if everyone appreciated their advantages the Road Fund would be ruined!

And so to Ruses Mill and its preface of car parks, refreshment booths and what not, all pointing to a large crowd turned out to see a shambles. But again "fast" went down in the reporters' notebooks. And so it was on Hustyn, which brought 97 four-wheelers to a standstill. We trickled through the water-splash at the foot, turned on the gas and disappeared over the summit.

On Bluehills Mine No. 117 was not so clever. A disgraceful error of judgment concerning the amount of lock available involved rounding the bend in "wall of death" fashion with the off-side front wheel high up on the rocky wall which flanks the outside of the hair-pin. The little car was tilted to a perilous angle, but its wonderfully low centre of gravity saved the situation. The back wheel bit deep into the loose stony surface and flung us over the top in the by then familiar all-conquering manner.

Soon the End was reached and No. 117, with its numbers removed, was pottering back along the road to Penzance fit and ready for the 320-mile return journey, which it comfortably laughed aside in 7½ hours' running time on the following day.

For the whole run 53 m.p.g. of petrol was averaged and about 1,500 m.p.g. of oil. The toolbox was touched but once—to look at a plug at the foot of Countisbury, in case the long descent should have oiled it.

With the Land's End run behind us and before returning it to its owner, the Morgan was put through its paces and found to have a top gear (5 to 1) maximum speed of 76 m.p.h. with two up on a good road, and a bottom gear (10 to 1) maximum of rather more than 40 m.p.h.

With higher gears, which are very easily obtained, of course, by merely changing the sprockets, about 55 m.p.h. in bottom gear and over 80 m.p.h. in top gear would be obtainable. The 5 to 1 top gear, however, appeared to suit the car very well and gave a comfortable cruising speed in the neighbourhood of 60 m.p.h., with excellent slow pulling and first-rate acceleration even from a speed so low as 10 m.p.h.

We now come to criticism. Starting with the engine, it has a wonderful power output, magnificent acceleration and very good slow running. It is on the rough side, however, and there is more vibration than there should be.

The brakes are very good, but would be improved if the ratchet of the hand lever were more positive in its action. The springing and steering are both beyond reproach, but the steering column, probably because the reduction gearbox had been over-filled, was rather addicted to dripping grease into the driver's lap. The electrical equipment was very well behaved and the starter proved itself always capable of dealing with the lusty engine. The non-trip speedometer, however, was very erratic in its readings.

It is, perhaps, unfair to continue in this strain. One cannot expect a £153 machine which can hold its own and give a trouncing to most of the fastest cars on the road to be perfect in all its details.

An Enthusiast Modifies His Morgan

ALTHOUGH the super-sports Morgan is essentially a two-seater, it is possible, by the exercise of skill and ingenuity, to provide a third seat for a small passenger. A modification of this kind has been carried out very successfully by Mr. A. Norman Thompson, 52, Leander Road, Brixton Hill, London, S.W.2, who is an enthusiastic and energetic private owner.

The extra seat is arranged above the bevel box, a cockpit being formed by cutting away part of the top of the hinged tail. Ample legroom is provided by cutting an inverted U-shaped opening in the front seat squab.

By re-fitting the hood farther back the extra seat is fully protected, whilst to make up the length an extension piece is fitted to the front of the hood and arranged to clip over the top of the windscreen or to fold back, thus providing a form of opening roof which should be very useful in showery weather.

Neat aluminium valve covers and a badge bar figure amongst the special fittings on this Morgan.

Several mechanical alterations have also been made to the Morgan—which is a 1929 model—by its owner. A new rear brake of the internal expanding type is fitted. It consists of a drum machined from the solid and providing a braking surface of 8 ins. by 1¼ ins. The drum is secured to the low gear sprocket and is fitted with cast aluminium shoes faced with Ferodo. A special re-arrangement of the control rods ensures a perfectly even braking force regardless of the vertical movement of the rear wheel on bad roads.

The need for periodically greasing the clutch has been overcome by Mr. Thompson by fitting an extension pipe to the crankcase breather so that oily vapour is blown into the clutch mechanism.

Another alteration in connection with the engine—a J.A.P.—concerns valve stem lubrication. Metal cups have been machined up to fit over the valve springs and under the bottom spring pads. The third, or inner, springs are discarded and thick felt washers are fitted over the valve stems and made a good push fit inside the inner springs. Oil is fed into the cups once a week, and Mr. Thompson finds that the stems remain effectively lubricated.

In the accompanying photograph can be seen the special aluminium valve covers which have been fitted, together with a neat cross-bar upon which the A.A. badge is mounted.

With regard to general running, Mr. Thompson says that his maximum timed speed has been 78 m.p.h. but that he has no difficulty in averaging 32 m.p.h. on a long journey without ever exceeding 45 m.p.h. Petrol consumption works out at 43 m.p.g. using a 175 jet and with the needle set in the second notch, not the third as is usually recommended.

It will be seen from the foregoing that Mr. Thompson is a skilled mechanic who makes his car his hobby—a sure method of obtaining a really satisfactory performance.

Morgans with Three Speeds

Famous Three=wheeler's Break with Tradition : Three = speed and Reverse Gears, with Single Driving Chain: Two=speed Models Retained: Cylinder Angle Changed: Dry=sump Lubrication

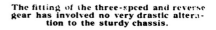

The fitting of the three-speed and reverse gear has involved no very drastic alteration to the sturdy chassis.

TO state that the Morgan Motor Co. have designed a new chassis for 1932 would be quite unfair to the amazingly simple design which has characterised this most successful three-wheeler from its earliest days. The essential features of the three-tube construction are unchanged, but so far as engine and transmission are concerned the design has been brought so much up to date that it is difficult to regard the machine as a whole as anything but new. Those who know and love the old two-speed Morgans will still be able to obtain this type unaltered from the 1931 design, at very modest

ensure adequate lubrication through the pumping action of the gear wheels. The reverse intermediate pinion is mounted on a separate stationary shaft.

Providing a reduction of just over 2 to 1, the worm wheel is mounted above the worm, and is housed in a circular aluminium casting formed in one with the gear box. The wheel is bolted to the cross-shaft and is carried on a deep-groove bearing on the near side and a roller bearing

further support for the first motion gear shaft, and also of shortening the propeller shaft, and thus avoiding whirl.

There is no change in the rear portion of the frame, except that the twin radius rods are bolted rigidly together with a solid forging mounted immediately behind the worm box. It will be remembered that the system of mounting the radius rods concentrically with the cross-shaft centre was introduced last year, and this system, which maintains unvarying chain centres under varying spring loads, is retained, as is the drop-out rear spindle and the large internal-expanding rear brake.

Since there are two sliding members on the main gear shaft, one for first and reverse, and one for second and top, a gate change is required, and this has been arranged in an extraordinarily neat and practical manner. The selector rods are attached to flat strip-steel members which lie parallel with the propeller-shaft enclosing tube. At their forward end they pass through a light sheet steel bracket clamped to the tube itself, and between the two flat steel members is a third, fixed to the supporting plate.

The change-speed lever is pivoted above this bracket and has a downwardly pro-

The 1932 three-speed o.h.v. super-sports model.

prices, but the main range for the future will include a three-speed and reverse gear box with a single driving chain, and a redesigned engine which is available in all the usual types.

The biggest change lies in the transmission. Except that the layshaft is mounted directly above the mainshaft, the new three-speed box is of conventional design.

Running in deep-groove ball bearings throughout, the mainshaft is very well supported, for, in addition to the spigot bush, which is surrounded by the front main bearing, there are two other bearings, one at the tail of the gear box and one behind the David Brown worm gear. The deep-groove bearings take both thrust and radial loads, and the excellent support for the shafts makes the box extremely silent in action.

Two long bronze floating bushes surround the fixed layshaft, and lie between it and a continuous sleeve carrying the four layshaft pinions. Here, again, the rigidity of the construction encourages silence, and holes drilled from the bottom of the teeth to the centre of the sleeve

on the drive side. The ball race takes both thrust and radial loads, and both bearings have large grease-proof packings on their outer faces. Each of these journals is carried in a circular bronze end-plate, the outer periphery of the bosses being used as bearings for the radius rods. Since these radius-rod bearings are 3⅝in. in diameter, they should last almost indefinitely, but, should wear take place after a very considerable mileage, the bronze end-plates are easily detachable and renewable.

On the near side is a fabric wheel for the dynamo drive, the dynamo itself being mounted on a casting rigidly bolted to the side of the gear box. On the off-side the front sprocket for the final drive is mounted on parallel splines so that it may be removed with ease if a change of ratio is desired.

Keyed into the front end of the gear box driving shaft is a forward extension shaft carrying at its foremost end a four-jaw dog drive, and immediately behind the dog is a ball race which is housed in the propeller-shaft tube. This extension serves the double purpose of providing a

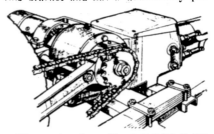

The new gear box with worm drive to the cross shaft. The dynamo is bolted to the side of the box. Note the section of the chain stay.

jecting lever of the same width as the strips. Sufficient rocking motion is provided at the lever pivot to enable the drop arm to engage with slots in either of the flat striking rods; this scheme provides a gate of the normal car type in a very compact way.

On the side of the tube opposite to the gear lever is clamped the hand-brake lever, which is of sensible length and is now provided with a spring-controlled ratchet.

In the forward end of the chassis there are no outstanding alterations except that the mudguards are now carried entirely on the chassis, having a rigid supporting bar at their rearmost extremities joining them to the lower frame tubes. It will be realised that the underslung worm arrangement permits of a slight drop in the rear end of the propeller-shaft enclosing tube, thus providing more room in the seating compartment.

Considerable changes have been made in the special J.A.P. engines employed. Though they embody all well known J.A.P. features, the cylinder angle has been altered from 50° to 60°. Dry-sump lubrication by Pilgrim pump is incorporated, and there are two separate camshafts, through one of which the starting handle is connected to the crankshaft, while the other is employed to drive the combined distributor and make-and-break for the Lucas coil ignition system which is now standardised.

The crank case of this unit will be the same for all the new models, as also will be the capacity of 1,096 c.c., but either side- or overhead-valve engines will be available, with water or air cooling. In the case of the air-cooled side-valve engines, the cylinder heads will be detachable above the valve seats as in modern car practice.

It is stated that the change of cylinder angle has enabled a vast improvement in balance to be attained, and that the tick-over and starting with coil ignition have been greatly improved. Incidentally, full electric starting is standardised on all new models.

The new chassis will be available in the following forms :—

	£
Family model, air-cooled side-valve engine ..	95
Family model, water-cooled side-valve engine	100
Aero model, water-cooled side-valve engine ..	115
Aero model, " 10-40 " water-cooled o.h.v. enging	125
Sports Family model, water-cooled side-valve engine	120
Sports Family model, " 10-40 " water-cooled o.h.v. engine	130
Super-sports model, specially tuned o.h.v. engine	145

All the foregoing models have Lucas electric starting and lighting, a speedometer, and screen-wiper. The Family model will also be available in two-seater form at the same prices. In this case the rear seats are replaced by a luggage locker, while the top of the tail provides ample space for further luggage accommodation.

Prices for the two-speed models, which remain unaltered in construction, are : Family model (air-cooled side-valve engine), £75; Family model (water-cooled side-valve engine), £80; Aero model (water-cooled side-valve engine), £95; Aero model (10-40 h.p. water-cooled overhead-valve engine), £110.

As already mentioned, the chassis which has been described is common throughout the new range, but in the case of the super-sports model the overall height of the chassis is decreased by dropping the axles and rear springing.

The new Morgans are a model of straightforward engineering practice, and it would be difficult to devise a more simple and practical chassis than that which is illustrated in these pages.

1935 Super Sports

1935 SUPER SPORTS—in wartime guise. The beautifully finished 50-deg vee-tw water-cooled, o.h.v. Matchless engine, with its 990c.c. and compression ratio of 6 to gave a maximum speed in the seventies, coupled with surprising smoothness and flexibili For several years this particular car gave much pleasure to the editor of this book . . . a price, new, of £130-odd and a Road Fund Tax of £4.

THE LATEST SPORTS TWO-SEATER MORGAN

The new body has a flat tail for luggage accommodation.

First Road Test of a New Fast Touring Type

AT the Show great interest was displayed in the latest Morgan chassis, incorporating a three-speed and reverse gearbox. For various reasons it has not been possible to carry out a road test until the present, and since the time of the Show other changes have been made.

The body of the model tested is of an entirely new type, to be known as the Sports Two-seater, and it is understood that this will replace the Aero model. In appearance, so far as the forward part is concerned, it resembles the Aero, but the tail is more reminiscent of the two-seater de luxe. A single door is fitted on the near side, but two doors are available to order, if they are required. In the same way, there is to be a choice of a vee-type windscreen, similar to that fitted on the machine illustrated, or a flat screen, more akin to that of the two-seater de luxe. This last variation naturally calls for different types of hood.

At the front of the machine two changes were noticed. The induction pipe of the 60-degree engine is now water-jacketed so as to improve the carburation. This jacket takes the form of a rectangular cast aluminium box, which is quite neat and which serves also to shield the body of the carburetter from the direct blast of cold air.

The other front alteration referred to is in the mounting of the headlamps. An additional tubular stay rises from the front axle framework to the mudwing, which is thus supported very rigidly. From the top of this tube a short bracket projects inwards and carries the headlamp.

Less obvious is the provision of an extra take-off spring for the rear brake. This spring is mounted on the cam lever and is, of course, auxiliary to the other springs which operate directly upon the shoes inside the drum. It serves to ensure that the shoes do not at any time drag and thus absorb power.

Inside the new gearbox there are one or two changes which, although they may appear to be of a minor nature, are, nevertheless, important in that they prevent oil leakage. Instead of the old type of felt packing, a special shaped leather washer is now employed. This has an L section so that part of it fits round the shaft like a bearing, and is held firmly against the shaft by means of a coil spring which surrounds it. In consequence, all leakage of the lubricant has been eliminated.

Washers of this type are now used on the propeller shaft where it enters the box, and on both ends of the cross-shaft which carries the worm wheel. A similar washer is also used on the brake side of the rear-wheel hub.

The model tested was fitted with a 10-40 h.p. o.h.v. water-cooled engine and is priced at £125. A similar car with a side-valve engine is to be marketed at £115 complete. Both engines, of course, are of the new 60-degree type introduced last year and have two-cam timing gear. The bore is 85.7 mm. and the stroke 95 mm., giving a cubic capacity of 1,096 c.c.

It will be remembered that the new three-speed gearbox follows conventional car practice, the indirect gears being engaged by sliding them into mesh and dogs being used for the direct drive. Behind the gearbox proper is an aluminium housing for the steel worm and its phosphor-bronze wheel mounted on a cross-shaft above. A single chain drives the rear wheel from the off side, and a helical-toothed pinion drives the dynamo on the other side.

Thanks to the chain drive it is, of course, a simple matter to raise or lower the complete range of gear ratios by changing the cross-shaft sprocket. An .18-tooth sprocket is standard and this provides ratios of 4.58. 7.5 and 12.4 to 1 forward, with a reverse gear of 16½ to 1.

Although not of the Super Sports type the engine of the model tested ran best on one of the various anti-knock spirits. In point of fact, National Benzole mixture was used during most of our test, and on this the Morgan behaved splendidly. Quite one of the most remarkable features of its performance is the excellent pulling in top gear at low speeds. To obtain the full benefit in this direction it is, of course, desirable to make proper use of the ignition lever, and the air lever should not be neglected.

Very much the same applies with regard to accelera-

tion. Given reasonable driving skill, it is doubtful whether the same standard of performance in this respect is obtainable on four wheels at anything less than three times the price of the Morgan.

With reference to the following figures, it must be borne in mind that the engine was not thoroughly run-in. Therefore a certain improvement might be expected later. Probably because of the 60-degree angle between the cylinders, the engine ran remarkably smoothly at low speeds. At about 45 m.p.h., however, considerable vibration was noticeable, and this was magnified by the drumming of something behind the dash. At higher speeds this unpleasantness disappeared.

With so new an engine—our test extended for a bare 300 miles—it was undesirable to leave the throttle fully open for long. In consequence, it is likely that the absolute maximum speed was not reached. Nevertheless, 65 m.p.h. was attained quite comfortably.

A Useful "Second."

The middle ratio is very well chosen, for really steep hills can be ascended at some 40 m.p.h. or more. The change from top to second is a particularly easy one. Taking all these things into consideration it is not surprising that the Morgan is capable of putting up some very respectable cross-country averages.

With regard to bottom gear, which, despite its comparatively high ratio of 12.4 to 1, is of the "dreadnought" variety, there was one defect on the particular model which we tested. Owing, probably, to some small fault in the gate mechanism, the change from second to first was accompanied by some uncertainty. On more than one occasion, in fact, the middle ratio remained engaged when the lever was moved through the gate. Fortunately, no harm was done.

While criticizing, reference must also be made to the position of the contact breaker. This is a matter which is admittedly unlikely to cause trouble in the ordinary way, but for those who ford an occasional stream additional waterproofing is desirable.

Although this particular car has the narrow track it looks as low and sleek as the Super Sports model. The close-up wings give very good protection and the front of the hood fits tightly to the screen.

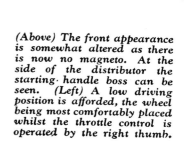

(Above) The front appearance is somewhat altered as there is now no magneto. At the side of the distributor the starting·handle boss can be seen. (Left) A low driving position is afforded, the wheel being most comfortably placed whilst the throttle control is operated by the right thumb.

Reverting to the transmission system, it was a great advantage to be able to reverse when manœuvring the Morgan in a restricted space. Even so small and handy a machine is all the better for being able to proceed backwards as well as forwards in such circumstances. Another factor which undoubtedly assisted very much on such an occasion was an experimental clutch of a new type which is being tested out. Of this for the present nothing more need be said. If, and when, it becomes available to the public, it will be fully described in *The Light Car and Cyclecar*.

Before leaving the mechanical side of the model, it must be said that the engine was invariably easy to start. From cold it is desirable to flood the carburetter and to operate the exhaust lifter before pressing the starter button. When the engine is warm the starter is capable of turning it over, even if the exhaust lifter is neglected, but it is, of course, a help

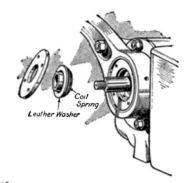

A spring-controlled leather washer is now used to prevent leakage of oil from the end of the mainshaft of the gearbox.

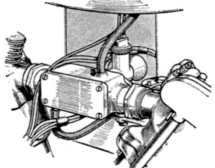

The induction pipe is provided with a water heated jacket which is connected to the radiator.

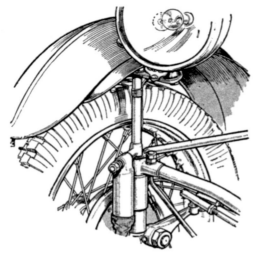

A substantial tubular support for the front mudguards cuts out all tendency to dither and forms a rigid headlamp bracket.

to the battery to lift the valves always. In any case the ignition should be retarded and the air lever brought back.

When taking over the vehicle at the works we were informed that the Amal carburetter needle was set rather high and that it should be lowered when the engine was run-in. Although this was not done, the consumption of fuel averaged about 55 m.p.g. in ordinary use.

Turning to matters affecting the body, access to the seats might possibly be a little easier if the door opening were carried farther forward. Once inside, however, there is plenty of room and reasonable comfort. Behind the seat squab is a space in which one large or two medium-sized suitcases can be carried.

For regular all-weather use it is probable that the flat screen, which is optional, would be somewhat better than the vee-type with the hood which accompanies it. Apart from the fact that the latter interfered with the action of the windscreen wiper, however, it was satisfactory, except in city streets, where it was found to restrict the driver's view of traffic emerging from side turnings.

On the open road or in country lanes the Morgan is a delight to handle. Its steering is accurate and, although not unduly heavy, it gives the driver the impression that he is driving a really big car. On rough roads the control is undoubtedly improved by the excellence of the suspension. Pot-holes and even railway crossings are scarcely felt by the occupants, and it is doubtful whether any light four-wheeled car gives one a more comfortable ride.

Above all, however, we must emphasize that the 1932 Morgan, although more ambitious in its specification, has lost none of its charm. It is still the nimble sporty little car that has enjoyed the enthusiasm of the keenest types of owner for a matter of 20 years.

SHELSLEY WALSH REGULATIONS

AS was mentioned in this journal last week, the regulations for the Open Hill-climb at Shelsley on June 25th are available on application to Mr. Leslie Wilson, hon. secretary of the Midland Automobile Club, 415, Stratford Road, Birmingham. Entries close on June 16th.

The regulations are not being distributed broadcast, so we give herewith a summary of their contents.

There will be seven classes—subdivided into "racing" and "sports"—as follow:—850 c.c., 1,100 c.c., 1,500 c.c., 2 litres, 3 litres, 5 litres and over 5 litres.

In addition to class awards there are eight special prizes: the Shelsley International Championship Cup and £105 for fastest climb of the day, the British Championship Cup and £25 for best time by a British sports car, the T.T. Cup for best performance by a car raced in any international event in 1931-32, the Open Cup for the best aggregate of two

runs, the Garvagh Challenge Cup for the best over-1½-litre sports model, the C.P. Type Challenge Cup for the fastest 1½-litre car, the Ladies Cup and the Fray Team Challenge Cup.

There is a separate entry fee for those making a bid for these trophies. In the ordinary classes the trade entry fee is £5 and non-trade £2, but there is no entry fee if entered for the Shelsley Championship Cup.

An inclusive fee of 10 guineas (trade) or 8 guineas (non-trade) entitles competitors to enter a car for all appropriate cups.

Practice runs will be allowed—in the car entered—on the day before the event. Three-wheelers are barred.

In the normal course of events each car will be allowed two climbs where it has clocked under 60 secs. (65 secs. for the "850s") on the first run.

Many Morgan Modifications For Next Season

A Single-plate Clutch and Entirely New Bodies on the Three-speed Chassis. Magna Wheels

A NEW MODEL. — *The Sports two-seater, which has a new design of two-door body whilst the tail is shaped to carry the spare wheel. The price, in o.h.v. form, is £120.*

A NOTABLE feature of the Morgan programme for 1933 is that, although the old two-speed chassis will be available to special order, only the three-speed model will be catalogued. It will be supplied with four different types of body, the Super Sports, the Sports two-seater, the Sports Family, and the Family model.

Several changes are to be noted in the chassis itself. Foremost amongst them is the use of a dry single-plate clutch instead of the cone clutch which has figured in the Morgan specification for just 21 years. The clutch pedal operates three toggle levers through the agency of a carbon bush which requires no lubrication.

The levers withdraw a metal plate which normally is forced by six helical springs against a light disc which carries two friction rings, one on each side.

Chassis Alterations.

The forward end of the chassis is improved, in that the wing stays have been increased considerably in size. They are tubular and continue right through the bearing for the sliding axle, which now has rather less camber. The connection from the steering box to the off-side front wheel is also modified, and as a result of these various changes it is understood that the steering is very much lighter than in the past.

In recent years two separate chassis frames have been used, one for the Super Sports and the other for standard models. There is now only one type, however, and this is half an inch higher at the front than was the 1932 Super Sports. The other 1933 models are consequently much lower than their predecessors.

In appearance the new Morgans differ very considerably from the earlier types, not only because of the new body designs, but also because they have Dunlop Magna detachable wheels. The hubs have been redesigned, of course, to suit the Magna wheels, and a spare is carried on the tail.

To change the rear wheel it must first be removed from the forks, exactly as in previous models. The hub can then be separated from the wheel and attached to the spare. The tyre size is 26 ins. by 4.00 ins.

Other chassis details which should be mentioned include the adoption of a new type of ignition distributor which is said to be completely waterproof. In the gearbox there is a different type of oil-retaining seal, and the dynamo is driven by a compressed fabric gear wheel instead of a fibre wheel.

So far as the Super Sports model is concerned, there are very few alterations to the bodywork. It is, however, rather wider at the front, so that there is more foot room. A stainless-steel radiator shell is used, and the chromium-plated exhaust pipes are carried back along the body waistline, the silencers being behind the seats. A spare wheel is carried on top of the tail.

At the other extreme is the Family model, which has been entirely redesigned so as to improve both comfort and appearance. Undoubtedly the bonnet lines are much better, and the tail is also a great improvement. Behind the rear panel is mounted the spare wheel, and the panel itself can be detached so as to gain access to the rear wheel. In the bonnet there is a small sliding door, so that the petrol filler-cap can be reached without lifting the bonnet.

The New Sports Models.

Between the two models just described are the Sports two-seater and the Sports Family. The former of these may be best described as having the front end of the Super Sports and a tail very like that of the Family model. Instead of the rear seats there is ample space for luggage and a fairly wide door is now provided on both sides. Except for the fact that it has rear seats and therefore less luggage accommodation, the Sports Family model is exactly like the Sports two-seater.

As already mentioned, the two-speed chassis will be available if specially ordered, but only with an air-cooled engine and Family body, its price with hood, screen and electric light being £80.

The prices for the 1933 models are as follow:—Super-sports, £135; Sports two-seater, side-valve, £110; Sports two-seater, o.h.v., £120; Sports Family, side-valve, £115; Sports Family, o.h.v., £125; Family model, air-cooled, £98; Family model, water-cooled, £103.

A RILEY DEVELOPMENT
Salerni Transmission Adopted

IN introducing the new 14 h.p. Edinburgh saloon on Tuesday last to a gathering of pressmen, Mr. Victor Riley, chairman and managing director of Riley (Coventry), Ltd., stated that all 1933 Rileys would shortly be available with fluid clutch and pre-selection transmission built under Salerni patents. The fitting is an optional extra on the 9 h.p. and 12 h.p. cars, and costs £30 in the case of the former and £50 on the six-cylinder models.

THE LATEST FAMILY MODEL. — *A new design of dummy radiator has been adopted for the Family models. Note the adoption of Magna wheels.*

Reprinted from THE MOTOR CYCLE *October 13th, 1932.*

ADVANCE DETAILS OF 1933 MODELS

Morgans with Detachable Wheels

Important Improvement for 1933: Car=type Clutch: Detail Modifications to Enhance Appearance

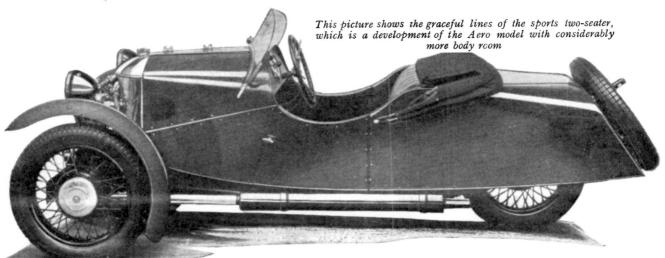

This picture shows the graceful lines of the sports two-seater, which is a development of the Aero model with considerably more body room

THE Morgan Motor Company, of Malvern, is celebrating its twenty-first birthday, and those whose motor cycling experience carries them sufficiently far backward will remember the excitement which was created at Olympia in November, 1910, by the appearance of the rakish single-seated three-wheeler with tiller steering.

In those days there was a single-cylinder model as well as a twin; but, in essentials, the design which appeared at that time has formed the basis of all the famous three-wheelers which have been produced by the Malvern works. The primary shaft drive, with bevel gear and two ratios provided by unequal size sprockets, and the amazingly simple and workmanlike tubular chassis, have persisted throughout the years; and, though three-speed and reverse gears made their appearance for the first time at the last Show, two-speed models were still listed. They disappear from the catalogue for the first time in 1933, but the two-speed "Family" model, selling at the very modest price of £80, will still be available for those who require cheap transport. This price includes a 976 c.c. air-cooled, side-valve engine, electric lighting, hood, and screen.

A Lower Chassis

For 1933 several changes have been made, all of which are of a highly practical nature. Of importance to both manufacturer and purchaser is the fact that the chassis of all models have been standardised. The super-sports model is now ½in. higher than before to provide improved clearance, while the standard models are 1½in. lower.

The reduction in height has been brought about in two ways, first, by a modification to the bend in the front axle supports, and, secondly, by a reduction in wheel size, all wheels now being of the 18×3in. Dunlop Magna detachable type, which carry 26×4in. tyres. Not only do these detachable wheels add considerably to the appearance of the machine, but both the tourist and sporting driver will have the satisfaction of knowing that they carry a spare which may be fitted with ease to any of the three wheels.

In order to change the rear wheel, it is necessary to detach the hub by means of a knock-out spindle, as was the case in the 1932 models, but the hub is of special construction, and, once removed, it is a simple matter to undo the retaining bolts and slip on the spare wheel. Incidentally, the bodywork has been

modified so as to provide far greater ease of access to the rear wheel.

In the clutch there is another departure from Morgan practice, for the fabric-faced cone has given way to a single-plate clutch, following normal car practice. A rigid pressure plate is held up to its work by six short springs, and may be withdrawn by a simple arrangement comprising three toggles upon which the thrust block operates. Actually, the driving face of the clutch is an extension flange of the starter gear ring. The clutch is very neat and simple, and should require the minimum of attention.

Lighter Steering

A further change of considerable importance has been brought about in the steering gear, for, by modification to the design of the steering levers to reproduce more accurately the requirements of the true Ackerman steering system, the power required for turning the machine has been greatly decreased. This ease of steering has been assisted by a slightly diminished rake to the sliding axles, and a considerable increase in the size of the wing stays, which now form the bearing for the sliding axle, should result in improved wearing qualities.

Though unchanged in essentials, the gear box is now fitted with a special oil-retaining seal, and a toughened compressed fabric wheel is fitted for the dynamo drive. Coil ignition remains a standard fitting, but a new distributor has been designed which contains the condenser, and is claimed to be completely waterproof.

Now as to the complete models which are mounted on this chassis :—The popular super-sports type has been altered but

A lowered chassis is now standard on all Morgan models and a modification to the points of attachment of the drag-link and track - rods has greatly improved the steering

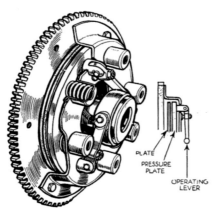

A single-plate clutch is now used. Note the interesting method of operation

little, but chromium-plated exhaust pipes, set at a high level, enhance the appearance. Access to the rear wheel is improved by the use of bonnet fasteners for the domed tail, in place of the six screws which were previously employed. On this tail is carried the spare wheel. A modification to the body has provided more foot-room, and the radiator shell is now of stainless steel. The price of this machine, with water-cooled o.h.v. engine and complete equipment, is £135.

The Sports Two-seater

Replacing the Aero model is the new sports two-seater, which has a particularly attractive appearance. Lower than the Aero, on account of the dropped chassis, the front of the vehicle is otherwise much the same, but large doors are fitted on either side, the tail is both wider and deeper, while the back panel forms a convenient carrier for the spare wheel. The extra width provides a considerable increase in the space available for luggage carrying, and the back panel is detachable, providing very easy access to the rear wheel. In addition to this increased luggage space on the outside, there is a considerable increase in locker space. The price, with a side-valve,

water-cooled engine, is £110, or, with the o.h.v. engine, £120.

One of the strongest lines ever produced by the Morgan factory has been the "Family" model, and this has been improved both in appearance and convenience to a very large extent. The bonnet shape has been modified, and the new dummy radiator, with its curved front, is a very great improvement from the appearance point of view. It is now unnecessary to lift the bonnet in order to refill with petrol, and the petrol tank itself is stronger and more easy of access. Low down under the rear seat is mounted the accumulator, which is more accessible than before. The spare wheel is carried on the detachable tail end, and a hood cover has been included in the standard equipment. There is now a door for the driver. Only side-valve engines are fitted to this model, and the price with the air-cooled type is £98, or, with the water-cooled, £103.

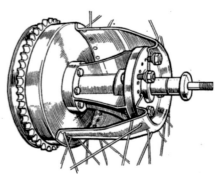

Dunlop Magna-type detachable and interchangeable wheels are now standardised. The new rear hub to suit this type of wheel is illustrated; the hub is located by a knock-out spindle as before

deeper tail. The price with side-valve, water-cooled engine is £115, or, with o.h.v. engine, £125.

All Morgan models are equipped with

A new dummy radiator has enhanced the appearance of the "Family" model

No change has been made in the "Sports Family" model, except for the chassis and body features already mentioned. That is to say, the four-seater is carried on the standard low chassis and carries the spare wheel on the wider and

electric starting and lighting, electric horn, and spare wheel. Hoods and screens are supplied in every case, together with suction windscreen wipers. In addition to this, the "Family" models have side-curtains.

The sports two-seater with the tail panel detached, showing the ease of access to the rear wheel

This view shows the cut-away scuttle of the super-sports model, and the new exhaust pipe

A "FOUR-WHEELED MORGAN"

An Interesting and Novel Conversion

The Allard Special has distinctly imposing lines, and, although still in somewhat of an experimental form, has a workmanlike appearance.

AFTER two years of experiment and really hard work a cyclecar enthusiast—Mr. S. H. Allard, of Keswick Road, Putney—has brought to fruition a pet idea which he has had in mind for years. It is what can best be described as a "four-wheeled Morgan."

By that we mean that various parts of a Morgan are utilized, such as engine, radiator, front suspension and portions of bodywork, but the rest of the car has been built from components of many makes.

The result, as can be seen from the pictures on this page, is a distinctly pleasing car, which, incidentally, is capable of a very fine performance, and holds the road like the proverbial leech.

The chassis frame consists of two straight channel-section members, cross-braced at four points. This frame is carried well below the wheel centres.

At the front end there are cross-members as on the Morgan, and between the extremities of these are carried the axle pins and helical springs; these are controlled by Newton hydraulic shock absorbers.

The rear suspension is by means of eight transverse quarter-elliptic springs after the manner of the f.w.d. B.S.A., and a large Hartford friction shock absorber controls each set of four. It will be seen that all wheels are independently sprung, and this makes the car ride most comfortably over very rough surfaces.

A pronounced crab track is used, the front being 4 ft. 8 ins. and the rear 3 ft.

10 ins. The wheelbase is 7 ft. 6 ins. and the overall height, to the top of the small glass screens, is only 3 ft. 7 ins. In spite of its low build and squat appearance the car has a ground clearance of 5 ins.

The engine is an 8-50 h.p. o.h.v. water-cooled J.A.P., and is, in fact, the actual unit which Mr. Allard used on his Morgan which from time to time has done very well at Brooklands. It is a highly tuned unit and has very good powers of acceleration.

An additional flywheel is mounted just behind the crankcase, and from this a short shaft takes the drive to a Moss four-speed-and-reverse gearbox. The "clutch housing" of this is bolted directly to a square steel plate, which forms additional strengthening for the frame.

Behind the gearbox the propeller shaft is guarded by a tubular casing

(Right) The "cockpit." The ingenious form of remote gear control can be seen, also the large array of instruments. Mounted also on the facia board is the hand pressure pump for the fuel supply.

where it passes between the driver and passenger. The shaft has Hardy disc joints at each end. The rear drive is very interesting and reflects great credit on Mr. Allard and those who have helped him to build this car.

The spiral-bevel housing is mounted direct on to the chassis, and from it run two short shafts, in which are incorporated Austin Seven mechanical universal joints. On each side of the casing there are two external-contracting brakes which were taken from a Chrysler. The front wheels have Morgan brakes and the pedal operates on all four wheels. The brake lever acts on the front wheels only. The rest of the controls are quite normal and the gearbox has a clever type of remote control.

The bodywork has attractive lines, but is, of course, at the moment still very much in experimental form. The tail is taken from an Aero Morgan, and in it is carried a large battery.

Starting, incidentally, is carried out by a Lucas dynamotor taken from a Morris car. This is connected to the clutch shaft by an inverted-tooth silent chain with positive lubrication. The space under the bonnet is used for the fuel and oil tanks, and the facia-board is a mass of instruments.

The car is a very fine effort and readers will have a chance of seeing it perform in the London-Exeter Trial which starts to-night.

For Workshops or Garages.

A very well-designed stationary petrol engine of about 3 h.p. and known as the Coborn, has been introduced by Kryn and Lahy (1928), Ltd., Letchworth, Herts.

The engine is of the air-cooled, single cylinder type; it has a balanced crankshaft, running on taper roller bearings, detachable cylinder head and barrel,

(Left) This view shows the transverse quarter elliptic rear springing and the way in which the battery is carried in the tail. Note also the twin exhaust outlets.

and side valves. A vaned flywheel working within a metal cowl ensures an adequate flow of air for cylinder cooling purposes, and it is claimed to be impossible to overheat the engine.

The mixture is supplied by a vertical car-type Solex carburetter which is coupled to a governor. Ignition is by an impulse-starter magneto. The power unit is entirely self-contained and a reduction gear of 2.54 to 1 can be fitted if desired. With the gear the Coborn engine costs £19 7s. 6d., or without it £17 15s.

Power to Spare
—and Speed too
with the
MORGAN
SPORTS
TWO-SEATER

A Speedy and Comfortable Three-wheeler Which Provides Plenty of Room for Luggage

SINCE the Morgan Sports two-seater was first introduced about a year ago, it has been improved in several respects. For example, two reasonably wide doors now make entrance and exit an easy matter and, on the model tested, a flat windscreen and a folding hood ensure an adequate range of vision, even when the hood is up.

On the mechanical side the new plate clutch is a great advance on its predecessor, and a new design of ignition distributor makes for greater reliability in that it is waterproof.

The body combines distinctly attractive lines with sufficient room for two people and their luggage; the legroom is generous. The seat itself is upholstered with Dunlop Latex cushions and is 34 ins. wide, the measurement from back to front being 17 ins. and the squab height 20 ins.; behind the latter is a locker in which two suitcases can be carried.

All the wheels are detachable and interchangeable and have large Magna hubs. These certainly give an appearance of solidity to the machine and the position of the spare wheel on the sloping end of the tail is also attractive. At the front the appearance is very similar to that of the famous Aero Morgan.

Acceleration Figures.

With its overhead-valve 10-40 h.p. J.A.P. engine, the sports two-seater has a high power-weight ratio and its acceleration is naturally good. Although it can be throttled down to about 10 m.p.h. on top gear, a lower ratio would normally be used to accelerate from so low a speed. Tests were therefore made from a steady 15 m.p.h., and it was found that 30 m.p.h. was reached in 5⅘ secs., while an additional 8 secs. sufficed to raise the speed to 50 m.p.h.

It must be stated that the car in question was not thoroughly run-in at the time of our test. Even so, it could exceed 65 m.p.h., and there is little doubt that after it has covered a greater mileage it will be capable of 70 m.p.h. or perhaps 75 m.p.h.; presumably there will also be an improvement in acceleration. The second-gear speed of the car, as tested, was about 45 m.p.h.

When driven as hard as is permissible with a fairly new engine, the petrol consumption worked out at about 40 m.p.g. At a more gentle gait this figure rose to about 50 m.p.g. Oil consumption in the ordinary way is at

Morgans are now fitted with spare wheels and on the sports two-seater the tail is specially shaped to accommodate this desirable fitting.

the rate of one gallon per 1,000 miles; this quantity also represents the capacity of the oil tank. The petrol tank carries four gallons.

As on previous Morgans, the rear brake is coupled to the pedal, while the two front brakes are connected to the lever, which is centrally placed. Consequently, in order to obtain maximum braking effect, it is necessary to use both controls. This is, in fact, to be recommended for general use, particularly if the road surface is at all slippery. From 30 m.p.h. the Morgan was stopped comfortably in 34 ft.

It is almost unnecessary to state that the sports two-seater is an excellent hill-climber; convincing testimony to this is supplied by the record of the Morgan in reliability trials. More ordinary gradients, such as those which are freely encountered in normal use, can generally be climbed in top gear. "Weatheroak," in Worcestershire, has an average gradient of 1 in 8, with a maximum of possibly 1 in 5. It was approached at 35 m.p.h. and at the top the speedometer showed 32 m.p.h., the whole ascent having been made in top gear.

Since the three-speed gearbox was introduced 12

months ago its control has been improved, and it is now both easy and certain. The new clutch is, of course, delightful, and its smooth take-up is a great advantage in traffic. Despite its unorthodox design the suspension system is remarkably good, and appears to be equally satisfactory on good main roads or on neglected by-ways.

The 1933 chassis, it will be remembered, is distinctly lower than that of all previous Morgans, except the Super Sports, and this alteration results in somewhat better road-holding. Moreover, the steering layout has been improved, and the car is remarkably controllable at all speeds and even on the roughest surfaces.

The electrical equipment is of Lucas manufacture and the headlamps gave a satisfactory beam which enabled quite high cruising speeds to be indulged in after dark. They are provided with pilot bulbs so that they can be used as side lamps.

The car had, of course, an electric starter, which was capable of turning the engine over when warm. On a cold morning, however, it was advisable to turn the engine through a few revolutions with the starting handle, which now fits into a boss on the timing case.

From what has been written it will be realized that the sports two-seater Morgan is a very satisfactory vehicle for general use. Naturally, it is especially attractive for "sporting purposes." Not only is it exceptionally lively, but it has an almost tank-like ability to cross quite rough country.

Given reasonable skill in driving it will propel itself over the "stickiest" course in a way which is very satisfying, and, once one has indulged in this pastime, all but the prematurely aged will seek for fresh fields to conquer.

Not the least attractive feature of the Morgan sports two-seater is that its high performance is coupled with very low running costs; 50 m.p.g. and a £4 tax spell cheap motoring.

AT A GLANCE.

ENGINE: o.h.v. Vee twin; 85.7 mm. by 95 mm. = 1,096 c.c.; tax £4. Thermo-siphon cooling; coil ignition; Amal carburetter.

TRANSMISSION: Single dry-plate clutch; enclosed propeller shaft with centre steady bearing; three-speed and reverse gearbox; ratios, 4.58, 7.5 and 12.4 to 1; worm drive to cross shaft and single roller chain to rear wheel.

GENERAL: Wheelbase, 7 ft.; track, 4 ft.; overall length, 10 ft. 10 ins.; width, 4 ft. 9 ins.; tyres, 26 in. by 4 in.

PRICE: £120, as tested; (£110 with s.v. engine).

THE MORGAN MOTOR CO., LTD., Malvern Link, Worcs.

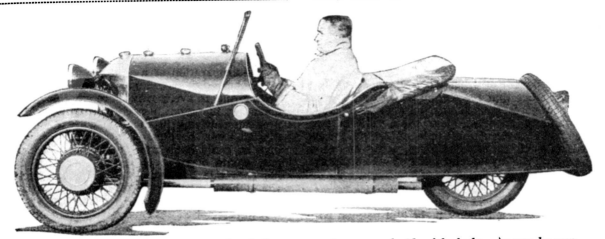

On the sports two-seater a large cylindrical silencer runs along on each side of the body. As can be seen from this photograph the addition of a spare wheel in no way detracts from the sporting appearance of the car.

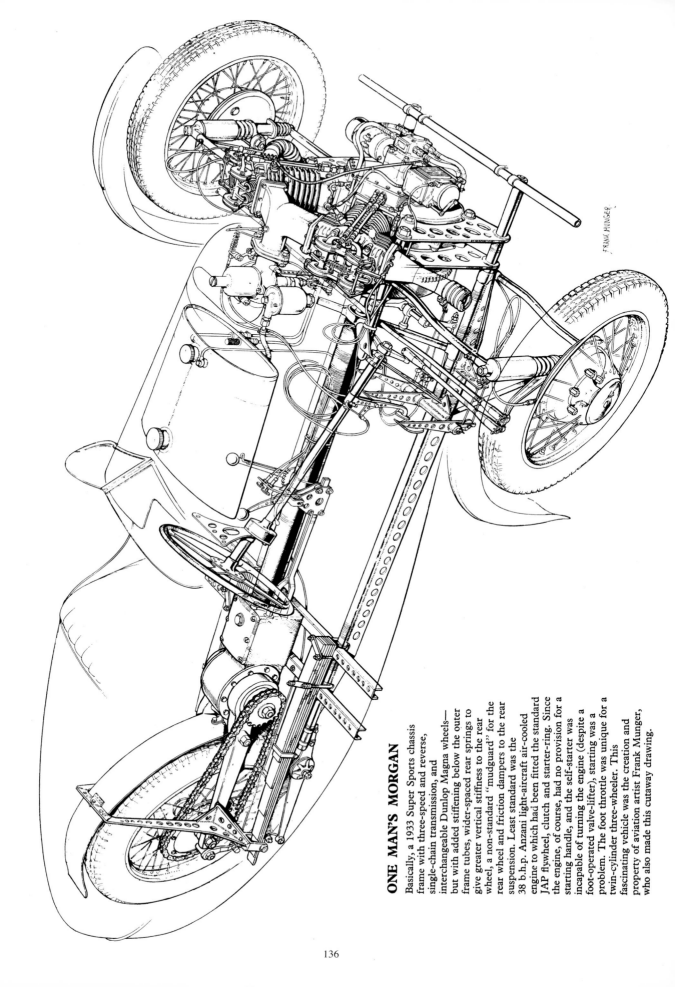

ONE MAN'S MORGAN

Basically, a 1933 Super Sports chassis frame with three-speed and reverse, single-chain transmission, and interchangeable Dunlop Magna wheels—but with added stiffening below the outer frame tubes, wider-spaced rear springs to give greater vertical stiffness to the rear wheel, a non-standard "mudguard" for the rear wheel and friction dampers to the rear suspension. Least standard was the 38 b.h.p. Anzani light-aircraft air-cooled engine to which had been fitted the standard JAP flywheel, clutch and starter-ring. Since the engine, of course, had no provision for a starting handle, and the self-starter was incapable of turning the engine (despite a foot-operated valve-lifter), starting was a problem. The foot throttle was unique for a twin-cylinder three-wheeler. This fascinating vehicle was the creation and property of aviation artist Frank Munger, who also made this cutaway drawing.

FRANK MUNGER

136

A MORGAN-MATCHLESS

New Model Listed at £110

A FEW days ago we were able to make a short run in a new Morgan model, fitted with a water-cooled 990 c.c. V-twin side-valve Matchless engine, produced by the well-known motorcycle concern.

Set at an angle of 50 degrees, the cylinders are fitted with detachable heads. The valves are enclosed. The new Lo-Ex alloy is used for the pistons, and a compression ratio of 5.4 to 1 is employed. The ignition is by coil.

The two-seater sports chassis follows conventional Morgan lines; features are the detachable and interchangeable wheels, brakes on all wheels, a three-speed-and-reverse gearbox, and electric starting and lighting.

The Matchless engine will pull smoothly in top gear at 15 m.p.h., and a smooth start can be made from rest on second gear, provided that the clutch is used carefully.

The maximum speed (by speedometer) appeared to be in the region of 68 m.p.h. —easily attained on a short stretch of

This new sports model Morgan is fitted with a 990 c.c. Matchless water-cooled engine which is characterized by a smooth power-output at low r.p.m.

road; on second a speed of 45 m.p.h. could be reached without undue fuss; 22 m.p.h. seemed to be the maximum in bottom gear.

A speed of 60 m.p.h. could be reached from rest in 18⅘ secs., which could be reduced to 17 secs. by accelerating from a start in second gear. From 40 m.p.h. to 65 m.p.h. the time taken was 12 secs.

The Morgan handled very easily and pleasantly, but with that innate "sporting feel" that all Morgans have. It is listed at £110.

Brooklands Loud Speakers.

A Philips 600-w. Public Address system has now been installed at Brooklands, and will be in operation to-morrow, May 6. There are 16 loud speakers, each with a ¼-mile range.

On Three Wheels

A MORGAN CLIMB *of* SCREW HILL?

A Promising Week-end Idea—Enthusiast's Specially Built Machine—Where Running Costs Count

By H. Sagar

NOW, you Morgan fans! I have had a letter from Mr. G. H. Goodall in which he expresses approval of my scheme for climbing Screw Hill, so it is up to you to rally round—in a double sense. Mr. Goodall thinks it would be a good idea for Morgan owners to rally somewhere in the vicinity, presumably before the so-called summer is over, so if you are at all interested, please write direct to the Morgan Motor Co., Ltd., Pickersleigh Road, Malvern Link. Action speaks louder than words, so do not spend a month endeavouring to

An interesting special three-wheeler powered by a K.M.A. racing engine. Its speed is in the neighbourhood of 90 m.p.h.

make up your minds, and then expect Mr. Goodall still to be interested.

It seems quite possible that Walna Scar, too, will be the scene of three-wheeler activities before long. A gentleman who knows quite a bit about handling three wheels is very interested in the idea and has definitely promised me that he will have a try "one of these fine days."

* * *

IF you have studied recent advertisements you will have noticed that the J.M.B. has been cleaned up considerably since the original experimental model appeared. This car, it will be remembered, is fitted with a 500 c.c. side-valve J.A.P. engine and other motorcycle components and will, I hope, attract many people who are still content with a sidecar although they could afford something better.

How many of you realize that there are now nine companies who have faith in three-wheelers? Although supplied purely for commercial purposes, the Fleet, James, Stevens and Croft cars are becoming increasingly popular, as is,

of course, the Raleigh—obtainable in a variety of forms for business use. To this list must be added Morgan and B.S.A., Coventry-Victor, who pin their faith to flat twins, and the J.M.B.

* * *

I HAD a letter from an enthusiast in Kensington recently, giving me details of a three-wheeler which has been built for him by Messrs. Taylor and Matterson. It employs Morgan clutch, bevel box, forks and transmission, but relies for its motive power upon a K.M.A. special racing engine, which gives it a speed of from 85-90 m.p.h. in standard trim. Its owner informs me that he is anxious to try it on the track, so it may be appearing at Brooklands.

How many enthusiasts are there who build their own machines? It would be interesting to compare idealists' varying opinions on the subect of the "ideal" three-wheeler, so if you have a home-built car, put your modesty on one side and let me know about it. There is, or was, a gentleman in the South country who converted a model T Ford into a three-wheeler. Whilst such conversions must be exceptional, I wonder if anyone else has found it possible to turn a four-wheeled car into a practical three-wheeler?

* * *

IT is always easy to do someone else's job—in theory, but I do think manufacturers are slow to make the most of their advantages. Take commercial three-wheelers as an example. You will find them advertised regularly in the

trade papers—in a fashion. One usually finds a sketch of the model, accompanied by the cold announcement that the tax is £4, the machine will do 50-60 m.p.g., and may be driven by a lad of 16. A photo would be a great deal better than a sketch, I am certain.

Now I have tried to persuade a business acquaintance to invest in a three-wheeler, as I am sure that it would effect a saving in his transport charges. I told him about the tax, which impressed him, and I believe I even conquered his long-standing objection to three-wheelers on the ground that they were unsafe; but when it came to the petrol consumption, he frankly regarded me as a liar.

If there is one business man of this kind, then there are others, and although I may not be a brilliant spokesman, I feel sure that three-wheeler sales in this sphere would benefit considerably were the A.-C.U., as the responsible body, to stage a demonstration on the lines of that arranged to show the capabilities of the 15s. tax motorcycle. The certificate issued at the conclusion of the test would give full details of performance, and potential customers would be able to see for themselves just what the running costs were.

It seems almost too good to be true, but a little bird which flew North recently informed me that we may see another four-cylinder three-wheeler making its bow next year. I am sure I am not alone in hoping that it may be so.

(Letters on topical matters addressed to Mr. Sagar, care of The Editor, will be forwarded immediately.)

A COMMERCIAL THREE-WHEELER. —— *One of a number of Fleet box-vans used by the L.M.S. Railway Company for their goods and parcels delivery services.*

MORGAN MODELS FOR 1934

Several Important Detail Refinements

(Above) The new o.h.v. Matchless engine which is available on the sports two-seater. (Left) A view of the 1934 Family model showing the improved tail.

NO changes in the basic Morgan models are made for 1934, but there are various detail alterations. The Family model is now listed only with a water-cooled engine, and a new air-cooled o.h.v. engine is available for the sports two-seater. In addition, there are various detail improvements.

On the Family model there is a new radiator of larger capacity. The header tank has a sloping front so as to deflect air downwards through the film block. At the other end of this model it is to be noticed that the tail is now very similar to that of the Sports two-seater, being rounded instead of having a square section as in 1933.

All 1934 Morgans have an oil filter placed on the side of the tank and connected to the return pipe. Consequently the oil scavenged from the sump is forced through a felt cylinder before it reaches the oil tank again. Another improvement to be found on all models is a Borg and Beck plate in the clutch. This plate, of course, has a flexible centre which cushions the transmission by smoothing out the engine torque.

No changes have been made to the mechanism of the three-speed-and-reverse gearbox, except that a better oil sealing washer is now fitted where the shafts leave the box. This is a composite device consisting of an L-section leather washer contracted on to the shaft by a coil spring surrounding it. The casting of the box itself is now appreciably wider at the back so that it holds more oil.

As before, the lighting dynamo is driven from the gearbox cross-shaft, but a change has been made to the gearwheels employed for this purpose. Straight teeth are now used to remove any end thrust and the larger wheel is made of a compressed fabric material of improved quality. The steel pinion on which most of the wear used to occur is now case-hardened.

As already indicated, the sports two-seater is now available with an air-cooled o.h.v. engine as well as with a side valve or o.h.v. water-cooled unit. The new engine is of Matchless manufacture and its lower half is similar to that of the water-cooled Matchless side-valve unit, but a separate lead is taken

1934 MORGAN PRICES.

Family model, s. v., water-cooled ...	£105
Sports Family, s.-v., water-cooled ...	£115
Sports Family, o.h.v., water-cooled	£125
Sports 2-seater, s.-v., water-cooled	£110
Sports 2-seater, o.h.v., air-cooled	£115
Sports 2-seater, o.h.v., water-cooled	£120
Super-sports, o.h.v., water-cooled	£135

Morgan Motor Co., Ltd., Malvern Link, Worcs.

(Above) How the header tank of the radiator on the Family model is shaped to deflect air on to the film. (Right) The Borg and Beck flexible plate now used in the clutch.

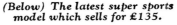

(Below) The latest super sports model which sells for £135.

from the oil pump to lubricate the overhead rockers.

These are enclosed in a box on each cylinder head and a short pipe is taken from the rocker box to the inlet valve guide for its lubrication. Each pushrod is enclosed in a telescopic tube which can be raised to reach the adjustment on the tappet. Generous finning characterizes the cylinders and the heads, and the whole unit has a distinctly businesslike appearance.

Most of our readers are familiar with the general specification of the Morgan, but for the benefit of those who are not the following brief details may be added. All models have a Vee-twin engine which drives through a plate clutch and short propeller shaft to a three-speed-and-reverse gearbox, whence the final drive is by a chain to the rear wheel. The front wheels are independently sprung by means of helical springs, whilst the rear wheel is carried in a stout fork, the suspension being quarter-elliptic. The brakes operate on all wheels and are of the internal-expanding type. The latest models will be on view at the Motorcycle Exhibition at Olympia (November 25).

RUBBER

SPLINED HUB

FRICTION LINING

Over ALPINE COLS with a MORGAN "SUPE[R]"

Two Members of the Fair Sex Prove that the Continent Holds no Terrors for a Modern Three-wheeler

(Above) The old fortress of Eze seen through the olives on [the] Grand Corniche. (Left) The harbour, Lake Iseo, taken fr[om] the Hotel Leon d'Oro.

LAST summer I was given an opportunity to put one of the new Morgan Super Sports models through its paces in the Alps, and having, in days gone by, driven many thousands of miles as an enthusiastic owner of earlier Morgans, I was much intrigued to sample the new vintage. Having heard that there were still in existence a few Italian lakes not totally surrounded by hotels and villas, we decided to risk the roads and have a look. So in the early summer we set off, myself and another girl, with a small quantity of compressed luggage.

We had mapped out a round tour; starting off easily with the marvellous motoring conditions of the Savoy Alps and Esterels, we would follow the Mediterranean to Italy, over the frontier at Sospel and from the Italian lakes north again over the real Cols of the Swiss Alps.

We crossed to Boulogne in perfect weather. The Morgan had done some 3,000 miles when we started and, running easily at 45 to 50 m.p.h., we made Soissons that night.

From there we followed the well-known road through Troyes—typically French and full of atmosphere, with its old buildings, winding cobbled streets

and still, dark canal—and on through Dijon to Tournus, where I have a pet hotel. As one walks out on to the crooked vine-covered balcony above the old courtyard one begins, for the first time, to feel again the atmosphere of the South!

Next morning a short run brought us to the foothills of the Alps. A rough calculation when we stopped for petrol in Grenoble showed that the big J.A.P. was doing about 50 to the gallon, which was satisfactory enough, but even so one could have done with a rather larger tank on the Continent, with Esso pumps so few and far between.

The Morgan, of course, revelled in the Col de la Croix-Haute: dropping into second on the corners, one accelerated some 30 yds. or so, then up into top again.

From Tournus, our next stop was Aix-en-Provence, and the following morning saw us swooping along the Grande Corniche—just under two-and-a-half days from Boulogne without undue haste.

After a few days by the Mediterranean, fresh oil and adjustment of the tappets saw the Morgan ready for the road again. Leaving Mentone, we climbed over the Col de Castillon to Sospel, whence more Cols followed and then the Italian Frontier, where there was a considerable military display and many formalities (including the careful sealing up of our aged Kodak in case we should be tempted to photograph any of " il Duce's " private frontier views!).

Shortly after this we had our first visitation of trouble, and it was of a rather nerve-wracking nature. The road was becoming distinctly "Alpine," the surface more loose and dusty, the hairpins sharper and steeper. The

panorama of Mentone Harbour and Cap Martin as seen from the Boulevard de Garavan.

By Lilian Fraser

Italian sun and the white road made the glare very trying as one climbed up, with a last final burst of really superb hairpins, to the entrance of the Col di Tenda Tunnel 4,331 ft. up at the summit of the pass.

Switching on the lights, we plunged into the blackness. For the first few yards my impression was that of impenetrable darkness and water—water dripping, water running down the jagged walls and rushing streams on either side, into which the narrow road dropped sheer. At this point the Morgan began to wag her tail with considerable violence, her single driving wheel waltzing wildly in about 2 ins. of greasy mud. I had just got back into the straight and narrow way by throttling down to the last ounce in top, when suddenly there was a fierce smell of burning and the whole of my lights blacked out. It was too dark even to attempt repairs and turning was also out of the question.

I will draw a veil, with a shaking hand, over the 3 kilos. which remained of that tunnel! There are faint lights that glow at intervals to guide one's direction—that is all.

Mobbed by Enthusiasts.

At Turin we filled up with petrol and the car was absolutely mobbed by Italians of all ages, shapes and sizes. (The inevitable question arises, why, if these Latin races are such super-enthusiastic sporting motorists, do they drive nothing but saloons like little black match-boxes bobbing along the roads?)

After Turin came our blissful introduction to the Autostrade (thinking bitterly the while of our own by-pass roads, converted into long dangerous streets by the new houses that line them). For 100 miles, driving at 52 m.p.h., we put up an average of 48 m.p.h. in the most perfect safety imaginable.

That night we stayed in Como—very fashionable, yet cheaper than I expected. Next day we found Lake Iseo, deep and still among the mountains; the old villages, clustering among the olives, gave contrast to the busy shores of Como, whilst, instead of smart steamers, the primitive sailing boats drifting lazily with their great striped sails, like Viking galleys, crept round the headlands of the tree-clad islands.

In the village of Iseo we stayed some weeks, spending much of the time rowing and swimming. The Hotel Leon d'Oro provided more than adequate comfort for the modest charge of 16 lire a day! Below the vine-covered terrace glittered the green shadows of the lake, whilst under our window our boat rippled softly at its

moorings. The days drifted by and so, at last, we dis-interred the Morgan and swung her head for the Swiss Frontier.

A long drive through the heat brought us to the Customs at Castasegna, where we arrived with every inch of our car and clothing coated thickly in dust, even our hair and eyelashes being powdered snow-white! Thereafter began the long sheer climb up to Maloja at 6,000 ft. After about 5,000 ft. the engine began to lose power slightly owing to the more rarefied air, but there was more than enough power in hand to compete with this, and a higher middle-gear ratio would, in fact, have been an advantage.

The cool air blowing off the snow-covered peaks was almost unbelievable after the heat and dust of Italy as we drove up the long line of lakes in the Engadine Valley. Stopping to wash off a little of the dust in the icy brown waters of Silvaplanasee, we pushed on to Silvaplana for the night.

Nearly 8,000 ft. Up.

Leaving the valley at about 2 p.m. the following day, and setting our features in stern lines, we resolutely commenced our highest climb, up among the snow of the Julier Pass to the summit, nearly 8,000 ft. above sea level. At this point the effect of the height on the car-buration became so noticeable that I seriously regretted not having brought some smaller jets in my tool kit. However, the big Hispanos and Isottas coming over from St. Moritz appeared to be feeling it also, for we slipped by them easily, the wide-tracked Morgan cornering beautifully.

Staying the night at a little village near Zurich, we reached Basle early next morning and crossed over into France. On through Alsace and the Vosges, we spent the next night in Rheims, to leave again at 7 a.m., bumping out over its cobbled streets, past the war-scarred buildings, on to N.44 to make the best time we could to catch the 2 p.m. boat from Calais.

At St. Quentin we made a really devastating mistake. Instead of the usual N.35 to Amiens, we decided to take the more direct road via Arras. For some miles the road was perfect; then suddenly the asphalt ended abruptly and we crashed down on to some 40 miles of soul-shattering cobbles of almost inconceivable antiquity! We were now in the late war zone, passing quite close to Vimy Ridge. The war must have passed many times over that road—I shall not do so again!

After averaging a steady 10 m.p.h. for most of the morning, our chances for the boat seemed very slender. However, striking civilized roads again soon after St. Omer, I got down to it and made the Morgan travel as she never had before. As we tore down the dead straight N.43, a sudden clatter and exultant roar denoted the violent departure of silencer number one! Having wasted some valuable minutes picking up the red-hot " bits," I then pushed the speedometer up to 65, whereupon silencer number two promptly followed suit!

At the end of its long trek the engine proved more than equal to the prolonged burst of speed, and ten minutes before the boat sailed we made our positively thunderous entrance into the streets of Calais!

THE ONE AND ONLY MORGAN

Minor Changes for Coming Season

FINE RANGE OF THREE-WHEELED LIGHT CARS

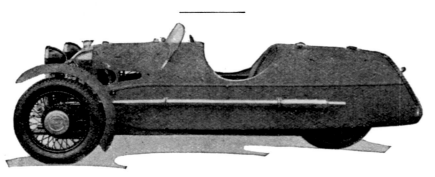

Two views of the striking bodywork which will characterize the Morgan Super Sports model for the coming season.

"NO change" is an almost accurate description of the 1935 Morgan programme. Were it not for the four-cylinder model and the super sports the phrase would be entirely correct, and even on these two there is very little alteration.

It is true that since the 1934 models were first described a year ago, there has been a change in the ignition system of all the twin-cylinder Morgans, but that change was made many months ago. It affects the contact breaker of the coil-ignition system. By a rearrangement of the high tension

<table>
<tr><td colspan="2" align="center">1935 MORGAN PRICES</td></tr>
<tr><td>Family Model, water cooled, s.v. .. .. ..</td><td>£105</td></tr>
<tr><td>Sports Family, water cooled, s.v. .. ..</td><td>£115</td></tr>
<tr><td>Sports Family, water cooled, o.h.v. .. ..</td><td>£125</td></tr>
<tr><td>Sports two-seater, water cooled, s.v. .. ..</td><td>£110</td></tr>
<tr><td>Sports Two-seater, air cooled, o.h.v. .. ..</td><td>£115</td></tr>
<tr><td>Sports Two-seater, water cooled, o.h.v. .. ..</td><td>£120</td></tr>
<tr><td>Super Sports, air cooled, o.h.v. .. .. ..</td><td>£127 10s.</td></tr>
<tr><td>Super Sports, water cooled, o.h.v. .. ..</td><td>£137 10s.</td></tr>
<tr><td>Four-cylinder Model ..</td><td>£120</td></tr>
</table>

leads and a new shape of distributor, this component has been made entirely waterproof.

Apart from that the Family model, the Sports two-seater and the Sports Family Morgan remain quite unaltered. Newest of all the Morgans is the four-cylindered machine, which made its first public appearance at the 1933 Motorcycle Show. Having lived with it for the best part of a year the good people at Malvern have decided that with just a little bit on here and the slightest bit off there, it would be even more handsome. And it is.

What it all amounts to is that the shape of the tail has been changed. Instead of sloping away as it did on

the 1934 Four, the tail retains a more circular section right to the end. The back panel or tail-end is recessed, and in this space the spare wheel fits. The result is a very appreciable improvement in the general appearance of the car.

This model, it may be recalled, has a four-cylinder engine with side-by-side valves and an aluminium alloy cylinder head. Its transmission system includes a single-plate clutch, a three-speed-and-reverse gearbox with worm drive to a cross-shaft from which a single chain drives the rear wheel. In this it resembles the twin-cylinder Morgans.

In many other respects it differs from them. For instance, it has a wheelbase longer by a foot, and the chassis frame is different, for the side members are Z-section pressings. Steering and front suspension are basically the same although the detail work is not. Further, all three brakes are connected to the pedal and the hand controls the rear brake only.

The Super Sports Model

As previously indicated, the only other changes for 1935 are to be found in the Super Sports. To prevent any possibility of the driver's or passenger's arm being scorched, the exhaust pipes are carried at a lower level along each side. This naturally makes a slight difference to the appearance.

Much more is to be noticed at the tail of the Super Sports. This is now barrel-shaped, something like the tail already described for the four-cylindered car. Moreover, the spare wheel fits into the end of the tail instead of sitting on top of it.

To finish the job off neatly, a polished aluminium disc covers the wheel except for the tyre and the edge of the rim. This disc carries the number-plate and the rear lamp. On top of the tail the space previously occupied by the wheel is now taken up by a simple luggage grid consisting of three aluminium strips mounted on wood bearers.

This model has an o.h.v. twin-cylinder engine, and there is the choice of either air cooling or water cooling. In both cases the unit is a Matchless, and the o.h. valves are operated by rockers and push rods, all enclosed and lubricated effectively.

Engines of the same make and design are used in some of the other Morgans, but those fitted to the Super Sports models are specially tuned. The Family model is an exception, for it has a water-cooled side-valve engine, and that unit is also available in the Sports two-seater.

Apart from the valve position, all these vee-twin engines are of similar design. They have a dry sump lubrication system with a separate oil tank which incorporates an oil filter.

These cars will not be on view at the Motor Show, but they will appear at the Motorcycle Show, which opens at Olympia on November 5.

IN BRIEF

TWO-CYLINDER MODELS

ENGINE : Twin-cylinder, s.v. or o.h.v.; 85.5 mm. by 85.5 mm. = 990 c.c.; tax, £4; coil ignition.

TRANSMISSION : Single dry plate clutch with flexible centre ; enclosed propeller shaft ; three-speed gearbox ; ratios, 4.85, 8 and 13.1 to 1; reverse, 17.5 to 1. Worm-driven cross-shaft and roller chain to rear wheel.

DIMENSIONS : Wheelbase, 7 ft. 3 ins. (Sports Family model, 7 ft. 7 ins.); track, 4 ft. 2 ins.; overall lengths, 10 ft. 4 ins. (Super Sports), 10 ft. 6 ins. (Family and Sports Two-seater), 10 ft. 10 ins. (Sports Family); width, 4 ft. 11 ins.

FOUR-CYLINDER MODEL

ENGINE : Four-cylinder, side valve; 56.6 mm. by 92.5 mm. = 933 c.c. Tax, £4 : coil ignition.

TRANSMISSION : As above.

DIMENSIONS : Wheelbase, 8 ft. 3 ins.; track, 4 ft. 2 ins.; overall length, 11 ft. 6 ins.; overall width, 4 ft. 11 ins.

THE MORGAN MOTOR CO., LTD., MALVERN LINK, WORCS.

On Three Wheels

By Triangle

FOR 1936 the four-cylinder Morgan shown here will sell at the reduced price of £115 10s., and there will be an additional four-cylinder model in the shape of a super-sports two-seater at £120 15s.

I WONDER how many of my readers are regarding the end of this month with rather dismal anticipation as the end of their motoring for the year. The plan of laying up machines for the winter on September 30 is nothing like so common as it once was, but there are still quite a few who do it.

Personally, I am all against the idea—at any rate so far as the last quarter of the year is concerned. For one thing, the Indian summer that we often get in October offers ideal motoring conditions, and for another, I hate to find myself with no form of transport at Christmas. Shopping can be the very devil if you have to rely on trams and buses, to say nothing of the awful business of getting to and from the various festivities that happen round about the end of December.

I believe, too, that winter motoring holds attractions of its own that are every bit as enjoyable as the summer can yield. In this I may differ from the views of the majority, but that, I always like to think, is because the majority are not so clever as I am in making the most of the cold shorter days.

However, it is early yet to think of winter days, so I will not continue that argument. All the same, I do advise anyone who is thinking of laying up his machine to reconsider the idea very seriously. If laying-up is a necessity for some period of the year, make it the January-March quarter. That is the time when the weather is at its worst and the three months concerned should give even those with quite elaborate plans for overhauling, ample time for whatever they have to do.

*   *   *

MY forecast last month that no startling changes were likely to be seen in three-wheelers for 1936 seems to be coming true. Already the Coventry Victor concern has announced the continuance of its luxury models with small improvements, and now comes the news that the Morgan range for 1936 remains the same with, however, the addition of a new super-sports four-cylinder model.

All About Morgans for 1936—Is Laying-up Worth While?— Useful Hints

The existing four-cylinder chassis will, I gather, be used and the body will be similar to that of the corresponding two-cylinder model. Exact details are not yet available for publication, but the price has already been fixed at £120 15s.

In addition I am able to pass on the welcome news that, with the exception of the side-valve, water-cooled Family model, prices of the remainder of the range have been substantially reduced. Here is the full list with last year's figures given in brackets for comparison:—

Two-cylinder two-seaters: Sports model with s.v. water-cooled engine £101 17s. (£110), with o.h.v. air-cooled engine £107 2s. (£115), with o.h.v. water-cooled engine £115 10s. (£120). Super sports model with o.h.v. air-cooled engine £126 (£127 10s.), with o.h.v. water-cooled engine £136 10s. (£137 10s.).

Two-cylinder four-seaters: Family model with s.v. water-cooled engine £96 12s. (£95). Sports Family model with s.v. water-cooled engine £110 5s. (£115), with o.h.v. air-cooled engine £115 10s. (£120), with o.h.v. water-cooled engine £120 15s. (£125).

In addition, of course, there is the existing four-cylinder model which now costs £115 10s. (£120), and the new super sports four-cylinder model at £120 15s.

At these reduced figures I should say that Morgan prospects for 1936 look very bright indeed.

*   *   *

AN owner of an o.h.v. J.A.P.-engined Morgan sends me a useful tip, which seems well worth passing on. In this engine, the ball joints between the tops of the push rods and the rockers rely for lubrication on oil mist blown up from the timing chest, but he noticed that, on his engine, these joints seemed absolutely dry. Puzzled, he tried running the engine on a fast tick-over with the rocker box covers removed, just to see what was actually happening.

To his surprise, several large lumps of hard grease were blown out of the push-rod tubes—and since then no further trouble with dry ball joints has occurred. The assumption is that the grease had at some time exuded from the rocker bearings and found its way down the tubes; as the tops of the push rods are thicker than the stems, it had been unable to return and had effectively screened the joints from oil mist.

*   *   *

HOW can fitting a new contact breaker spring cause pinking?—was a poser set me by a four-cylinder B.S.A. owner the other day. Apparently he had broken the spring, fitted a new one, carefully adjusted the gap, and then found to his amazement that the engine showed a pronounced tendency to pink.

The problem is not so difficult as it sounds. It all depends on the adjustment of the gap and its effect on the ignition timing. If the gap is very wide the points will open much earlier and the ignition will be correspondingly advanced. A small gap, on the other hand, will retard the ignition.

Obviously, in the case in question, the gap, before the spring was replaced, was too small and the ignition had been permanently retarded. Possibly the small gap had been brought about by wear on the fibre heel-piece that bears on the cam and had been reduced gradually, so that its effect was not noticed. At the same time carbon was forming in the head—also without its effect being noticed owing to the slow and progressive retarding of the ignition.

So soon as the ignition timing was advanced to its correct point, however, the effect of the carbon accumulation immediately became apparent by pronounced pinking.

Simple!

Reprinted from "Motor Cycling," January 29, 1936.

Road Tests of 1936 Models

THE 10 h.p. FOUR-CYLINDER

MORGAN

A Fast and Comfortable Sports Three-wheeler of 1,172 c.c.

With its radiator fitted well forward, in latest car practice, the Sports Morgan Four presents a handsome appearance.

(Above) The cockpit is arranged to give a good view of the road ahead and to provide easy control. (Right) The four-cylinder, s.v. engine is water-cooled and has a down-draught carburetter and coil ignition.

THE combination of a flexible and efficient power unit of no less than 1,172 c.c. capacity with a vehicle weighing, all told, less than 8 cwt., is obviously one which will appeal to the sportsman as giving promise of exceptional performance on the road.

Morgan enthusiasts who were at the Motorcycle Show last year will no doubt have admired the appearance of the new Sports four-cylinder two-seater which made its début there, and it was one of these models, fitted with the 10 h.p. engine (available in place of the well-known 8 h.p. unit at an extra charge of 7 guineas) which was the subject of this test.

The Chassis Layout

In view of the fact that the model is a new one, it will be as well, perhaps, to refer briefly to the specification and layout before actually going into performance details.

The chassis, with its channel-section members, although a breakaway from the practice followed in the twin-cylinder models, is a thoroughly tried component and follows the lines of the well-known 8 h.p. four-cylinder four-seater model. The engine, again on lines similar to the 8 h.p. type, but of somewhat larger dimensions, is an up-to-date water-cooled side-valve unit, with such modern features as a down-draught carburetter and a detachable cylinder head of turbulent internal formation.

Transmission of power to the rear wheel is in accordance with Morgan practice by means of an enclosed propeller shaft to the three-speed-and-reverse gearbox,

which lies between the seats, and thence via a bronze worm and wheel to the heavy weight final chain.

All three brakes are coupled to the pedal and the independent suspension of the front wheels by means of helical springs is damped by a pair of subsidiary coil springs. The body follows the lines of that fitted to the twin-cylinder sports models, and, combined with a large and handsome bonnet radiator, gives not only a speedy but also a distinctly imposing appearance to the little vehicle.

Turning now to the performance. Although a maximum of 74 m.p.h. (corresponding to engine r.p.m. of 4,540) could be quickly attained and was comfortably held, the outstanding features were undoubtedly the phenomenal acceleration and hill-climbing propensities of the engine. So good were these that even the fast solo motorcyclist could hardly be disappointed, and the ease and celerity with which other cars could be passed on the road was a delight. It is no exaggeration to say that, even by Morgan standards, this new model is unusually rapid.

All out in "second," the maximum speed obtained was 55 m.p.h. (5,630 r.p.m.), and a comfortable cruising speed in top of anything up to 60 m.p.h. could be maintained whenever road conditions permitted. At speeds of over 67 m.p.h. both power unit and transmission were inclined to be somewhat noisy.

Road-holding and steering were of the true Morgan variety. On good main-road going the model could be accurately placed and it cornered splendidly. Unless the surface was unusually treacherous, there was a pleasing absence of excessive tail-wag.

VO-SEATER

Comfort is a strong point about the latest Morgan Four and this has been in no way sacrificed to provide attractive lines. Although no doors are fitted entry and exit is easy when the hood is down.

The steering is, by modern car standards, high-geared and very direct. When first handled, this is apt to lead to the impression that it is heavy. Actually, however, only a short acquaintance is necessary before the driver comes to appreciate it at its true worth. At speed the motor is guided, not by turning the wheel, but simply by a gentle pressure on it.

The arrangement is almost ideal for a sports model and quite effortless to handle over long distances. Thanks to correct layout at the front, the steering wheel, which is, by the way, of the spring-spoked variety, showed very little tendency to kick back even under unfavourable circumstances.

In traffic the four-cylinder engine was most pleasant to handle and the minimum speeds of 10 m.p.h., 6 m.p.h. and 3 m.p.h. in top, second and first gears,

although they were quite satisfactory, were probably not so low as would have been possible had the engine been more fully run-in. The power output at low r.p.m. was excellent and, in consequence, the model was easy to handle on hilly going off the beaten track.

Silent Speed

As was to be expected, in view of such capabilities, a capacity for maintaining high average speeds over give-and-take roads was a pronounced characteristic of the model which should have no difficulty in keeping up with anything but the fastest of the solo men.

The power unit, despite the performance which it delivers, was delightfully smooth and silent up to within about 7 m.p.h. of its maximum speed. Following up-to-date car practice, all its working parts are fully enclosed and automatically lubricated, a point of interest being that no means of tappet adjustment is provided.

On a 48-mile run at an average speed of 25 m.p.h., the petrol consumption was 41 m.p.g. The same journey at an average of 38 m.p.h. resulted in a consumption figure of 37 m.p.g. In each case a passenger was carried in addition to the driver.

Oil consumption was quite negligible, and after 300 miles there was no perceptible change of level shown by the dip-stick. The ignition timing is automatically controlled, and, on the model tested, unless a leaded fuel was used there was a tendency towards detonation if the throttle was suddenly opened wide at anything below about 35 m.p.h. This characteristic became less apparent as the test proceeded and the engine became freer.

Starting

Starting was always easy provided the strangler was used when the engine was cold, an excellent feature being the rapidity with which the starting motor would

Reprinted from "Motor Cycling," January 29, 1936.

Brief Specification of the 1,172 c.c. Model F Morgan

Engine: Four-cylinder, side-by-side valves, water-cooled. Down-draught carburetter. Lubrication by a combination of forced-feed and splash. Detachable cylinder head. Belt-driven dynamo. Automatic ignition control. 8 h.p.: Bore 56.6, stroke 92.56 = 933 c.c. 10 h.p.: Bore 63.5, stroke 92.56 = 1,172 c.c.

Transmission: Enclosed propeller shaft with centre bearing to three-speeds-and-reverse gearbox, thence via worm and wheel and final chain to rear wheel. Gear ratios, 4.58, 7.5 and 13.1 to 1. Reverse, 17 to 1.

Chassis: Steel channel of deep section. Coil-type front springs; quarter elliptic rear. Geared steering. Internal-expanding brakes on all wheels.

Bodywork: Coachbuilt two-seater; wood framing and sheet-metal panels. Moseley Float-on-Air cushions. Choice of colour schemes.

Equipment: Lucas 6-volt dynamo lighting and coil ignition set, with electric starter. Four Dunlop Magna detachable and interchangeable wheels. Tyres 26-in by 4-in. Hood, with envelope. Full kit of tools. Speedometer and number plates. Spring-spoked steering wheel.

Dimensions: Wheelbase, 8 ft. 3 ins.; track, 4 ft. 2 ins.; overall length, 11 ft. 6 ins.; overall width, 4 ft. 11 ins.

Weight: 7 cwt. 3 qrs. 21 lb.

Price: With 8 h.p. engine, 115 guineas. With 10 h.p. engine, 122 guineas.

Makers: Morgan Motor Co., Ltd., Malvern Link, Worcs.

Tax: £4.

ROAD TEST OF THE MORGAN FOUR (Contd.)

swing the engine, no matter what its temperature. Dual control is provided for the throttle, there being a lever on the steering wheel working via a Bowden cable, in addition to the usual car-type auxiliary pedal. The down-draught carburetter and the ignition distributor are both accessibly placed.

A short vertically mounted lever in a remote gate controls the gearbox, and this worked excellently, very little experience being necessary before rapid and certain changes could be made, either up or down. In top gear the box was quite silent, although the indirect gears produced perhaps rather more noise than is usual nowadays. The transmission as a whole was at times a trifle harsh, although the clutch was light and smooth, and the final chain seemed well up to its work, as it showed no sign of requiring adjustment at the conclusion of the test.

Gears and Brakes

The gear ratios have undoubtedly been well chosen. "First," although amply low enough for all ordinary requirements, is sufficiently high to enable a really smart get-away from rest to be made, and the step up to "second" and again to "top" is such that the engine never seemed to be labouring against too high a ratio when rapid acceleration was required. It was, therefore, always possible to make the fullest use of the Morgan's high power-to-weight ratio.

All three brakes are coupled to the pedal, the hand-lever operating the rear one only. Normally, therefore, apart from when parking, the pedal is used exclusively. From 30 m.p.h. on a dry, level road, with two up, the Morgan could be pulled up in 38 ft. A satisfactory feature was the complete absence of any locking of the wheels or of a tendency for the car to pull across the road. We were impressed with the fact that, even under unfavourable weather conditions, the vehicle showed no desire to get out of hand, even when the brakes were applied suddenly.

The movement of the pedal necessary to secure maximum results was rather greater than some would like, although this is a characteristic to which the driver quickly became accustomed. Fairly heavy pressure was required to secure a sudden stop.

The Lights

Lighting by means of a pair of combined head and side lamps was ample for all ordinary requirements. The lamps are mounted fairly high up, which is a good feature, and the dip switch controls both of them. A Lucas Altette horn is standardized, and both dynamo and battery can be got at easily for periodic inspection.

One does not have to drive this model far before it is realized that the degree of protection afforded by the dash and windscreen—the latter, incidentally, of the folding type—is above the average. This is due to sensible planning of the body, the driver sitting close up to the windscreen and well down in the cockpit. For the same reason, the support and protection afforded to the back and shoulders is also above the average. All the facia-board instruments are within easy reach and the amount of leg room should satisfy the tallest of drivers or passengers.

Visibility Good

Although it was necessary for the driver to sit bolt upright in order to see the near-side mudguard, visibility in general was good. Side curtains are not provided, but the hood buttons snugly round the windscreen, and, when folded down, is neatly enclosed in an envelope. There is space behind the seat, the squab of which hinges forward, for tools and a limited amount of luggage, a smart chromium-plated grid on the tail being capable of accommodating a further quantity of luggage.

With its attractive finish—the model tested was in cream and scarlet—the Model F looks what it is, a genuinely fast vehicle of the true sporting type. It can fairly, and without exaggeration, claim to be very fast, yet it is economical to run and easy to handle. In the course of the test we found that the faster it was driven the more it appeared to like it, and really long journeys could be undertaken with the certainty that they could, if necessary, be accomplished in a time normally associated with some of the faster and more expensive of large sports cars.

MORGAN THREE-WHEELERS for 1937

Three Main Types Retained Without Alteration in Price or Design

The Morgan models shown on this page are representative of the three main types—sports, super-sports and four-cylinder.

EXCEPT for the fact that Family models no longer figure in the list, the Morgan range of three-wheelers is being retained without modification for the coming season; that is to say, the super-sports, the four-cylinder and the sports models are all continued for

1937 without any alteration either to price or to specification.

The super-sports model is, of course driven by an o.h.v. twin-cylinder Morgan-Matchless engine, which can be either of the air-cooled or water-cooled variety. Much the same applies to the sports two-seater, which, however, can also be obtained with a side-valve engine. The four-cylinder three-wheeler is offered with either a two-seater body or as a four-seater.

The full list of models and prices is as follows:—

	£	s.
Sports 2-str., s.v., water-cooled ...	101	17
Sports 2-str., o.h.v., air-cooled ...	107	2
Sports 2-str., o.h.v., water-cooled ...	115	10
Super Sports, o.h.v., air-cooled ...	126	0
Super Sports, o.h.v., water-cooled ...	136	10
Four-cylinder, 4-str., 8 h.p. ...	115	10
Four-cylinder, 2-str., 8 h.p. ...	120	15

Extra for 10 h.p. engine in four-cylinder models £7 7s.

Extra for two-door body on Sports 2-str., £5.

Although all these models have much in common, apart from the engine, there is a considerable difference between the chassis of the four-cylinder types and that of the twin-cylinder models, the difference mainly lying in the fact that the former have two deep channel-sectioned frame members, one on each side of the central propeller shaft tube, whereas the two-cylinder types have a tubular chassis.

The suspension, transmission and braking systems are similar on all types. The suspension includes the well-known independent Morgan system employing helical springs at the front and two quarter elliptics, one on each side of the rear wheel, at the back. So far as the transmission is concerned, the drive is taken through a dry-plate

clutch fitted with a Borg and Beck flexible centre and thence by a propeller shaft to a three-speed and reverse gearbox fitted just forward of the rear wheel, the final drive being by a roller chain on the off side. Internal expanding cable-operated brakes are used, the pedal taking effect on the rear wheel and the central brake lever on the two front wheels.

Representative examples of the three types are shown on this page. The four-seater, four-cylinder model, it will be observed, provides generous accommodation in the rear for two children, but there is room, when occasion demands, to carry adults in the back seats. The sports two-seater on the four-cylinder chassis is similar in frontal appearance, but has a tail somewhat after the lines of the two-cylinder sports model. This type, it will be recalled, was introduced just before the Motor Cycle Show last year. For those who want extra lively performance a 10 h.p. engine can be fitted to either of the four-cylinder types at an extra charge.

It will be noticed in each case that a spare wheel and tyre is provided, and this feature nowadays is standard on all Morgan models. Other items of equipment common to all types are a windscreen wiper, speedometer, hood and electric starter.

Morgan three-wheelers have, of course, always been famous for their acceleration, hill-climbing and lively turn of speed, and the satisfaction they have given in the hands of their owners is proved by their long period of popularity, which dates back to well before the war. An announcement regarding the four-wheeled Morgan, introduced some time ago, will be made next week.

IN BRIEF

Sports and Super Sports

ENGINE: Two cylinders; overhead or side valves and air-cooled or water-cooled (see price list); 85.5 mm. by 85.5 mm. (990 c.c.). Tax, £4.

TRANSMISSION: Single dry-plate clutch; enclosed propeller shaft to three-speed gearbox; ratios, 4.58, 7.5 and 12.4 to 1; reverse, 16.5 to 1. Final drive by worm gear and roller chain.

DIMENSIONS: Wheelbase, 7 ft. 3 ins.; track, 4 ft. 2 ins.; overall length (sports), 10 ft. 6 ins.; (super sports), 10 ft. 4 ins.; overall width, 4 ft. 11 ins.

Four-cylinder Models

ENGINE: Four cylinders; side valves; 56.6 mm. by 92.5 mm. (933 c.c.) or (see price list) 63.5 mm. by 92.5 mm. (1,172 c.c.). Tax, £4.

TRANSMISSION: As sports above.

DIMENSIONS: Wheelbase, 8 ft. 3 ins.; track, 4 ft. 2 ins.; overall length, 11 ft. 6 ins.; overall width, 4 ft. 11 ins.

MORGAN MOTOR CO., LTD.
Malvern Link,
Worcestershire

A TWIN-ENGINED MORGAN

"Triangle" Describes an Interesting Conversion Featuring Two Scott Motorcycle Engines

The pair of two-cylinder two-stroke engines fits neatly in the usual place and, as this photograph shows, they do not look unwieldy.

IMAGINE a super-sports Morgan m which the cylinders have somehow become spread out into a much wider Vee than usual and have been individually distorted into oval section. Imagine also the machine travelling along with an unusual degree of silence and a very multi-cylinder purr about its exhaust.

If you can do that you have an excellent first impression of the machine described on this page; but, perhaps, if you live down Weybridge way, you have no need to imagine these things but have actually caught a glimpse of this strange three-wheele and wondered at its odd-looking "engine" and the unfamiliarity of its exhaust note.

If you have, here is the explanation. The "engine" is not one engine at all, but two, and its exhaust is explained by the fact that they are Scott two-stroke motorcycle engines combining the power of their 596 c.c. two-cylinder units into one harmonious 1,192 c.c. whole. Each delivers something like 30 b.h.p., so there is no need to explain why they are to be found where they are. Smooth torque and unbounded power (for all practical purposes) have ever been the aim of enthusiasts.

The enthusiasts in this case are Mr. J. Granville Grenfell, M.I.B.E., the well-known racing engineer and tuner, of Brooklands Aerodrome, and Mr. K. S. Alderton, of Harpenden, Herts, who conceived the idea of fitting two reconditioned Scott engines into a 1934 super-sports Morgan.

It did not quite prove a case of "no sooner said than done," for although the two engines sat nice and comfortably on the front of the Morgan frame with their crankcases back to back, the problem of how to combine the power of those 1,192 c.c. into the harmonious whole just mentioned was not quite so straightforward.

How it was eventually done can be seen in the sketch at the foot of this page.

The engines, it should be explained, run in opposite directions—which enables their respective torque reactions and vibrations to wage a nice little civil war, leaving the rest of the chassis in a pleasant state of non-intervention.

The near-side engine drives direct by means of a roller chain on to a central shaft coupled to the clutch. Power from the off-side engine takes a rather more complicated course and four sprockets are concerned in sending it the way it should go.

If you follow a link of the chain round, on its journey from the engine sprocket, you will find that it first passes downwards round an idler sprocket, then upwards round a sprocket on a countershaft (from which another chain drives the magneto), downwards again and round the underside of the clutch shaft sprocket and then back again to the engine once more. The whole drive is enclosed and runs in an oil bath.

The rest of the transmission—in fact the rest of the car, apart from the engine, is of normal Morgan type and the whole job cost something in the region of £200 to build.

On the road, the machine possesses the attraction of remarkable flexibility and smooth running (four two-stroke cylinders, remember), terrific acceleration (bear in mind the 60 b.h.p. and the light weight of the Morgan) and a reserve of maximum speed under all but the most exceptional conditions (*second* gear suffices for a mere 70 m.p.h.). In short, a "special" of more than usual interest and attraction.

(Left) A sketch showing how the two engines are ingeniously arranged to drive a common shaft connected to the clutch. Normally, the drive is totally enclosed.

The MORGAN 4-CYLINDER THREE-WHEELER

A Machine for Those Who Like Open-air Motoring and a "Car with a Kick in It"

These two pictures give an excellent idea of the trim lines and low build of the four-cylinder version of the famous three-wheeler which forms the subject of this test report.

ALTHOUGH the subject of this test report was a two-seater Morgan of the four-cylinder variety, much of what is said applies equally to the four-seater model. Both cars differ from other Morgans not only in the type of engine employed, but also, of course, with regard to various features of construction. The chassis frame, for instance, is entirely different.

Since the arrangement of the various controls must be known before a car can be driven and because they have much to do with the pleasure of driving, let us discuss them first. On the facia board is an oval panel carrying the ammeter on one side and the ignition and lighting switch on the other. In between is a trip speedo-meter of which the "30" mark can be seen without difficulty from the driving seat.

Just below the steering wheel and operable by the right hand is a dipping switch. Above the steering column on the facia board is a pull-out control for the starter motor and in the corresponding position on the near side is a similar knob which brings into action the easy starting device on the carburetter.

Three pedals, arranged as usual, operate the clutch, brake and accelerator, but there is also a Bowden lever attached to one spoke of the steering wheel and connected to the throttle so that the engine can be accelerated by hand. The horn button, by the way, is placed near the bottom of the instrument panel, within easy reach of the left hand.

The gear lever is mounted centrally above the prop.

shaft tube and operates in a neat gate. First gear is engaged by pressing the lever towards the off side and pulling it back towards the seat. For second ratio the lever is moved forward and over towards the near side, while to engage "top" it is pulled straight back from that position. For reverse, the lever is moved into a position directly forward of the bottom gear location.

A point of difference from twin-cylinder Morgans is that the brake pedal is connected to all three wheels. The lever, however, operates the rear brake only and is intended for parking. It is placed a little to the left and slightly forward of the gear lever and its ratchet is controlled by a sliding trigger mounted on its front edge and easily moved by the fingers.

In spite of the low seat, there is no difficulty in judging the width of the vehicle, because the headlamps are mounted on the wings and both can be seen easily by the driver. On the score of visibility, the Morgan should be particularly good in fog because its screen can be folded down on to the scuttle.

Each seat consists of a padded cushion resting on thin three-ply, which gives a resilient effect. At the back is a one-piece squab which can be hinged forward to disclose a large space in which tools and small parcels can be carried. Underneath each seat also there is a shallow compartment which can be used for this purpose.

On the particular car tested there was no door, but one can be fitted on the near side at no extra cost. A folding hood stows neatly away behind the seats and is enclosed in an envelope when not in use. It can be erected very quickly simply by removing the envelope and pulling the hood fabric forward so that its front edge can be attached to the windscreen by means of Lift-a-dot fasteners.

As to accessibility, the engine oil filler and dipstick are both conveniently placed on the near side. The plugs, distributor and carburetter also can be reached without difficulty. A neat mounting for the spare wheel is obtained by recessing it into the back panel of the tail, where an aluminium disc keeps its spokes free from dust or mud and acts as a rear number plate.

Although the rear wheel may seem to be not too accessible, actually it can be reached with very little trouble. When the spare has been removed, the panel on which it is mounted can also be taken away by undoing four nuts and the driving wheel can then be detached.

Wheel removal at the rear is not quite so easy as

Important features of the model F two-seater Morgan shown in these pictures are the four-cylinder side-valve engine, the snug all-weather equipment and the accessible controls.

but appears to follow motorcycle practice, in which any ratio can be "crashed" into engagement without let or hindrance.

The brakes are good. It is true that they require a fair pressure on the pedal, but when this is applied the

IN BRIEF

ENGINE: Four cylinders; side valves; 56.6 mm. by 92.5 mm.=933 c.c. Tax, £4; power output, 24 b.h.p. at 3,500 r.p.m.

TRANSMISSION: Single dry-plate clutch; three-speed gearbox. Ratios, 4.85, 8 and 13.1 to 1; reverse, 17.5 to 1. Final drive by enclosed propeller shaft and single roller chain.

GENERAL: Cable-operated brakes; independent helical springs front and quarter-elliptic rear; 5-gallon petrol tank under bonnet.

DIMENSIONS: Wheelbase, 8 ft. 3 ins.; track, 4 ft. 2 ins.; overall length, 11 ft. 6 ins.; overall width, 4 ft. 11 ins.

PERFORMANCE: Flying ¼-mile, fastest one way, 66.2 m.p.h.; mean speed, 64.8 m.p.h.; standing ¼-mile, 24¾ secs.; petrol consumption, 40 m.p.g.

PRICE: £120 15s.

MORGAN MOTOR CO., LTD.
MALVERN LINK,
WORCS

car stops promptly and without any trace of misbehaviour. Also commendable is the steering. It is highly geared so that only a small movement of the wheel is necessary for all ordinary purposes.

Its self-centring action is sufficient to straighten the car after a corner, but not so pronounced as to make the steering unduly heavy. Cornering is, in fact, a pleasure, and contrary to the idea (which should have died years ago) that a three wheeler is liable to overturn, we found that this Morgan can be turned as quickly as most cars of any build and that its limit is imposed by tyre grip only. In short, it will slide before it dreams of capsizing.

To judge by the growth in popularity of the closed car, there may be fewer people to-day than there used to be who enjoy the masculine style of motoring. For those, however, who do like plenty of fresh air and a car with a kick in it, a Morgan such as this four-cylinder model should certainly fill the bill. If still more verve is desired, a 10 h.p. engine is available at an extra cost of £7 7s.

on a normal car owing to the fact that the wheel is carried in a fork and has chain drive, but the provision of a knock-out spindle which enables the wheel to be detached, complete with the chain sprocket, reduces the work to fairly simple terms.

A high power-weight ratio makes the Morgan a very lively little vehicle. As our test figures show, it accelerates rapidly and the time taken for the standing start quarter-mile is appreciably better than would be recorded by any four-wheeler short of an expensive sports car. Part of the credit for this result is undoubtedly due to the easy gear-change. The latter incorporates no synchromesh or other special device,

NEW MORGAN THREE-WHEELER

Super Sports Four-cylinder Model with Girling Brakes

CHIEF interest in the Morgan three-wheeler programme for the coming season is centred in the new four-cylinder super-sports two-seater. Basically similar to the other four-cylinder models, it is mounted on a somewhat shorter chassis, whilst the body, as can be seen in an accompanying photograph, is very like that of the super-sports twin-cylinder model.

More important, however, than the new body is the fact that Girling brakes are fitted. There is no need

(Right) The "old faithful" Morgan with a twin-cylinder Matchless engine is continued unchanged.

(Left) The new model has attractive lines and its performance should be in keeping. (Below, centre) A "close-up" of the near-side front wheel, showing (A) the connection of the operating cable and (B) the adjusting nut of the Girling brakes.

here for us to describe this system at length, as readers should already be familiar with it. In the case of the Morgan, however, the conventional rods connecting brake pedal and wheel units are replaced by Bowden cables—an eminently satisfactory substitution since, by the design of the brakes, all the cables will be in tension. Moreover, cables are somewhat lighter than rods, and this is important when one considers the 8 cwt. legal limit.

The power unit is actually a four-cylinder side-valve affair with a Treasury rating of 10 h.p. Other features are the downdraught carburetter, three-bearing crankshaft and the single-plate clutch. Where, however, in a four-wheeled car the gearbox would be mounted with the engine, it is, in the case of the Morgan, mounted at the rear of the chassis, whence it drives the single rear wheel by means of a chain. A three-speed and reverse gearbox is incorporated in the transmission.

Suspension, both front and rear, is of the type already well tested on Morgan three-wheelers. At the front it consists of vertical helical springs encased in telescopic tubes, whilst the rear wheel is carried on swinging arms controlled by quarter-elliptic laminated springs.

As for the other three-wheeler

models, they are all unchanged from the 1937 designs. It should be noted, however, that the water-cooled sports two-seater has been dropped. There remain, therefore, the super-sports two-seater fitted with an o.h.v. 990 c.c. air-cooled Matchless twin engine and the two four-cylinder models (two-seater and four-seater), which are available with either 8 h.p. or 10 h.p. power units. It should be emphasized at this point that the new super-sports in no way replaces the twin engine super-sports; this latter model will continue to hold its popularity.

IN BRIEF

FOUR-CYLINDER MODELS

ENGINE: (10 h.p. model) four cylinders, side valves, 63.5 mm. by 92.5 mm.= 1,172 c.c. Tax, £4. (8 h.p. model) four cylinders, side valves, 56.6 mm. by 92.5 mm.=933 c.c. Tax, £4.

TRANSMISSION: Single dry-plate clutch; three-speed and reverse gearbox. Ratios, 4.85, 8 and 13.1 to 1; reverse, 17.5 to 1. Final drive by chain.

GENERAL: Mechanical brakes; helical front springs, ¼-elliptic rear; 4-gallon petrol tank.

DIMENSIONS: Wheelbase, 7 ft. 3 ins.; track, 4 ft. 2 ins.; overall length, 10 ft. 8 ins.; overall width, 4 ft. 11 ins.

PRICES: Two-seater, £120 15s.; four-seater, £115 10s. (both are available with either 8 h.p. or 10 h.p. engines).

SUPER-SPORTS FOUR-CYLINDER

ENGINE: As 10 h.p. above.

TRANSMISSION: As above.

GENERAL: As above, except that Girling brakes are fitted.

DIMENSIONS: Not yet available.

PRICE: 10 h.p. two-seater, £136 10s.

TWO-CYLINDER MODEL

ENGINE: Two cylinders (50-degree V-twin); overhead valves; 85.5 mm. by 85.5 mm. = 990 c.c. Tax, £4.

TRANSMISSION: As above, except that gear ratios are—4.58, 7.5, and 12.4 to 1; reverse, 16.5 to 1.

GENERAL: As four-cylinder models.

DIMENSIONS: Wheelbase, 7 ft. 3 ins.; track, 4 ft. 2 ins.; overall length, 10 ft. 4 ins.; overall width, 4 ft. 11 ins.

PRICE: Super-sports two-seater, £126.

THE MORGAN MOTOR CO., LTD., Malvern Link, Worcs.

Reprinted from "Motor Cycling," March 23, 1938

Road Tests of 1938 Models

FOUR-CYLINDER S.V.
MORGAN

A Comfortable Sporting Model for Two

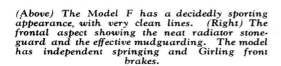

(Above) The Model F has a decidedly sporting appearance, with very clean lines. (Right) The frontal aspect showing the neat radiator stone-guard and the effective mudguarding. The model has independent springing and Girling front brakes.

ENTHUSIASTS at the Earls Court Exhibition must have gazed with admiration upon the handsome lines of the latest Model F Super Sports Morgan. Fitted with a four-cylinder engine of 1,172 c.c. capacity, Girling brakes, interchangeable wheels and adequate weather protection, the machine gave promise of a fine all-round performance, coupled with a degree of comfort and companionship to both driver and passenger, which it would be hard to beat on any other form of three-wheeled transport. Therefore, it was with more than usual interest that we looked forward to road testing the latest model. And the results did not disappoint us.

Excellent Suspension

Comfort was equal to almost any four-wheeler and, we would go so far as to say, better than many, particularly with reference to the seating accommodation and the springing. The seats themselves were very ample air cushions, which could be inflated to suit individual tastes, whilst the rear squab was thick and high enough to give full and very comfortable support to one's whole back and shoulders, thereby enabling distances of nearly 150 miles to be covered non-stop without even a trace of fatigue; in fact, after such a journey, there seemed no apparent reason why double the distance should not have been travelled in the same manner, with the exception of a stop to take on fuel.

There is no doubt also that the layout of the controls had a lot to do with this tireless long-distance travel, and, for a man of normal build, no additional cushions were necessary to bring the steering wheel into the best and most natural position; also there was ample leg room to allow easy manipulation of the accelerator, brake and clutch controls, which were nice and progressive in action. A stronger throttle-return spring would have been an improvement for the individual needs of our tester. Another point which it did not take long to appreciate was the degree of protection afforded by the dash and the windscreen, which was well above the average and brought about by the sensible planning of the body, which allows the driver to sit well up to the windscreen and down in the cockpit. Incidentally, the screen was of the "fold-flat" type. A door is provided on the passenger's side, but none on the driver's side—a fact that made entering or leaving the body a matter of some difficulty when a passenger was seated, particularly with the hood up.

Suspension must needs be closely linked up with

A close-up of the car-type water-cooled power-unit, a four-cylinder engine of 1,172 c.c. capacity. The down-draught carburetter and the general accessibility can be clearly seen from this view.

comfort, and in this respect the independent front-wheel springing has for some years past made the Morgan famous as a good road holder. The ability of these

Super-sports Model F

(Below) The tail-end of the Morgan showing the spare wheel and the detachable plate that gives access to the rear wheel. The chromium-plated luggage grid will be seen surmounting the tail and it will be observed that twin screen wipers are fitted.

(Above) The Model F was amazingly steady at all speeds, and would hold the road well when cornering fast or on bad surfaces.

A view of the cockpit showing the layout of the controls, and the spring steering wheel. The windscreen can be folded flat for fast motoring.

little machines to give a comfortable ride round Brooklands at high speed is ample proof that the springing is well able to do its work under normal road conditions,

and the new Model F is no exception to the rule. Sections of road which normally give cars a good shaking at 50 m.p.h. could be traversed in the Morgan without any excessive bumping at well over 60 m.p.h., whilst certain wavy parts of the Watling Street were covered with the greatest of ease at 65-70 m.p.h.

Judged by modern car standards the steering was high geared and almost direct; however, this arrangement is ideal for the sports model and was quite effortless to handle. Thanks to the correct layout of the front end, the steering wheel showed very little tendency to "kick back" even when cornering fast on a curve covered with potholes, whilst on ordinary main roads it was almost uncanny the way in which the model could be flung round bends with the tyres squealing their protest.

Powerful Brakes

All three brakes are coupled to the pedal, the hand brake, simply intended for parking purposes, operating only on the rear wheel. From 30 m.p.h. on a dry road with two up, the Morgan could be stopped in 29 ft. During the period of coming to rest the front wheels were just on the point of locking; the rear wheel cannot lock under ordinary circumstances due to the design of the system and the distribution of the braking effort. From this it might be misinterpreted that the front Girling brakes were fierce; on the contrary they were exceptionally powerful, but, at the same time, typically "Girling" in their progressive action, so that even on greasy cobbles they inspired the greatest confidence. We cannot pass the brakes without giving a word of praise to the easy adjustment of the shoes; a matter of two minutes is sufficient to "take up" the brakes on all three wheels.

Turning now to performance, although a maximum speed of 71 m.p.h. could be quickly attained and held on the level, the outstanding feature was the effortless manner in which a speed of just over 65 m.p.h. could be maintained along some of our good main roads. The ability with which main-road hills could be dealt with, and the excellent acceleration would not have disappointed even a fast solo motorcyclist.

In the first case the gearbox-driven speedometer was

Brief Specification of the 1938 Model "F" Super-sports Morgan

Engine: Four-cylinder four-stroke; bore, 62.5 mm.; stroke, 92.5 mm.; capacity, 1,172 c.c.; 32.5 b.h.p. at 4,300 r.p.m.; 6.6-1 compression ratio. Side valves. Down-draught carburetter. Electric starter and coil ignition.
Transmission: Shaft drive to gearbox; worm and countershaft to final drive. Chain of ¾-in. pitch. Gear ratios,

4.85, 7.9, 15.3; reverse, 18.3 to 1.
Frame: Pressed-steel channel-section side members, with tubular front and large tubular backbone. Independent suspension. Coil springs on front wheels and quarter elliptic on rear wheel.
Wheels: Interchangeable, with four-stud fixing. One spare. 18-in. by 4-in. Dunlop Magna wheels.

Tank: 4½-gallon capacity, situated under bonnet. Oil carried in engine sump.
Equipment: Lucas lighting. Fold-flat windscreen and hood. Door on passenger's side. Luggage grid.
Makers: The Morgan Motor Co., Malvern Link, Worcs.
Price: £136 10s.
Tax: £4 per annum.

ROAD TEST OF THE MODEL "F" MORGAN (Contd.)

checked over subsequent to changing a sprocket in the final drive, and found to be nearly 10 per cent. fast; accordingly all the figures printed are corrected and represent genuine speeds.

In second gear (7.9-1) the maximum speed obtained was exactly 51 m.p.h. At this speed there was a considerable amount of vibration from the propeller shaft which runs at engine speed; no reading was taken in bottom gear. Economy was a strong point, most particularly as regards fuel; even when putting up high average speeds over long distances the consumption remained as high as 37 m.p.g. For all-in running, which included a lot of town work, the average figure was 35 m.p.g. Oil was consumed at the rate of 1,600 m.p.g. At one time during the test this increased at an alarming rate, but a bad leakage was found from the front timing cover, which had come loose; however, after this had been well tightened, a further 350 miles were covered, during which time the consumption remained normal. The absence of any form of oil-indicator gauge was a detail which may be thought worthy of criticism. A reserve position was provided for the petrol tap, but the distance one could run on the reserve supply was really too short to be of practical value—a point which the manufacturers would, perhaps, consider.

Starting from cold after the machine had been standing all night was best and most easily accomplished by means of the handle. If the starter was used the motor was apt to fire on one cylinder, thereby throwing the starter-motor pinion out of mesh. The best procedure

with the handle was to pull the strangler on to full choke, wedging the choke handle in the absence of any means for locking it. Then swing the engine over three or four revolutions with the ignition switched off; then having turned the ignition on, the first or second pull up usually effected a start. There was no need to touch the throttle control.

Lighting was by means of a pair of combined head and side lamps, which were amply powerful for all ordinary uses, the side-lamp to head-lamp switch was combined with the ignition switch on the dash, whilst the dipper is clipped on the steering column.

Finished in red with cream wheels, the Model F Super-sports Morgan looked a fast and attractive sports vehicle; these looks were not belied, and, in spite of a very strenuous test, it was impossible to tire out this game little machine. The fact that long journeys could be accomplished by two people in a degree of comfort and at such a speed as would have done credit to cars costing many times as much, must make the purchase price of 130 guineas a proposition worthy of serious consideration, annual tax, of course, being only £4.

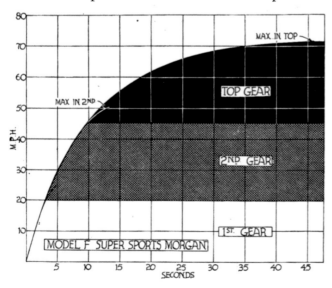

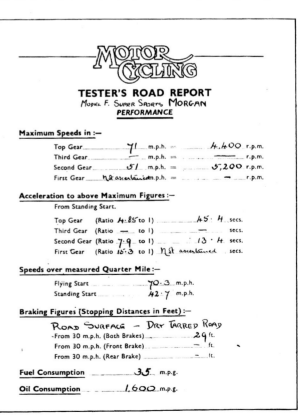

TESTER'S ROAD REPORT
Model F. Super Sports Morgan
PERFORMANCE

Maximum Speeds in :—

Top Gear	71 m.p.h. =	4,400 r.p.m.
Third Gear	— m.p.h. =	— r.p.m.
Second Gear	51 m.p.h. =	5,200 r.p.m.
First Gear	not ascertained m.p.h. =	— r.p.m.

Acceleration to above Maximum Figures :—
From Standing Start.

Top Gear (Ratio 4.85 to 1)	45.4 secs.
Third Gear (Ratio — to 1)	— secs.
Second Gear (Ratio 7.9 to 1)	13.4 secs.
First Gear (Ratio 15.3 to 1)	not ascertained secs.

Speeds over measured Quarter Mile :—

Flying Start	70.3 m.p.h.
Standing Start	42.7 m.p.h.

Braking Figures (Stopping Distances in Feet) :—
Road Surface - Dry Tarred Road

From 30 m.p.h. (Both Brakes)	29 ft.
From 30 m.p.h. (Front Brake)	— ft.
From 30 m.p.h. (Rear Brake)	— ft.

Fuel Consumption 35 m.p.g.
Oil Consumption 1,600 m.p.g.

The SUPER-SPORTS MORGAN

High Performance and Comfort are Features of the Latest Model of a Famous Series

Built for speed and comfort, the Morgan has an attractive streamlined body. In the picture below is shown the spare wheel mounting; luggage may be carried on the grid on the tail.

UNDOUBTEDLY, one of the most exhilarating vehicles we have tested in recent months is the Super-sports Morgan, naively described on its licence as a "tricycle." The writer had not experienced three-wheeled motion for some time past, and during the long week-end in which he had the car it was a constant source of pleasant surprise.

It is generally acknowledged that a three-wheeled sports car is not everyone's ideal of perfect transport. It has been pointed out that it is a vehicle with definite limitations. This is true. It is a car in which white tie and tails might be out of place ; on the other hand, the Morgan fulfils a very definite function.

Here is a conveyance for the enthusiast, the man who enjoys developing "urge" in a big twin. It is a car which offers high speed and really rapid, safe cornering. It gives performance the equal of many four-wheeled sports cars, but with a new thrill. Its acceleration is astonishing, its braking powerful and its road-holding superb.

In appearance, this latest product of the Morgan works follows the well-tried lines of its very successful predecessors. The body is carefully streamlined, and is beaten from a single sheet of metal. The spare wheel is housed in a recess in the tapered tail, on which is a luggage-grid, capable of carrying one or two suitcases. A broad, vee-shaped screen gives the occupants complete shelter from wind and rain. A further measure of protection for the passenger is provided by the extension of the scuttle.

Both seats are comfortable. The squab is deep and well sprung, and the cushions are pneumatic. There is ample legroom on the passenger's side, but, although there are only two pedals, the driver's footroom is rather restricted. The driving position is eminently satisfactory, at once imparting a feeling of confidence. Admirably raked to come into the lap, the steering wheel, of flexible type, carries manual controls for ignition, air and throttle. The dipswitch is mounted on the steering column. Visibility is excellent: the near-side wing can be seen without effort, but a rear view mirror would be appreciated.

The remote control gear-lever is placed very conveniently where the left hand drops on to it. Alongside is the brake lever. Beneath the driver's legs, and protruding through the floor is the electric starter button, which is operated in conjunction with an exhaust lifter.

Power, in large quantities, is derived from an o.h.v. water-cooled vee-twin Matchless engine of 990 c.c. Transmission is by shaft to a sliding-pinion type of gearbox, thence to worm and wheel. Final drive is taken by a short chain of ¾-in. pitch.

To start the engine from cold requires careful adjustment of the ignition and mixing controls and a few moments' work with the crank. Practice reveals that little difficulty is experienced when the Amal carburetter has been flooded, the ignition fully retarded and the air lever moved to the "closed" position. The compression ratio is in the region of 6 to 1; some care should be exercised in using the starting handle.

When the engine is once firing, the ignition may be advanced, and the air control opened. Here it may be remarked that the exhaust note, whilst pleasing to some, can be regarded somewhat gravely by officers of the law and anti-motorists. It is possible, however, to proceed comparatively quietly in town traffic when the revs. are kept down to "tick-over" speed.

Suspension at low speeds has all the firmness of the four-wheeled sports car. Steering is high-geared and, therefore, apparently heavy at low speeds, but it is exactly right on the open road, when it is immediately responsive. The certainty of control at high speeds is one of the most attractive features of the car; coupled with the front-end stability provided by the famous Morgan helical springing, fast cornering becomes almost a matter of course.

The Girling mechanical brakes fitted on all three wheels are powerful and smooth in action. All wheels are interchangeable, and little more than 10 mins. is required to remove the spare wheel and replace the driving wheel.

In traffic the Morgan is perfectly tractable, and showed no tendency to oil plugs. Tramlines present no particular difficulty, and the three-wheeler is surprisingly steady, even on such surfaces as wet wood blocks.

It is on the open road, however, that the Super Sports model shows its true colours. This is a car which really does thrust the driver in the back as it gets away from traffic hold-ups. With such widely spaced gear ratios as 12.4, 7.5 and 4.58 to 1, a quick change is almost impossible, but the fraction of time lost in closing the hand throttle and snicking into another gear is amply compensated for by the heartiness of the acceleration.

Best results were obtained when second gear was selected at about 15 m.p.h. and top at 40 m.p.h. It is possible to reach 50 m.p.h. in second, but at this speed the engine goes through a noisy period. Once in top gear, one has the gratifying impression that the car is impatient of restraint.

Cruising speed is in the region of 55 m.p.h. This can be maintained indefinitely with a very small throttle opening. Acceleration at this speed is as rapid as in the lower speed range, and the car reaches its maximum in a very short time. Over a timed flying

Removal of the floor-boards reveals the gearbox, dynamo and battery. Rear suspension is by quarter-elliptic springs.

(Above) Accessibility: engine maintenance is made easy by the forward mounting of the power-unit. The layout of the front suspension remains unaltered on the latest model.

IN BRIEF

ENGINE: 50-degree watercooled V twin; pushrod overhead valves; 85.5 mm. by 85.5 mm. = 990 c.c. Tax, £4.

TRANSMISSION: Single dry-plate clutch; three-speed gearbox. Ratios, 4.58, 7.5 and 12.4 to 1: reverse, 16.5 to 1. Shaft drive, with centre bearing, to gearbox, worm and countershaft to final drive chain.

GENERAL: Tubular frame; independent front wheel suspension (helical springs); quarter-elliptic rear; 4-gallon forward petrol tank, 1-gallon oil; 6-volt electrical equipment.

DIMENSIONS, Etc.: Overall length, 10 ft. 4 ins.; overall width, 4 ft. 11 ins.; track, 4 ft. 2 ins.; weight, 8 cwt. 58 lb.

PERFORMANCE: Flying ¼-mile (best), 73 m.p.h.; mean, 70.87 m.p.h.; standing ¼-mile, 21.0 secs. Petrol consumption (average), 40 m.p.g. Braking, by Ferodo-Tapley meter, 88 per cent.

PRICE: £136 10s.

THE MORGAN MOTOR CO., LTD.
MALVERN LINK
WORCS.

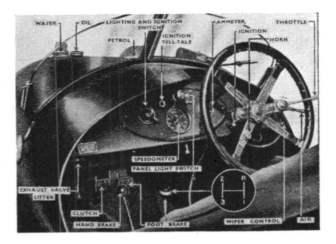

quarter-mile, the Morgan averaged 73 m.p.h., but the zest in driving the car lies more in the manner in which it reaches its maximum than in merely motoring with the taps wide open.

The stability of the three-wheeler at high speeds deserves more than a perfunctory word of praise. On fast bends (and to a Morgan most bends are fast) the car is rock-steady. There is no tendency to slide, nor for the tail to swing, and the steering is such that a flick of the wheel is sufficient to maintain a straight course over the roughest of surfaces.

Mounted on the wings are head lights which are well up to their job. For wet weather driving, a suction-operated windscreen wiper is fitted, but the low hood restricts visibility. It was found, however, that rain tended to be deflected over the heads of the occupants, and the enthusiast will probably dispense with the hood except when parked.

At £136 10s., the Super Sports Morgan represents a form of motoring which is rare enough in these days of small car luxury. It is a real sports car, combining high performance with economy.

JUNE 1935.

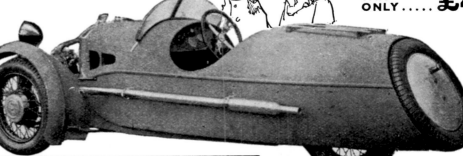

The Morgan

"THE LIGHT CAR" gives you first details of the post-war version of—

A three-wheeler, the Model F Super.

TWO four-wheelers and two three-wheeled models are already in production in Malvern. So far as the latter pair is concerned, there are no alterations from the 1939 specification. The four-wheelers, however, have one or two small changes as well as a new engine which, although delivered in a few of these cars just before the war, has not been described hitherto.

Manufactured specially for the Morgan Motor Co., Ltd., by one of the largest Coventry car makers, this new power unit has all its valves overhead and operated by push rods. Dimensional details will be found in a separate data panel. With a larger capacity at 11½ per cent. more power (40 b.h.p.) at 4,300 r.p.m. instead of 4,500 r.p.m., the new engine is also appreciably lighter than its predecessor.

This unit is mounted, it may be recalled, in a remarkably low chassis. (The floor boards are only 7½ ins. above ground level.) A short enclosed shaft drives a four-speed synchromesh gearbox located amidships, where its stubby lever is very conveniently placed.

Suspension at the rear is conventional except that there are no shackles for the semi-elliptic springs; instead, the master leaves slide in trunnions. At the front there is independent suspension of the type which has been used in Morgans for some 35 years, each wheel being arranged to slide vertically under the control of a helical spring to carry the load and a smaller spring as a necessary check on rebound.

Here some modifications are to be found. As a result of alterations to the springs themselves and particularly to the rebound springs, shock absorbers are no longer necessary and are not fitted at the front.

Another change is the incorporation of very simple steering dampers which have eliminated wheel wobble. A flat strip of saw steel, suitably tempered, is attached at one end to the chassis frame. At the other, bronze washers are riveted to it and these are placed between the main spring and the sliding axle where they provide enough friction to prevent oscillation but do not tend to make the steering heavy. A third change is the radiator mounting. This unit now rests on a pair of brackets attached to the front of the chassis frame.

Two body types are to be available on this chassis—an open two-seater with large luggage space, which also houses a concealed hood, and a drop-head coupé. Both have two spare wheels carried in a special trough.

The three-wheelers are unchanged. The four-seater has an 8 h.p. engine and the Model F Super a 10 h.p. unit, both being water-cooled. The single rear wheel is carried in a robust swinging fork, with a pair of quarter-elliptic springs.

The Super is a two-seater with a high performance, and the four-seater is more of a family vehicle designed to provide a fair measure of liveliness with highly economical transport for four.

These, incidentally, appear to be the only three-wheelers likely to be available on the British market at present, and they should be of very considerable interest, particularly in these days of high taxation. There will, indeed, be a warm welcome for the Morgan both in three- and four-wheeled form.

The 4/4 Two-seater

Engine.—O.h.v. 4-cyl., 63.5 mm. by 100 mm. (1,267 c.c.). Tax, £12 10s. Thermo-siphon cooling. Solex carburetter; A.C. mechanical fuel pump from 9-gallon tank.

Transmission, Etc.—Dry-plate clutch, gears 5.0, 7.1, 12.1 and 17.1 to 1. Steering, Burman-Douglas. Suspension, independent at front with helical springs; semi-elliptic at rear with Hartford shock absorbers. Girling brakes. Tyres, 4.50-17.

General.—12-v. electrical equipment; wheelbase, 7 ft. 8 ins.; track, 3 ft. 9 ins.; length, 11 ft. 4 in. width, 4 ft. 6 ins. Unladen weight, 14½ cwt. Price, £355 plus £99 15s. 1d.

The 4/4 Coupé

Same as Two-seater except length, 11 ft. 7¾ ins.; height, 4 ft. 1¾ ins. Unladen weight, 15½ cwt. Tyres, 5.50-16. Price, £395 plus £110 18s. 3d.

Three-wheeler, Model F (4-seater)

Engine.—S.v., 4-cyl., 56.64 mm. by 92.56 mm. (933 c.c.). Tax, £5. Thermo-siphon cooling. Zenith carburetter, 4-gallon gravity tank.

Transmission.—Dry-plate clutch; enclosed propeller shaft to gearbox; gears 4.85, 7.9 and 15.3 to 1; reverse, 18.8 to 1. Worm gear and ¾-in. pitch; roller chain drive to rear wheel. Steering, Morgan, with 2 to 1 reduction. Suspension, independent at front with helical springs; quarter-elliptic at rear. Brakes, Girling. Tyres, 4.00-18.

General.—6-v. electrical equipment, wheelbase, 8 ft. 3 ins.; track, 4 ft. 2 ins.; length, 11 ft. 6 ins.; width, 4 ft. 11 ins. Unladen weight, under 8 cwt. Price, £205 plus £57 13s. 10d.

Three-wheeler, Model F Super

Same as Model F Four-seater except 62.5 mm. by 92.5 mm. (1,172 c.c.). Gears, 4.58, 7.45 and 14.4 to 1; reverse, 17.8 to 1. Wheelbase, 7 ft. 11 ins.; length, 11 ft. Price, £245 plus £68 16s. 1d.

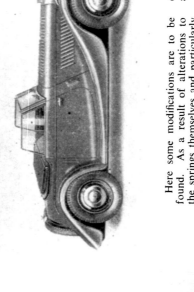

(Right) Four seats, three wheels. This is the Model F—very popular before the war. (Below) The attractive 4/4 drop-head coupé. Another illustration appears on page 28.

Outline for speed and sport: the 4/4 two-seater.

1949 MORGAN THREE-WHEELERS

Two-model Four-cylinder Range Unaltered

The 1949 F. Super Morgan listed at £260 plus £72 19s. 5d. P.T.

THE sole manufacturers of passenger three-wheelers now in production in this country, the Morgan Motor Co., Ltd., of Malvern Link, Worcs., are continuing unaltered their programme of four-cylinder water-cooled models. There are two types, the Model F-4, occasional four-seater, and the Model F-Super, a plus-70 m.p.h. two-seater.

Morgan "four" details are almost too well known to necessitate reiteration, but for the benefit of those who may not be familiar with the construction of these two machines it may be briefly stated that both are generally similar, with "Z" section steel chassis incorporating a central tube between engine and gearbox and a side-valve engine of 1,172 c.c. The latter incorporates thermo-siphon cooling, dynamically balanced crankshaft, automatic control to the coil ignition system, turbulent cylinder head, and down-draught carburetter. The compression ratio is 6.2 to 1. Transmission is from a single dry-plate clutch with a flexible centre, by shaft to the three-speed-and-reverse gearbox. the ratios being 4.58, 7.5 and 12.4 to 1; reverse is 16.5 to 1. Final drive is by worm and wheel built into the rear of the gearbox and thence by a ¾-in.-pitch, slow-speed chain to the single rear wheel.

Independent wheel suspension is on the well-known Morgan system coil springs being used at the front and long, leaf springs at the rear. Wheels are of Dunlop Magna type, detachable and interchangeable with a spare carried at the rear of the body. Tyres are 18-in. by 4-in. Dunlops. Girling brakes are fitted on all wheels. Lucas 6v. electrical equipment, including starter and horn, is employed and car-type steering, very light in operation, is featured. The fuel tank holds four gallons and the oil capacity of the sump is one gallon. A pneumatic windscreen wiper is fitted.

The single-door body of the four-seater is fitted with all-weather equipment and adjustable front seats. Lamps, radiator shell and fittings are chromium plated, and the standard colour is Saxe blue with black wings and wheels. The short-wheelbase sports model has two doors, folding windscreen, and hood, while finish is red, black or British Racing Green.

Both touring and sports models are equipped with Moseley Float-on-Air cushions.

Morgan prices for 1949 remain at £246 15s. (plus £69 5s. 10d. purchase tax) for the Model F-4, and £260 (plus £72 19s. 5d. P.T.) for the Model F-Super. Deviation from standard finish costs an additional £3 10s. in each case. Tax is £5 per annum.

Two Morgan Three-wheelers

Two-Seater and Four-seater Models With Water-cooled, Four-cylinder Engines for 1951

MORGANS, the extremely lively three-wheelers, famed for 40 years for their combination of snappy motor cycle performance with sports-car comfort, remain unchanged for 1951. The programme comprises two models, the "F" Super, a two-seater sports machine, and the "F4", which has a four-seater body.

Independent suspension of the front wheels is provided by means of coil springs

In each case the power unit is a Ford Ten car engine, especially adapted for Morgans. The engine is a side-valve, water-cooled four in-line of 1,172 c.c., with a compression ratio of 6.2 to 1. Power output is claimed as being 32.5 b.h.p. at 3,500 r.p.m.,

and when it is realized that the total weight of the Morgans is in the 8-cwt region it is not difficult to see the "wherefore" behind the high performance! Good power-to-weight ratio pays dividends all along the line—especially so in terms of acceleration and economy. The two-seater is said to have a cruising speed of about 65 m.p.h.

Transmission is via a single-plate dry clutch with a flexible centre and a shaft to the gear box, and thence by worm wheel and a ⅜in-pitch roller chain to the single rear wheel. The gear box has three forward speeds and reverse. In the case of each model the ratios are 4.58, 7.5, and 12.4 to 1, with 16.5 to 1 reverse.

Light, and possessing immense strength, the chassis has side members of deep Z-section steel and retains the all-important tubular member between the engine and gear box. Independent suspension of the front wheels is provided by means of coil springs. Suspension of the rear wheel is by quarter-elliptic leaf springs. Brakes are Girlings, the front pair being coupled to the pedal; the rear brake is connected to the hand lever and is intended for parking purposes only.

The body is coach-built from seasoned wood and sheet metal. It is entirely separate from the chassis and, indeed, is easily detachable. Standard finish of the four-seater is a saxe-blue body with black wheels and wings. The two-seater is available in black, red or British racing green. Deviations from the standard finishes are available at extra cost. Morgans, incidentally, come under the £5-a-year Road Tax ruling.

Makers are The Morgan Motor Co., Ltd., Malvern Link, Worcs. Prices are as follows:—

	Basic Price	Total Price		
	£	£	s	d
Model "F" 4	270	345	15	0
Model "F" Super	285	364	18	4

Both Morgan models have a four-cylinder engine; this is the "F 4" four-seater

Road Tests of Current Models—

The 1,172 c.c. Four-cylinder F-Super TWO-SEATER MORGAN

Smart and clean of line, the F-Super offers sports-car facilities with the performance of a fast motorcycle. (Right below) The model has car-type controls.

Tested in its Modern Form, a Popular Make of Three-wheeler is Shown To Possess High Performance With Reliability

WHEN, in 1908, Prebendary Morgan watched the production of his son's original construction of a vehicle—an engine, two driving chains and three wheels—he could hardly have realized that he was witnessing the foundation of a cult that was to grow into something almost akin to a religion amongst three-wheeler enthusiasts, and had he been alive to-day he might nearly have experienced a twinge of clerical guilt at the idolatry which the Pickersleigh Road, Malvern, product arouses amongst its worshippers. Furthermore, had he accompanied the writer on a trip to the Scottish Six Days Trial this year, he would surely have been disturbed by the wave of covetousness which a snappy, scarlet 1950 F-Super Morgan aroused in the breasts of men wherever it appeared!

For the truth of the matter is that Morgan three-wheelers have been in short supply since the war and their absence has tended to increase the fond regard in which they are held by many ex- and would-be owners. Never made in large quantities, and seldom exported, this vehicle was badly hit in the matter of steel quotas and material allocations when peace-time production was resumed.

Consequently, the aforementioned " Scottish " journey was something of a *tour de force*, for few people, judging by the interest and comment the machine caused, had had an opportunity of examining a post-1939 model other than at Earls Court.

The amazement expressed by garagemen when they opened the bonnet to discover beneath a 1,172 c.c. Ford engine, was a never-failing source of amusement, and the following discussions on the comparative values of twins and fours and the reminiscences thereby provoked, often turned a simple two-gallon fill-up into a 15-minute flood of memory in which all the points of the latest job were compared with " the ' Super-Sports ' I ran in 1935 "!

Older Morgan fans will recall that the earlier models possessed a main frame which was virtually composed of three tubes in triangular disposition.

In the modern Morgan the central tube is retained, but those at the sides are replaced by Z-sectioned steel members. The after-end of the propeller shaft terminates in a three-speed-and-reverse gearbox and worm and wheel drive, and the big bearings on which the forged-steel rear fork arms pivot are concentric with the cross-shaft; thus the radial movement of the fork maintains constant tension of the $\frac{3}{4}$-in. by $\frac{7}{16}$-in. final drive chain.

Underslung quarter elliptic leaf springs look after the rear suspension, while at the front the vertical plunger springing arrangement, long characteristic of Morgans, is retained. For 1950 this layout has been slightly altered to

give increased spring length—a " mod." which, by the way, can be carried out to all earlier models. The steering gear is a straightforward Akerman layout with a 2-to-1 reduction gearbox.

All three wheels have 7-in.-diameter cable-operated Girling brakes, the two front drums being controlled by the pedal and the rear one by a lever mounted alongside the gear-shaft on the propeller-shaft housing tube.

The perfectly standard Ford 10 engine has coil ignition, a Ford carburetter and a six-volt belt-driven dynamo. The starter motor is cable-operated from the dashboard and the Lucas battery is stowed behind the driver's seat. As most people know, the Ford 10 has a three-bearing crankshaft, long-life, non-adjustable tappets and a highly efficient force-feed lubrication system.

The electrical equipment includes chromium-plated head lamps, with a dip switch on the steering column, a two-stage charging switch, dash lamp, ammeter and inspection lamp sockets. The crackle-finished instrument board also embodies a gearbox-driven Jaeger trip speedometer, horn button, and starter and choke controls.

Flared, valanced mudguards have been adopted since the war and a further body change is the addition of a door on the driver's side; both doors have map pockets and there is a glove cubby-hole in the varnished oak facia board.

All the wheels, of Dunlop " Magna " pattern, are interchangeable and the standard tyre size is 4 ins. by 18 ins

M.A.G.-engined Morgan at Stile Kop hill-climb (56.8 sec.) and P. Houel's pre-war G.P. Morgan won the cyclecar class of the Circuit de l'Eure race at 34.5 m.p.h. for the 178¾ miles. H.F.S. gained a "gold" in the A.C.U. Six Days' Trial in his 980-c.c. 759 lb. Morgan, in organising which T. W. Loughborough of the A.C.U. had tried out the hills with a Morgan and a 3½ h.p. Sunbeam. On Oct. 16th, 1919 new works of 38,400 sq. ft. were opened at Pickersleigh Road, Malvern Link, but the machine shop, carpenters' shop and tinmens' shops remained in the old building near the Link station. This gave a total of over 50,000 sq. ft. and the aim was 40-50 cars a week.

Harry Martin had a special Morgan with o.h.v. J.A.P. a/c. engine and type-Z Claudel Hobson carburetter.

1920.—For 1920 a ball thrust in the clutch, longer bearings for the steering heads, and stronger bevels of different tooth formation were adopted. Awards continued to be won by Morgans in competition events of all kinds, and some 20 cars a week were being turned out in spite of a shortage of engines. Mr. Morgan owned a big Studebaker but still covered an appreciable mileage in Morgans and had patented a detachable rear wheel.

When racing was resumed at Brooklands Ware drove a single-seater Morgan-J.A.P. with a cut-down G.P. radiator and Hawkes a stripped 2-seater model built for the abandoned 1914 Cyclecar T.T., with an 82 × 104 mm. (1,098 c.c.) 8-valve M.A.G. engine and now known as the "Land Crab." Ware's was the more reliable, lapping at 59½ m.p.h. to win the 3-wheeler B.M.C.R.C. race. It had an abbreviated tail, disc wheels, a big cut-away 4-spoke steering wheel, bracing tubes from the tops of the steering heads back to the cockpit and a hoop across the back-wheel to give the spindle rigidity.

Mr. Morgan now owned an Austin 20, which made light work of the 1 in 3 Old Wyche Cutting in Malvern carrying three passengers. Success after success was won by his 3-wheelers, such as H.B. Denley's "gold" in the Scottish Six Days, five "golds" in the Edinburgh, etc., and a couple of Morgans served officials well during the I.O.M. motorcycle T.T. races. Hawkes eventually beat Ware at Brooklands, but Ware won a later race at 69½ m.p.h., Hawkes' engine proving unreliable. H. George Morgan continued to bombard the Press with letters!

In the very tough A.C.U. Six Days' Trial the Morgans of H.F.S., S. Hall and F. James gained "golds"; respectively they drove 980 c.c. 756 lb., 1,000 c.c. 756 lb., and 1,100 c.c. 812 lb. cars. J.A.P.'s built Ware a special w/c. o.h.v. 90 × 85-mm. Morgan for the Cyclecar G.P. at Amiens but a piece blew out of one cylinder and it finished the course slowly on one "pot."

A private owner wrote to say his Morgan-J.A.P. won its class by 10 sec. from a G.N. in the Northants M.C. Speed Trials without any special tuning whatsoever, and a census on the North Road gave a count of seven Morgans, six G.N.s, three Rover 8s and two Tamplins amongst the light cars and cyclecars. *The Light Car & Cyclecar* then had the idea of a freak climb at Nailsworth Ladder; as in 1914 and in 1919, an 8-h.p. Morgan made a clean ascent, Hall's car getting up on an 11 to 1 bottom gear. The Morgan was now in production in France, taking fifth, sixth, ninth and tenth places in the Gaillon Hill-Climb. Advertisements proudly announced gold medals in the Scottish International and English Six Days' Trials of 1920.

THE SIMPLICITY OF GENIUS.—A diagrammatic picture of a vintage Morgan, showing the tubular chassis, the two tubes of which served as exhaust pipes for the motorcycle-type V-twin engine, strengthened by the central backbone within which ran a propeller shaft, with squared ends soldered and rivetted in, taking the drive from a cone clutch with exposed thrust-race to the bronze bevel-box soldered to a cross tube. Final drive was by 2-speed chain-and-dog transmission to the single rear wheel, and even in the late vintage period the gear-lever was just a piece of bent metal topped with a primitive wooden grip. The coil-spring i.f.s., with phosphor-bronze castings doing duty as steering pivots and suspension plungers, can be seen, mounted on transverse cross-tubes. An "X"-formation of tubular bracing at the front of the frame was extended to support the engine plates. There were contracting band brakes on the rear wheel. Steering for many years was direct—very direct!—and the starting handle was at the side. With some 30 b.h.p. to propel less than 7 cwt., the vintage Morgan was no sluggard, but jealous rivals said it combined the discomfort of a motorcycle with the cost of a car!

1921.—The 1921 Morgans shown at Olympia in 1920, when 30 a week were being built, had several important improvements. The new easily-detachable back wheel by means of a re-styled fork and chains of equal length was introduced, the high gear now being 18 × 33 (4½ to 1), against the former 14 × 25. Low gear remained at 8 to 1. The hand-brake now had a larger drum, 6½ in. in diameter, and the back wheel had a Leo Swain rim band to stop the cover creeping. Flat wooden guards over the chains protected them from mud off the tail and the back fork hinged on an improved, taper bearing. Bigger front-wheel taper hubs on ⅜ in. ball bearings, spun brass covers in two halves enclosing the springs to stop the upper crowns coming adrift from the upper cylinders, a guide and support for the starting handle, and a simplified clutch facilitating engine removal were other improvements, while a small flywheel pulley enabled a Lucas dynamo lighting set to be fitted (£25 extra). The dynamo clipped to the n/s. tube behind the engine and was driven by Whittle belt. The battery was under the seat, the switchboard on the left of the dash, over an oddments tray. The dash carried a clock.

A new model was the Aero, with V-air-deflector behind the radiator and streamlined tail. Prices were up to £228 for the De Luxe, the least-expensive being £206 for the a/c. Sporting Model with hood and screen but no lamps. H. F. Edwards of South Kensington offered a special streamlined model at £226 and Barkers Motors of Balham a detachable tail seating one adult or two children for £12 10s. in one flat coat of paint ready for the colour of the customer's car.

It was claimed that the entire 1921 output had been ordered in advance by Morgan's agents. Incidentally, while car tax was up to £1 per h.p., 3-wheelers paid £4 a year. Yet another variant of extra seating was the Pillionette, costing 18s 6d. and enabling a child to be carried on the tail of a Morgan, the invention of L. Marcus of Golders Green.

It is interesting that amongst Morgan drivers in the 1921 Paris-Nice Trial were Darmont and Sandford, both later to bring out their own versions of this 3-wheeler in France, while in England Eric Longden who eventually brought out his own 4-wheeled cyclecar, raced a 988-c.c. Morgan.

In the A.C.U. Six Days' Trial this year H.F.S. Morgan's 983-c.c. Morgan which weighed 814 lb., Boddington's 1,090-c.c. 928-lb. model and Elce's similar Morgan which scaled 782 lb., all won "golds," H.F.S. doing 67 m.p.g., 44 m.p.h. and 2,596 m.p.g of oil in the various tests—it still carried Reg. No. CJ 743!

In spite of the post-war slump the factory was working at full capacity, turning out "close on 120 machines per month," *vide* one Press cutting. In listing the competition successes scored in June alone the Company proudly coined the slogan "The Private Owner can win on a Morgan." Douglas Hawkes had evolved a very special racing single-seater, "Flying Spider," built at Malvern, which dispensed with the frame tubes, relying only on the backbone, had the 8-valve M.A.G. engine set far back in the extended chassis with its crankcase streamlined, and so slim a body that the driver could only just get into it after removing some side panels. The B.A.R.C. no longer allowed 3-wheelers to compete at its meetings, so the car was confined to mixed club days and B.M.C.R.C. races, and its hey-day was yet to come.

Although Ware's Morgan was supported by four French-built Morgans in the G.P. de Cyclecars at Le Mans it broke a push-rod and in the end only Stoffel finished, fifth and last. However,

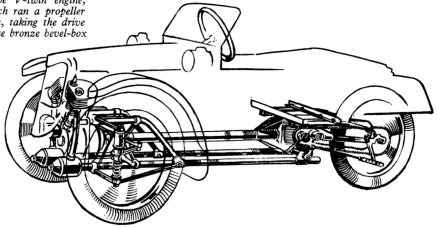

The 1918 Morgans

The De Luxe model.

The Sporting model.

The Grand Prix model.

Ware's 1,096-c.c. Morgan-J.A.P. held Class H2 records from 1 kilometre to 50 miles, its best speed being 86.04 m.p.h. over the kilometre, but in the J.C.C. 200-Mile Race his w/c. Morgan-J.A.P. retired with clutch failure. But racing Morgans were certainly doing the knots!

Although the "Aero" Morgan had been briefly mentioned, it was not among the 1922 models, being built to special order, with ship's ventilators, snake horn, aero-screens and nickel fittings. The range comprised the new Standard 2-seater at £150, with shortened wheelbase and no running-boards, the G.P. costing £180, the a/c. and w/c. De Luxe models, priced respectively at £175 and £186, and the Family jobs, costing £180 with a/c. engine, £191 if water-cooled. Equipment included hood, screen, acetylene lamps, horn, tools and mats! And so the Morgan was able to hold its own with L.S.D., T.B., Castle Three, New Hudson, Reynolds Runabout, Economic, Scott Sociable and other 3-wheelers when it appeared on Stand 63 at the 1921 Motorcycle Show, which opened at Olympia in a London fog.

1922.—Morgans continued to be as active as ever in trials and speed events, H.F.S. setting the example to drivers like F. W. James, N. Norris, W. A. Carr, G. H. Goodall, W. H. Elce, H. Sawtell, S. Hall, F. W. Dame, A. G. Gripper, R. Whiffen, A. C. Maskell, H. Beart, S. McCarthy, H. Holmes, the disabled P. Garrard, and others too numerous to list, while Ware continued to race his trim Morgan-J.A.P. against the motorcycle combinations and Hawkes' single-seater "Flying Spider" won a Surbiton M.C. Brooklands' race at 73.56 m.p.h. H. Martin's 1,074-c.c. Morgan-Anzani also beat the sidecars in a B.M.C.R.C. race won at 70.58 m.p.h. Morgan advertisements in April proudly showed the A.C.U. "Stock Car" Trial team of six cars lined up outside the Worcester Road works. H.F.S. won the premier award and Norris the highest cyclecar award. The Rev. Prebendary Morgan went on letter-writing, defending his son's 3-wheelers, for instance, against the £100 4-wheeler, which, he remarked, " one meets more often in the correspondence column than elsewhere." An article headed " Will the 3-Wheeler Survive ? " spurred him to statistics. Taking " the outstanding events of the past 12 months—the English and Scottish Six Days, the three great M.C.C. trials and the A.C.U. " Stock ' Trial," the Rev. Morgan emphasised that the under-£200 4-wheelers, numbering about a dozen, had won two " golds,"

five " silvers," whereas the 3-wheelers, a mere half-dozen of them, took 23 gold and 12 silver medals, as well as six special certificates—and, he added magnanimously, " these include the awards (three " golds," one " silver ") obtained by the Castle Three and New Hudson, which should perhaps be excluded, as they cost over £200." His letter brought a rebuke from A. Frazer-Nash of G.N.

In mid-1922 *The Light Car & Cyclecar* tested a w/c. Morgan-M.A.G. between Malvern and London, getting close on 60 m.p.g. from the still-stiff engine, at an average of 25 m.p.h. Eight gold medals were won in the London-Edinburgh and for the 1,100-c.c. class of the second J.C.C. 200-Mile Race at Brooklands Hawkes had a Morgan with 8-valve twin-carburetter a/c. Anzani engine with a shaft-driven o.h. camshaft over each cylinder and a Best & Lloyd oil pump driven from the n/s. camshaft. No bonnet was fitted and a flat tank was mounted on a fairly normal tail. Ware had a s.v. Morgan-J.A.P. with open-ended tail, Martin a push-rod o.h.v. Morgan-Anzani, all three having a hoop over the back wheel to give anchorage to a Hartford shock-absorber. Alas, all these retired, Hawkes' with a cracked cylinder, while Ware gave up the unequal struggle of trying to repair a leaking water jacket with tin-tacks!

An assortment consisting of H.F.S.'s 978-c.c. Morgan-J.A.P., S. Hall's 1,096-c.c. Morgan-M.A.G. and W. Carr's 1,090-c.c. Morgan-Anzani, normal 2-seaters, not G.P. models, came through the A.C.U. Six Days' Trial with flying colours and three gold medals. By October prices were down to £135, £155 and £160 respectively for the a/c. Standard, De Luxe and Family models, and £160, £165 and £170 for the Grand Prix, De Luxe and Family versions with w/c. engine, either 8-h.p. J.A.P. or 10-h.p. Blackburne. A w/c. M.A.G. cost an extra £7, an o.h.v. w/c. Anzani £5 extra. Someone in Wakefield put a lofty coupé body on a Morgan, not the first incidentally, two proprietary reverse-gear conversions were announced, and for 1923 prices were again lowered, the Standard costing only £128, the w/c. G.P. £155.

A year which had opened with 3-wheeler owners in trouble with the Law unless they displayed car-size number-plates, ended with Hawkes taking several records with his 200-Mile Race Morgan-Anzani, the fastest the Class H2 f.s. kilometre, at 86.94 m.p.h. At Olympia, the Morgan Company showed eight cars and a stripped chassis on Stand 139, finished in green, white, dark mauve, dark red, yellow, grey and royal blue. The brakes on all models were now cable-operated. The star attraction, however, was an 8-h.p. o.h.v. w/c. Anzani-engined 200-Mile Race replica with Binks 2-jet carburetter, M.L. magneto, K.L.G. plugs and exhaust-heated induction pipe, the body being of polished aluminium, and radiator and tank nickel-plated. Priced at £200, it was called the Aero model in the Press but Morgan advertisements as yet made no reference to it.

1923.—By 1923 the conventional small car had already made life difficult for cyclecar manufacturers and many had expired. Now Sir (later Lord) Herbert Austin dropped that bombshell amongst them, the 4-cylinder, water-cooled, 3-speed, 4-wheel-braked Austin 7.

" Omega," writing in *The Auto*, strongly attacked the 3-wheeler, remarking that he would rather have a Rover 8, for example, " than the finest 3-wheeler Mr. Morgan's Company could produce, with all the " knobs " imaginable, and I feel now so bold as to predict that the number of people like me will steadily increase." This led to correspondence with both H.F.S. and his father, although I cannot trace that this journalist, who had road-tested a G.N. in 1918/19, ever had his request for a trial run " in a representatively good Morgan " granted. Mr. Morgan was able to remark that " a 3-wheeler has never overturned at Brooklands " and that " the G.N., which Omega knew, is no longer with us," while he countered the suggestion of *The Auto*'s correspondent that he might " kick away the ladder which has served him so well " and make a 4-wheeler (an " Omega " prediction 13 years ahead of its time!) by commenting whimsically that " Some day, perhaps in the dim and distant future, it is possible that I (or perhaps my son, if he shall have taken my place) may duplicate the three wheels, and concentrate on a 6-wheeler! "

Meanwhile, the Morgan 3-wheeler continued to amass awards in all the leading trials. The Austin 7, in tourer or Chummy form, cost £165, and Morgans £128 to £153 in a/c. and £155 to £163 in w/c. form. The provision of front brakes on the new Seven was countered by Morgan announcing at the end of March that Bowden-cable-operated internal-expanding hand-applied front brakes could be fitted to existing Morgans at a cost of £6. A Standard-model £140 Morgan-J.A.P. fitted with these new f.w.b. scored one of its most convincing victories at this time.

A RACING MORGAN OF 1923.—E. B. Ware, of J.A.P.s, at the pits during the J.C.C. 200-Mile Race.

Driven by Ware, it won the Westall Cup for best performance in the searching J.C.C. General Efficiency Trial, a success Morgan was to repeat in 1924. In gaining maximum marks, 1,743.15 out of a possible 2,000, the Morgan achieved 56 m.p.g., lapped Brooklands at 55.71 m.p.h., averaged 13.4 m.p.h. up the Test Hill (fastest time), was best in the brake test, best on top-gear acceleration, and best in the s.s. acceleration test. It weighed 715 lb. unladen, the only lighter contestant being a 670-lb. Tamplin. This was a convincing performance, in a contest in which three G.N.s and Gordon England's 957-lb. Austin 7 (48 m.p.g., 47.4 m.p.h. lap speed, 6.2 sec. slower up the Test Hill) took part. The final placings put Ware 76.55 marks ahead of Frazer-Nash's G.N., Chinery's Gwynne third. At the time Ware was greeted by a car-icature in *The Light Car & Cyclecar* reading :—

Did he once ride a tricycle,
Cool as an icicle?
Who knows? Perhaps.
Were his legs much too slow for him;
Not enough go for him?
Who knows? Ask J.A.P.s!

The Morgan went on winning races as well, A. Horrocks, the Bolton agent, producing a nicely streamlined version, with curved nose behind the engine and the seats dropped below the prop-shaft tunnel, and Martin demonstrated his 1,074-c.c. Morgan-Anzani on the 503-yard Herne Hill Cycle Track (1 mile in 1 min. 30.2 sec.). The Stratford Wireless Co. fitted up a G.P. Morgan with an overhead aerial and twin Magnavox speakers in front of the engine, the valve panel being placed vulnerably outside by the driver, to receive 2LO, Norris' car with the new w/c. Blackburne o.h.v. engine did well at Kop and H. V. Hughes' s.v. racing-bodied Morgan cleaned up four firsts and a second at Southport.

Towards the end of 1923 Hawkes' Morgan-Anzani took the British Class H2 f.s. kilometre record to 92.17 m.p.h., the mile to 90.38 m.p.h., and secured s.s. and longer distance records as well, while Norris' Morgan-Blackburne cleaned-up the 1,100-c.c. Three-Wheeler Championship Race at a B.M.C.R.C. Brooklands' Meeting, at 86.77 m.p.h. This atoned for Norris' misfortune in the J.C.C. 200-Mile Race, when his car was destroyed by fire in London on the eve of the race. A normal w/c. Aero-Blackburne was substituted, but it retired with a broken valve rocker, but not before it had harried the Salmsons, lapping at 84 m.p.h. Ware's s.v. w/c. Morgan-J.A.P., after some laps with its steering tie-rod trailing after a hurried wheel change(!), managed 70 laps but was unplaced, and Hawkes' w/c. 8-valve o.h.c. Morgan-Anzani retired after 30 laps with a broken valve cotter. It had the radiator moved back 8 in. to accommodate twin carburetters, the fuel tank carried oil, and there was a 14-gallon petrol tank under the chassis.

To offset these " 200 " disappointments, at the end of the year Morgans held the Class J1 (750-c.c. single-seaters) f.s. kilometre record (Poiret on 668 c.c. in the Bois de Boulogne—77.92 m.p.h.), the 10-mile, 50-mile and one-hour honours in this class (Ware, at Brooklands, with J.A.P. engine, at 47.26 to 59.5 m.p.h.), the Class H1 1-mile to 5-mile records (for 1,100-c.c. single-seaters) by Hawkes' 1,078-c.c. Morgan-Anzani, at 76.85 to 89.5 m.p.h. (the fastest British records did not count as World's records), and the Class H2 (1,100-c.c. 2-seaters) 1-kilometre to 10-mile records, by Norris' Aero Morgan with Blackburne o.h.v. 1,095-c.c. engine, at 85.78 to 90.82 m.p.h.

The Motorcycle Show saw the price of the a/c. Standard model reduced to £110 (lighting £8 extra), while amongst the exhibits was a very exciting single-seater Morgan-Blackburne for which 75 m.p.h. was guaranteed. The Aero-model, which now had an external gear-lever, beside the brake-lever, was listed officially, at £150 with s.v. w/c. engine, although the Grand Prix Morgan was still available, at £145, or £135 in a/c. form. By December a s.v. Aero was advertised at £148, an o.h.v. Aero at £160, the w/c. De Luxe was down to £140 and the w/c. G.P. cost £138. This Aero model, especially in later a/c. versions, was aptly named for, as C. E. Allen has observed, the cockpit was reminiscent of that of a radial-engined 'plane, " that merry twinkling of the rocker gear, the odd sparks which fly from the exposed exhaust ports at night, the odd spot of oil and grease thrown back onto the aero-screens, and on a bumpy road it's rather like taxi-ing over a grass aerodrome. . . . No wonder they called it the Aero model! "

H. F. S. Morgan driving in an early A.C.U. Six Days' Trial.

THE VINTAGE YEARS OF THE MORGAN 3-WHEELER

FIRST TO EXCEED "THE TON."—Harold Beart's Morgan-Blackburne which took records at Brooklands at over 100 m.p.h. during the 1925 season, and averaged 91.48 m.p.h. for an hour. The protruding pipes gave a mild boost effect to the carburetter air intake.

1924.—By 1924 the popular four-wheeler was very much established and the 3-wheeler was more than ever forced to base its appeal on sporting performance and low running and first costs. Morgan faced the light car opposition with five basic models, ranging from the a/c 976-c.c. Popular (£110) to the 1,098-c.c. s.v. Aero (£148), a single-seater o.h.v. racing version of the latter being listed at £160.

The Aero was a truly sporting proposition, with petrol and oil fillers inline along the brief bonnet behind the tall radiator cap. The cockpit, protected by two adjustable aero-screens, was pretty stark. The dashboard had a central oil drip-feed, its exposed pipe running under the scuttle, a Lucas ammeter-cum-switch panel on the left, a speedometer on the right, Bowden levers clipped to the steering wheel, ship's-type ventilators on the scuttle, and a snake bulb-horn lying along the o/s. mudguard.

Normally, Morgans still had 700 × 80 tyres, a 6-ft. wheelbase (the Family model was a foot longer), two speeds of 4½ and 8 to 1, and the simple chassis was said to weigh 2¼ cwt. The chassis backbone ran above the floor and the brake-lever was clipped to it, exposed cables running forward to the front brakes, if fitted, and providing some degree of compensation. Ignition was by M.L. magneto and there was a choice of Amac or B. & B. carburetter. "Omega" of *The Auto* was still attacking the Morgan, stating at the time of the 1923 Show that he was puzzled "that sensible people, with babies, could ignore the appeal of the 4-wheeler against the 3-wheeler, price for price and running-cost for running-cost."

Certainly the £165 Austin 7 was now very firmly established, and well publicised by racing successes. (The Trojan 2-stroke cost £157 10s., the Rover 8 £160, an A.V. cyclecar £105, a Tamplin £120, the revised 4-cylinder G.N. £250, while amongst 3-wheelers the Bramham cost £145, a Scott-Sociable £135.) There were three vehicles costing less than £100, namely the belt-drive Bleriot-Whippet (£82 19s.), Gibbons (£65), Harper (£80 17s.), and L.A.D. (£60.) The Morgan was to outlive them all. . . .

The Light Car & Cyclecar published a survey of readers'

A side view of H. Beart's 107 m.p.h. Morgan. It was developed from the car he raced during 1924.

experiences—shades of *Which?*—to indicate the comparative cost of running a cyclecar versus a light car. From this it was estimated that running costs over 6,000 miles, including a J.C.C. subscription, would work out at £54 12s. 3d. in a Morgan, £68 15s. 5d. in a Rover 8, £65 18s. in a Jowett and £65 14s. in an Austin 7. (Petrol was 1s. 6½d. a gallon, oil 6s. 9d. per gallon, tax £4 on a 3-wheeler, £9 on the Rover.) The fuel and oil m.p.g. were : Morgan 50/1,540; Rover 43/740; Jowett 42/1,500; Austin 45/1,800. Repairs equalled 3s. a week, a comprehensive Lloyd's policy £8 5s.! A tiny point in Morgan's favour—Frank Spouse, who drove a T.B. 3-wheeler in trials, had been appointed sole Morgan Distributor for Scotland!

At the 1924 Scottish Show all the Morgans on view had w/c. Blackburne engines, the new o.h.v. version of which gave approx. 35 b.h.p. and was supplied to the Morgan Co. with the flywheel balanced with the engine. A funnel-like air-intake was used close up behind the radiator.

In the J.C.C. General Efficiency Trial E. B. Ware's s.v. De Luxe Morgan (ME 4835) again made the best performance, gaining 330 out of a possible 385 marks. A Gwynne 8 was second (321 points), G. N. Norris' w/c. o.h.v. Aero Morgan Blackburne with oversize tyres third (306 points). Ware recorded the best petrol consumption, speediest acceleration in top speed and won the brake test. Norris made best time on the "Brooklands' Test Hill, best acceleration "through the gears" (his two speeds!) and fastest lap of the Track. This time the actual figures were not published and there was some controversy as to the validity of the various tests and the manner in which they had been organised. *The Light Car & Cyclecar* was tactless enough to suggest that the little 269-c.c. tiller-steered Harper Runabout, a 3-wheeler with single front wheel, could have won. This brought long and involved correspondence from H. F. S. Morgan and the Rev. H. G. Morgan, from which I will refrain from quoting at this late date.

At Brooklands, Norris' Morgan-Blackburne won a 5-lap Passenger Handicap from scratch, at 87.22 m.p.h., during the B.M.C.R.C. Easter Meeting. H. F. S. and G. H. Goodall tied for fastest cyclecar time at Kop Hill (28.6 sec.), and H. F. S., driving a Standard model Morgan, made f.t.d. in the acceleration test in the Midland C.C. Economy Car Trial. But at the Neath & Dist. M.C. Margam Park Speed Trials, Parsons' Morgan repeatedly gave best to Sgonina's G.N. In Malay, an Anzani-Morgan made f.t.d. in the passenger class of the speed trials.

Although a busy manufacturer, H. F. S. continued to drive in a variety of events, but the J.C.C. took him to task for not supporting theirs. Harold Beart, the Croydon Morgan agent, had begun his Brooklands career, finishing a good second to Dunfee's Salmson in a J.C.C. race.

The Morgan was again prominent in the A.C.U. 1,000-Mile Stock Trial (it was barred from the R.A.C. Six Days), being the only competing machines to be driven North to the start, accompanied by an A.C.U. observer—the motorcycles all went by

The Morgans of 1924

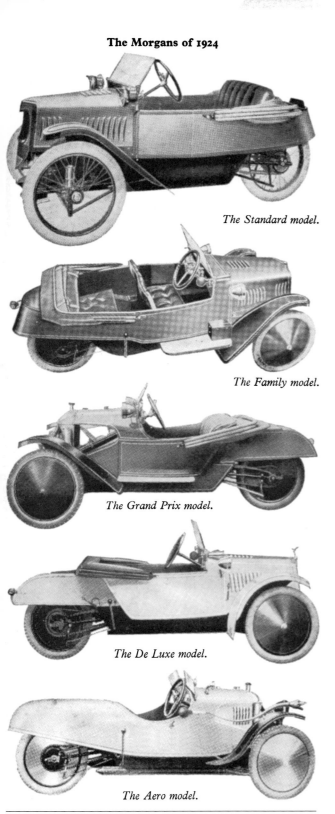

The Standard model.

The Family model.

The Grand Prix model.

The De Luxe model.

The Aero model.

WELL-KNOWN MORGAN EXPONENTS.—*E. B. Ware and his passenger Allchin, in their 1922 s.v. Morgan-J.A.P. They were both badly hurt in the accident depicted below.*

Indeed, successes continued to come in from all quarters, so that my ambition to quote them all, with Reg. Nos. of the successful Morgans, is defeated by space restrictions. For the Hereford Speed Trials H. F. S. used a Morgan-Blackburne with new, enlarged front brakes, and covered the ½-mile, from a f.s. of 50 yards, at 70.2 m.p.h., beating Goodall's red Morgan and even Harvey's new racing Alvis. In Tcheco-Slovakia (contemporary spelling) Meyer's o.h.v. Aero won its class in the Kralon-Pole-Sobesice hill-climb. Beart won at Brooklands from a McEvoy-Anzani to which his Morgan-Blackburne gave 3 sec. start, at 84.7 m.p.h., but in another race had fuel-feed trouble, leaving N. A. Lowe's similar car to beat Baragwanath's P. & P. combination, although Spring's Norton and sidecar was the winner. At the Madresfield Speed Trials H. C. Lones won his class in a stripped o.h.v. Aero and Norris easily won a 50-Mile B.M.C.R.C. Handicap in which an Austin 7 was competing, after Beart had retired with plug trouble. In the Scottish Six Days' Trial, H. F. S. won a silver cup in his smart blue 8-h.p. Morgan-J.A.P., he and Mrs. Morgan attired in spotless white and the car still carrying Reg. No. CJ 743, Spouse, now Aero-Blackburne mounted, a silver medal, but Carr's Morgan-Blackburne De Luxe (NP 65) retired after hitting a wall on Tornapress. R. R. Jackson had made an appearance in sprints, in an Aero-Blackburne (NP 3394), Bullough was going well at Southport, R. T. Horton was driving

train! This time H. F. S., accompanied by his wife in matronly dress, who helped polish the car before the start, drove a s.v. Aero-J.A.P. (NP 3871), Goodall a s.v. Aero-M.A.G., Carr a Standard-model Morgan-Blackburne (NP 4080). All three won gold medals. All used standard ratios of 10¾ and 5 to 1.

In France the Darmont-Morgan was in active production at Courbevoie, and at speed trials in the Forest of Senart near Paris Dhome's French Morgan, Darmont's very slim single-seater 750-c.c. Darmont-Morgan and Pierpont's 750-c.c. 2-seater Morgan set new records over the f.s. kilometre, respectively at 97.23, 125.742 and 119.8 k.p.h.

DISASTER.—*Ware's o.h.v. Morgan-J.A.P. after its crash in the 1924 J.C.C. 200 Mile Race, which resulted in a ban on 3-wheelers racing with 4-wheelers at Brooklands.*

a Morgan in trials. The Morgan Club was holding social runs, as it does today, eleven members rallying to the "Red Lion," Hatfield, for a run to Bedford, and a 500-c.c., using one twin Blackburne o.h.v. cylinder, ran in the French Cyclecar G.P. Someone had rigged up an Aero with streamline prow, disc wheels, searchlight and Motometer, etc.

Then, in the J.C.C. 200-Mile Race a most unfortunate blow befell Morgans, and, indeed, the whole sporting 3-wheeler world. The Morgan had never been particularly fortunate in this long-distance Brooklands race. For 1924 three cars, outwardly like Aero models, but with the big (external) silencers now demanded by the Track authorities, were entered, the "works" cars with Blackburne engines, for Norris and Beart, Ware's naturally J.A.P.-powered. Although these 2-seater Morgans were reported as capable of lapping at around 90 m.p.h., they had much trouble in practice, Ware's engine blowing gaskets, the driving chains breaking, and one car having a narrow escape when a steering arm broke. In the race Ware's engine refused to pick-up, and when it did get going, a top-gear dog broke and had to be changed. Norris, however, was duelling with Zborowski's Salmson, which it passed, only to coast in, the top-gear chain having broken. Beart was delayed long at *his* pit while a flat rear tyre was changed, after which his engine resolutely refused to start.

Then it happened! Ware had got going again, lapping probably at over 85 m.p.h., but on his 33rd lap his rear wheel appeared to be wobbling. (Parry Thomas, having troubles of his own in the Marlborough-Thomas, had reported a smell of scorching rubber when he overtook Ware.) Two more laps, and the Morgan suddenly swerved as it was crackling across the Fork, hit the fence and spun round, flinging out the occupants before it overturned. Ware and his mechanic, Allchin, eventually recovered, but Ware died some years ago.

The race went on, the Salmsons victorious in spite of overheating. Beart, understandably, stopped to increase the clearance between the tail of his Morgan and the tyre! This accident caused the J.C.C. to ban 3-wheelers not only from the 1925 200-Mile Race (which incorporated artificial corners) but from their High Efficiency Trial (also over a "road" course) which replaced the General Efficiency Trial and which Morgan was naturally anxious to win for the third time in succession. The B.A.R.C. was firmly behind the ban.

Meanwhile, H. Beart beat Norris in the B.M.C.R.C. 3-wheeler Championship race, averaging 83.99 m.p.h. for three laps and later he broke Class H2 records in his o.h.v. Aero-Blackburne, at speeds of 96.33 m.p.h. for the f.s. kilometre to 89.88 m.p.h. for 10 miles.

Commercially, the year ended well for the Morgan Motor Co. Correspondence in *The Light Car & Cyclecar* from owners who purported to have been held up in their 40/50 Mercedes and 50-h.p. Daimlers "by those beastly 3-wheelers" resulted in a lively response in favour of the Morgan (could H. F. S. or his father have compiled both sides of the argument?), and for 1925 improvements were made and prices drastically reduced—in time for competition from the 4-cylinder D'Yrsan tricars, the chassis of which was very like that of the Morgan, but used a conventional gearbox with reverse gear. At the Motorcycle Show on Stand No. 53 a canary-yellow Grand Prix Morgan with spotlamp between its aero-screens attracted attention. Spiral-bevels running on double-row ball-bearings, a higher bonnet forming a straight-line to the scuttle, and the latest J.A.P. engines and body-work improvements were adopted. 20 in. × 3½ in. Dunlop S.S. balloon tyres with flared front mudguards, and metallic-lustre paintwork were available on the Aero model, in which flexible exhaust pipes ran into external silencers, this arrangement costing £1 extra.

The Standard model now cost £95, or £105 with Lucas dynamo lighting set, the w/c. Grand Prix-J.A.P. with electric lighting £128, the De Luxe £120 or £130 in w/c. form, the Family £3 more than the De Luxe, and the Aero was priced at £135 with J.A.P., £140 with o.h.v. Anzani, and £147 with racing Blackburne engine. All the Aeros would exceed 70 m.p.h. and you could get a hood for them for £3. Front brakes cost £6, wheel discs £2 10s., hood covers 15s., a speedometer £4, special colours £2, and the oversize Dunlops £2 per wheel extra. The Standard model was supplied only in grey at normal cost, but, like the Family, had slightly raised body sides (as had the G.P.), the other models being in a choice of grey, red, blue, purple or green. Incidentally, the 1925 Austin 7 cost £155, the Carden £90.

By the end of 1924 Morgans held all the British Class H1 and

Morgan 3-wheelers lined-up for a race on Southport sands.

H2 records, the fastest being Beart's one-way f.s. mile, at 97.32 m.p.h. (mean = 94.21 m.p.h.), and the year closed with H. F. S. in the chair at the Morgan Club dinner at Ye Olde Cock Tavern, Fleet Street, which 70 people attended.

1925.—For some time controversy raged about the J.C.C. ban, but the Club remained adamant and it was not until four years hence, with the formation of the New Cyclecar Club, that 3-wheelers were to race against 4-wheelers at Brooklands, and only last month that the V.S.C.C. relented sufficiently to allow Morgans to race, on their own, at one of their meetings. . . .

This did not deter Morgan drivers from competing in any events open to them. Goodall, for instance, drove a Standard model (NP 636) *sans* bonnet, to take a "silver" in the Victory Cup Trial, in which H. F. S. gained a "gold" and Chippendale's Morgan overturned without damage in the brake test. And in the last of the public road speed trials, Goodall's Morgan "Jim" won its class at Hereford, being 1.4 sec. faster than Taylor's Brescia Bugatti, the fastest 4-wheeler, and in those near Tavistock on the same day, H. Dobbs' Morgan Blackburne beat Grogan's Frazer Nash.

As ever, the "Land's End" attracted Morgan exponents, Maskell running a stripped Aero (XR 11), the trilby-hatted Marshall a Standard (CJ 5649), a dozen Morgans winning between them four "golds," three "silvers" and a "bronze." The rest retired, as did a lone D'Yrsan. In the 1925 A.C.U. Stock Trial Carr drove a s.v. w/c. Standard (AB 9602), Goodall a w/c. Aero-Anzani (AB 16); both taking gold medals.

About this time experiences of readers and professional testers began to be published. Gordon Oxenham wrote of his 1925 w/c. Grand Prix-J.A.P., which would do 60 m.p.h. when the engine was clean, 56 when it was "full of carbon and pulling a load of 20-stone." It gave 60 m.p.g., climbed Brockley Hill at about 35 m.p.h., Kop Hill at 20-25 m.p.h. *The Light Car & Cyclecar* reported on the latest Aero-Blackburne (XX 8647), which weighed 7 cwt. 1 qtr. 21 lb. and developed over 40 b.h.p. at 4,500 r.p.m. This gave an easy 70 m.p.h. "on reasonably smooth roads. The tester decided that "the anticipation of a skid (on tramlines) was more terrifying than its reality" but that " getting away in low gear on a greasy road tends to throw the rear of the car sideways until the back wheel can obtain sufficient grip to drive the machine." The hood was criticised for cutting off all visibility to sides and rear and making hand-signalling impossible, the fabric-lined cone clutch was fierce until treated with engine oil, and overall fuel consumption was about 45 m.p.g., while roughly 2,000 m.p.g. of oil was obtained, at about 20 drips per minute from the Best & Lloyd drip-feed. (The handbook recommended 30, but owners used anything from 15 to 90 d.p.m.) The direct steering was disliked and it was thought that a simple form of reduction gear would be a distinct advantage. (From driving my 1927 Family Model I couldn't agree more, but it was many years before the Morgan Co. relented and fitted a reduction box, or a reverse gear!) As tested, the Morgan cost £167.

Up at Southport, Bullough in what I suspect was the ex-Hughes Morgan, A. Moss (Stirling's dad?), Ron Horton (in OM 4000) and S. Keary were successfully mixing it with the G.N.s, which tended to be superior. Morgans were out in force in the "Edinburgh," even to Hall's 1912 model (CB 88) bought for £12 a few days beforehand. It did not gain an award, but neither did H. F. S. However, the other Morgans collected six "golds" and two "silvers." In the International Six Days' Trial Carr's lone Morgan (NP 15, with spare wheel carried in a well in the n/s. running-board), teamed with an Ariel and a Humber motor-

Beart and Norris about to contest the Cyclecar Championship at a 1924 B.M.C.R.C. Meeting—Beart gained an unexpected victory at 83.9 m.p.h.

cycle, won the B.M.C.R.C. Championship, and 13 Morgans took part in the Morgan Club's own trial, in the Hatfield area, for two cups presented by H. F. S. (where are they now?)—why doesn't the present Morgan 3-Wheeler Club repeat it? *The Motor Cycle,* commenting on Carr's performance in the Six Days', remarked that he lost one time mark only and climbed all the hills splendidly, adding " His passenger deserves special praise."

Meanwhile, Harold Beart had evolved a very special racing Morgan at his Croydon works. The frame was strengthened and each rear spring had seven graduated leaves, a single Hartford shock-absorber being mounted over the rear wheel on a bracket above the bevel box and a stirrup secured to the fork-ends. At the front cast-steel sliding axles replaced the normal bronze ones, so that forward-projecting brackets could take Hartford shock-absorbers anchored at the bottom to steel brackets, and swivelling with the wheels. The axles slid on hardened and ground Ubas-steel pins screwed-in and grease-gun lubricated. Spring-loaded ball-joints on the track-rod, and a Ford epicyclic reduction gear on the top of the steering column, further improved control. A 4-to-1 ratio was achieved, with a forged-steel drop-arm slightly longer than standard.

The rear wheel was brakeless, the foot-brake having been dispensed with, and was shod with a 27 × 4.20 Dunlop. The front tyres were 26 × 3.75 Dunlops, on wellbase rims.

This Beart Morgan had ratios of 5.95 and 3.33 to 1, a magneto button on the top of the external gear-lever facilitating gear-changing without the need to slip the clutch or ease the throttle. A spring-loaded selector mechanism prevented the dogs coming out of mesh. Chains and bevels were oiled, *via* a drip-feed and copper pipes, from a pressure-fed tank. The engine was a 1924 w/c. o.h.v. 85 × 96.8 mm. (1,096 c.c.) Blackburne with racing cams, c.r. increased by machining the heads, a B. & B. " mouse-trap " carburetter controlled by a foot accelerator, and M.L. magneto. A bowl behind the air intake, fed by two projecting pipes, maintained atmosphere pressure to the carburetter irres-

pective of speed. Fuel was carried in a tank under the frame, supplemented when required by a tank in the body, giving a combined capacity of approx. 14-gallons. The large oil tank fed two drip-feeds, adjustable by the riding mechanic, and the radiator was special. No attempt was made to reduce weight but the body, which cowled-in the engine, weighed only 43 lb.

This fascinating Morgan could do over 60 m.p.h. in low speed, and 100 m.p.h. in top at about 4,300 r.p.m. on the tachometer, which was driven from the bevel-box countershaft. Yet in a season's Track work, it averaged 24 to 25 m.p.g. Beart brought it out in July at Brooklands and set Class H2 records for 5 miles and 10 miles and the equivalent kilometre records, the 5-kilometre record being at fractionally over 100 m.p.h., *the first time a 3-wheeler had been timed at this speed, officially or unofficially.* A *one-way* kilometre was clocked at 104.63 m.p.h. and the f.s. 5-mile record fell at 99.67 m.p.h. In August Beart took the f.s. kilometre and mile records at 103.37 and 102.65 m.p.h., respectively, and the following month captured the 50-kilometre, 100-kilometre and one-hour records, his speed for the hour being 91.48 m.p.h. In October Robin Jackson filled in, as it were, with the s.s. kilometre and mile records in his Morgan-Blackburne, at 64.04 and 71.03 m.p.h., respectively. Beart also raced Horton for the B.M.C.R.C. Cyclecar Championship, starting slowly but winning by six yards, at 83 m.p.h.

" Shacklepin," who wrote " Cyclecar Comments " in *The Light Car & Cyclecar,* bought an Aero-Blackburne in April and, giving his experiences after 7,000 miles, complained of clutch slip oil running down the tappet rods, and an inadequate dynamo output, but generally praised the car, which had been fitted with Bentley & Draper shock-absorbers to the back wheel. Morgans met 4-wheeled cars again in the M.C.C. High-Speed Trial at Brooklands and, required to average one m.p.h. more than a 1½-litre car to get a " gold," nine Morgans started and eight won gold medals.

The only alterations for 1926 were better bodywork on some of the touring models, the De Luxe model having 1-in. higher body sides and, in company with the Family model, a better hood and 2-pane screen. The latest 1,086-c.c. J.A.P. engine with big valves was available for the Aero and the new Blackburne engine had stronger valve gear with the cups in the top of the push-rods instead of in the rockers. All models now had dynamo lighting sets, and an electric horn was fitted to all except the 980-c.c. Standard model. Front brakes, now only £4 extra, were by no means universal. The 1926 prices were £115 for the a/c. De Luxe, or £125 in w/c. form, £123 for the w/c. Grand Prix-Anzani, the Family costing £116 with a/c., £126 with w/c. J.A.P. engine. The Aero cost £130 with s.v. w/c. J.A.P., £135 with Blackburne and £142 with Anzani engine. The Standard still sold for £95. Thus the Morgan challenged the Austin 7, now down to £149, while interest in 3-wheelers was by no means waning, for the famous Malvern make was joined at the 1925 Motorcycle Show, where it occupied Stand No. 32, by the flat-twin w/c. Coventry-Victor and the Omega-J.A.P.

(To be continued)

THE VINTAGE YEARS OF THE MORGAN 3-WHEELER

ONE-LUNGER.—*The Morgan was given engines of various sizes for racing, including small vee-twins and single-cylinder power units. This is Eric Fernihough's 500-c.c. Morgan-J.A.P. of 1926, described in* MOTOR SPORT *of that year.*

1926.—Enthusiasm for Morgan was unabated, in spite of one unkind cartoon which depicted a Grand Prix Morgan and two kids in a pram, the caption reading " The Two-Seater They Talk About Before Marriage—And The One They Get!" One Aero owner made a replica of his car to a scale of ¾ in.= I ft. and set it up on the Morgan's radiator cap, and in the serious sphere of speed events R. T. Horton was racing at Southport sands where Bullough's Morgan was in winning form while R. R. Jackson and Eric Fernihough, in the Inter-Varsity Hill Climb, gained first and second places in the unlimited sidecar class. Fernihough, later to become one of the World's fastest motorcyclists, then still an undergraduate at Cambridge, had built a single-cylinder Morgan Special (*see* MOTOR SPORT, August 1926), using a 1925 494-c.c. a/c. push-rod o.h.v. J.A.P. engine which ran up to 5,700 r.p.m. With this he was very successful. At Brooklands on March 31st he covered five miles (f.s.) at 73.12 m.p.h., five km. (f.s.) at 73.37 m.p.h., ten miles (s.s.) at 69.65 m.p.h. and ten km. (s.s.) 70.37 m.p.h., passing Pratts spirit through the Amac carburetter and using Castrol oil and Avon tyres. These were new Class I records, and in June Fernihough was out again, clocking 71.81 m.p.h. for a f.s. km., 71.91 m.p.h. for a f.s. mile. On the last day of August, taking his *fiancée*, Miss Butler, as passenger, he went after long-distance records in the half-litre Morgan. He set up new records from 100 km. to 6 hours, at speeds around 57/59 m.p.h., although for the six hours the average had dropped to 49.51 m.p.h. Best speed was 59.7 m.p.h. for 100 miles. But unfortunately the rear tyre burst and the driver and his girl passenger who had been sharing two-hour spells at the wheel, were thrown out as the Morgan overturned, but were not badly hurt.

This was the age when record breaking paid well in respect of bonus money, so the very next day G. E. Tottey, the New Imperial rider who still turns up at B.M.C.R.C. Brooklands Re-Unions, took out a 490-c.c. Omega-J.A.P. 3-wheeler and raised Fernihough's 50-mile, one-hour and 100-km. records, respectively to 60.09, 60.52 and 60.52 m.p.h. However, Fernihough put a 599-c.c. J.A.P. engine in the Morgan, and covered 50 km. at 62.29 m.p.h., 50 miles at 62.61 m.p.h., 100 km. at 62.72 m.p.h. and averaged 62.69 m.p.h. for the hour, new Class I records. (J. J. Hall, with the 1,100-c.c. Omega-J.A.P., took Class K records for three hours (58.84 m.p.h.), four hours (58.64 m.p.h.), five hours (57.9 m.p.h.), six hours (57.34 m.p.h.), seven hours (56.59 m.p.h.), 200 miles (59.14 m.p.h.) and 500 km. (57.88 m.p.h.)—happy days !)

In trials, naturally, Morgans went on scoring successes, and it was estimated that since 1920 they had won 27 gold, 14 silver and nine bronze medals in the " Land's End " alone. H. Beart & Co. of London Road, Kingston were fitting steering reduction gears and foot throttle controls to Morgans, the Aero owned by " Shacklepin " of *The Light Car & Cyclecar* being amongst them, and Jackson and Booth of Congleton sold a proprietary reverse gear. (At least one policeman was obviously unaware that

3-wheelers were not compelled to have a reverse gear, incidentally!) In the Scottish Six Days' Trial the 1,096-c.c. Morgans of Spouse and Watson gained silver medals but H.F.S. and Carr retired, the former with leaky water joints, the latter damaging his chassis on Loch Losgoinn. In the strenuous International Six Days Trial Goodall (NP 636), Horton (CJ 6343) and Carr (NP 65), using w/c. Aero-J.A.P.s with the new 10-h.p. o.h.v. engine, did magnificently, all winning " golds " and the Team Prize in their class. Their total loss of marks was only 20, whereas the sole surviving team of sidecars lost 310 marks.

Performances like this were excellent publicity and in the face of fierce competition from 4-cylinder small cars the Morgan remained extremely popular, Homac's advertising that they could not give delivery in under 14 days. The *Motor Cycle & Cycle Trader* reported that the 10.4-h.p. w/c. o.h.v. Blackburne-Aero would do 10-30 m.p.h. in 5.2 sec. on the 4.6 to 1 top speed, or in 2.8 on the 7.9 to 1 low speed, had a top speed of 72 m.p.h., and would stop in 34 yards from 40 m.p.h. using only the foot brake, in 26 yards if hand and foot brakes were both applied (this apparently with front brakes). Alternative ratios of 5 to 1 and 10 to 1 were spoken of, the tyres were 700 × 85, the petrol tank held three gallons.

Up to October 1926 a 349-c.c. Villard 3-wheeler held the km. and mile f.s. 3-wheeler records in Class H (up to 750 c.c.,) at 55.49 and 55.12 m.p.h. respectively. Class I (up to 500 c.c.) records were shared by Jackson (498-c.c. Morgan-Blackburne), Fernihough/Miss Butler (494-c.c. Morgan-J.A.P.) and Tottey (494-c.c. Omega-J.A.P.), Fernihough holding the majority, the fastest being Jackson's f.s. km. at 72.44 m.p.h., Class J (up to 750 c.c.) was Tottey's preserve, with a 730-c.c. Omega-J.A.P., but Sandford's 747-c.c. Sandford had the s.s. km. and mile records and the Omega's f.s. km. at 78.29 m.p.h. Class K (up to 1,100 c.c.) was almost a Morgan monopoly, cost by Beart's 1,096-c.c. Blackburne and 1,097-c.c. J.A.P., except for the s.s. km. and mile records held by Jackson's Blackburne and the 200-mile and 3-hour records held by Hall's 1,097-c.c. Omega-J.A.P., fastest being the f.s. km. at 103.37 m.p.h. Passengers were carried in all classes.

At Olympia in 1926, with Morgan showing a dozen cars and a chassis on Stand No. 53, Omega and Coventry-Victor continued to exhibit and were joined by the single-cylinder £65 H.P. For 1927 the Morgan was grease-gun lubricated, 7-in. front brakes were standardised on the De Luxe, Family and Aero models, and the bevel-box was redesigned to allow a larger ball-bearing behind the pinion, while the rear fork and bearings, countershaft, dogs and rear axle were strengthened, and there was ample clearance for the largest rear tyres. The Standard model, now with double screen, electric horn and celluloid-covered steering wheel, cost £89. More commodious bodies figured on the De Luxe, Family and Aero models, and 4-in. Dunlops were standard. Prices were, respectively, a/c. £110, w/c. £120; a/c. £111, w/c. £121; w/c. Aero

It's clear that John Shealy II is a Morgan nut; in fact, he may well be the leading Morgan proponent in America. He owns five Morgans (including a 1933 Beetleback 3-wheeler he bought the day he was leaving California to fly home), he races Morgans, is writing his third book on the marque, sponsors the John H. Shealy II Award for Best Morgan of the Year at the annual conclave, and simply is totally immersed in Morgan romance, history and technical data. But unlike many people who carry on automotive love affairs, Shealy believes his cars are meant to be driven and enjoyed—no up-on-a-pedestal lover is John. And that's one of the major reasons why he set out on his madcap cross-country jaunt: "I did it to show that 3-wheelers are not fragile little things; they're sturdy cars that can be used. Most of the Morgan people at the Fullerton meet didn't really expect us to make it all the way across the U.S." Shealy adds that he knew it could be done, and his riding mechanic, Tim Hund, while not a Morgan man, was reasonably confident they would succeed.

Such confidence may have seemed entirely misplaced on the first day of the 3328-mile journey, as Shealy hit a 100-lb sack of

across the desert, like with a sailboat, while the blowing sand was scouring most of the paint off the car."

Eight days from the start, near-disaster struck as they were leaving Tucson, Arizona following a fuel stop. An oil line ruptured, having been badly chafed by the leaping and landing in Georgia, and Shealy and Hund found themselves facing 2-3 ft flames from the engine. Shealy recalls that his first inclination was to scoop up dirt from alongside the highway to quell the blaze, only to discover that sunbaked Arizona soil doesn't scoop, whereupon he started beating at the fire with various articles of clothing. Hund remembers that the fire was burning directly beneath the gravity-feed fuel tank, and when it began to whistle like a teapot, he had visions of the promised land.

Unfortunately, among all the people who stopped to gawk, no one had a fire extinguisher, but just prior to what Hund is sure was the moment when the whole thing would blow and Morgan 3-wheeler pieces would shower the desert, a trucker showed up with an extinguisher and the fire was smothered as the local firefighters were arriving on the scene. The singed trike was

 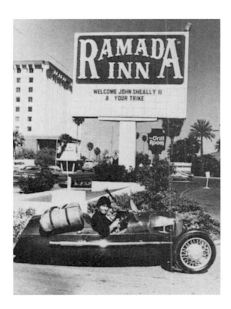 

cement in the dark of night on the interstate near Charlotte, North Carolina. One doesn't make sudden darting maneuvers in a 3-wheeler, so Shealy and Hund held on tightly while the trike was airborne for about 30 yards, making a 2-wheel landing but staying upright. There was little apparent damage, but the effects of the flight were enough to stress the Morgan's parts and systems. The most immediate problem was that the engine had jumped its timing, which led to overheating, glowing exhaust pipes that burned both men's jackets, a broken valve, scored piston and damaged valve guide. This was all put right the next day in Atlanta at the Harley-Davidson dealership by a man named Ray Lyttle, one of those mechanics you always hope you'll meet on just such an occasion. The valve was replaced by one from a Harley 74, the guide was trimmed, and the piston was practically remade through the heliarc welding talents of a local shop teacher.

A variety of niggling mechanical problems plagued the cross-country effort as Shealy and Hund pushed on through the southern states, fighting a soaking rain (no top, of course, on the 3-wheeler) from Atlanta to Birmingham, Alabama; the generator threw a pulley between Birmingham and Shreveport, Louisiana, an 18-hour day fraught with minor repairs and adjustments. The crossing of Texas was uneventful until they were west of Dallas, headed for Abilene, where they encountered 30-40 mph crosswinds. The ever-smiling Shealy, who seems to thrive on misadventure, recounts, "I was tacking and jibing

pushed two miles up the road to a service station, and a passerby invited Shealy and Hund to use his shop for repairs.

"All the way across the country, the camaraderie and help from people were simply terrific," Shealy says. "The television station in Virginia had filmed our departure and sent tapes to various other stations along our route, and it was amazing how many people we met who told us they had seen us on the news."

The two Virginians spent the next day rewiring and repairing the Morgan, and then set off for Phoenix, where they took a day off to relax and recuperate. The last leg of the trip took them across the desert to Palm Springs, fighting crosswinds up to 70 mph this time, and as the end of the adventure was almost in sight, the demon of things mechanical got in one parting shot as the engine threw a valve spacer and bent a pushrod. Once more into the breach, lads, and all that. So Hund and Shealy pulled the pushrod and straightened it by beating it with a rock against the freeway guardrail, but they had no replacement spacer. Would the whole adventure come to an ignominious conclusion on the Riverside Freeway just a few miles from their destination? Not a chance! Shealy eyeballed the size of the pushrod end and guessed that the 7/16 socket in their repair kit would fill the gap, which it did. With a flashlight taped on the front of the car (the headlights had not worked since the Tucson fire), Shealy and Hund motored on to their destination. And Shealy, in his boyishly enthusiastic way, sums it all up: "My only regret is that we don't have time to drive it back home to Virginia."

Triple treats

Just what is the attraction of driving a three-wheeler?
Mick Walsh compares the authentic Morgan with its modern equivalent,
the Norfolk-built Triking; pictures by Julian Mackie

I've long had a desire to find out what three wheelers are really like. Tales of my father capers using a Morgan trike to commute ov the Chilterns, in the early sixties – much to th amusement of his neighbours – plus years watching the antics of racing trikes at VMCC an VSCC meets, has proved that these demon machine are about serious fun.

Sadly their appeal to collectors – much like that the nearest four-wheel counterpart, the Chain Gan Nash – has meant prices are well beyond my budge but my inability to resist the charm of these wonde ful creations prompted planning a week samplin historic Mogs, and their natural successor, th Triking.

I must confess I have certain trepidations abou three-wheelers, having turned a Reliant Robin on i

GX 3170

of during my first week on CLASSIC AND SPORTSCAR, nting my ego more than the motorised glass-fibre rambulator. I'd also watched Morgan trikes defy- the laws of physics lifting wheels cornering at dwell Park and Angoulême and on occasions pping over. Did you need to be completely batty to nt to drive trikes, or was it the secret of a heady otoring experience that neither motor bikes or rs could match?

The prospect of finding a genuine Morgan Super orts which I could play with for longer than an ernoon seemed fairly slim, particularly last April, on most of these prized toys were still in

hibernation. The natural alternative was to contact Tony Divey, a cheery Norfolk Morgan enthusiast who had the vision to create a modern alternative to the classic Morgan trike. His creation, christened the Triking, makes no pretence to be a replica, but more a substitute. A former technical illustrator with a background working for such high-tech companies as Lotus, Porsche and Dornier, Tony has long had a passion for Morgan three-wheelers, having owned eight over the years. The prospect of commuting

from his Norfolk home to Munich, where he was working at the time, didn't bear thinking about without his Mog, but the reliability of his venerable trike made the trip just a shade impractical. For him there was only one alternative, and with 25 years of practical engineering experience behind him, he set about the challenge

The result is for me a perfect reincarnation of Henry Frederick Stanley Morgan's wonderful machines. Like many of its owners (and with a production so far of under 40, they're a rare breed), it's a totally unpretentious machine. To drive one regularly I'm sure requires a huge sense of humour. The rigours and discomfort of these machines are all part of the total experience, making every journey an adventure. Some folk just have to travel that way. I may be determined never to buy a closed car, and I adore old motorbikes, but I'm not convinced a trike is the perfect solution. Could it encompass the best or worst elements of each? I had to find out.

The rigours and discomfort of these machines are part of the experience, making every journey an adventure

Even though we left the full address of the Triking factory back in the office that overcast April afternoon, I somehow knew we wouldn't have any trouble finding Tony Divey's production line. As we headed into Marlingford village, near Norwich, I spotted his bungalow with a drive and gardens looking more like a Triking club gathering. The factory is annexed to his home in an enlarged garage, where he and his son construct these three-wheeled gems. As with most English cottage industry crafts the workmanship is superb, and you quickly realise why the Triking is priced so highly.

For the rest of the afternoon he entertained us with his three-wheeler experiences as we examined the construction in concept of a new chassis, built up using square section tubes, not far removed from the steel backbone chassis design of a Lotus. This is clad in stressed alloy side panels, all dressed in beautifully-made glass-fibre bonnet, rear body and front cycle wings. Sitting proudly at the bow, like a ship's figurehead, is a Moto-Guzzi 950cc V-twin. Not only is this beautiful Italian engine aesthetically perfect for the task, it performs with the reliability and durability earned by years of endurance racing on two wheels. Such performance traditions and associations with a classic two-wheeled product make the 70bhp unit a perfect counterpart to the Morgan's JAP.

The front suspension uses double wishbones, coil springs and shocks to support inspiring 11in disc brakes. The rear is a simple swinging fork with shaft drive, also borrowed from the Guzzi motorbike

Above: Low-slung and bobbed-tail profile of the Triking helps aerodynamics. Below: Speedboat style dash, with superb Italian instruments and modern rocker-style switches

Mechanics at Chalkpits Museum bus garage admire trike trio. The 1913 model was a favourite

Owner David Pittuck at speed in 1932 Aero Jap. Lines and detailing are exquisite. Below: Cord-bound steering wheel with hand-throttle and advance lever. Right: exquisite stork mascot

design. All this adds up to a power-to-weight ratio of 200bhp per ton and 0-60mph in seven seconds. If that doesn't excite you…

As ever, we couldn't stop talking, and it was almost dark before I ventured back to the dreaded A11 trunk road for the Big Smoke, having donned flying jacket, leather helmet and goggles. I soon came to terms with the in-line motorcycle gear-change, with first forward and the other four progressively back. Compared to a car, the selection seems a little imprecise, but a sensitive clutch and familiarity makes for a rapid, instant change. You have to remember to slip down all the gears to find neutral again at traffic lights.

My first real sensation with the Triking was most of the contents of a deep muddy puddle

I expected the acceleration to thrust you back in the seat, but it's more like a high-speed simulator, with the hedgerows flashing by beside you. As with most beefy big V-twins, the Italian engine really delivers low down the rev range. With 62lb ft on tap it will happily slug along in fifth when you feel lazy.

But my first real sensation with the Triking was most of the contents of a deep muddy puddle. Cutting the apex on a country lane just after leaving Marlingford I turned the front wheels into the roadside bath, forgetting that angled wheels on a fixed wing equalled an instant shower as I leaned out of the cockpit VSCC racing style. After a brief halt to wipe my face and goggles, I charged away again.

The rest of the route was not the most suitable introduction to sporting three-wheelers. The novelty and romance which ought to come from the combination of man, trike and the elements, vanished about Newmarket, when I realised I really wasn't wearing enough clothes or – more importantly – the *correct* clothes. Sheepskin flying jackets are fine in freezing, dry conditions but in the wet you might just as well be wearing a sponge. Fortunately the rain only lasted until Royston, where a succession of slippery roundabouts entertained me as I whistled up alongside unsuspecting normals in snug tin boxes. Suddenly you understand this crazy machine's charm…

That is until the dark silhouette of a Sainsbury's artic cuts you up, and you entertain morbid thoughts of getting lost under its intimidating trailer. Then you feel small and lonely.

Peaceful rural road disturbed by editor let loose in 1913 Morgan trike, one of the earliest

A brief halt at my parents' home provided welcome refreshment, but Dad's enthusiasm for most motoring oddities couldn't tempt him out for a quick spin round the block. Mum was less convinced about my sanity than the Triking, and insisted I ring in when I reached Clapham. Having discouraged (not forbidden) me from riding motorbikes through my youth, I think she saw the trike as some awful revenge.

Slogging back down the A1(M) to London, I couldn't help thinking the Triking would be better suited to California, the ideal transport for a nutty professor at LA university. I used the Triking to commute across London for the rest of the week but had the feeling most pedestrians and road users who witnessed the Trike were reather bemused by it, regarding the driver as loony. Motorcycle messengers, however, showed great interest, often chatting at lights about Moto Guzzis, and instantly spotting the origin of the engine.

Keen to sample 'the real thing', we planned to take the Triking to meet its ancestors (in spirit if not heritage) at the collection of David Pittuck. A true enthusiast for the originals, particularly French-built Darmonts, David now finds these marvellous machines the perfect diversion from his hectic business. When you discover that his first bike after he had passed his test on a 50cc moped was a Brough Superior, and that his first memory of a Morgan trike was of one being towed by his uncle's vintage Voisin, you begin to understand his passionate interest. On meeting him for the first time, I thought his face looked oddly familiar, and it wasn't until later in the day it clicked: I'd seen him recently as one of the first starters in the Pioneer run on his 1904 Bolée. He'd generously offered me a drive of his superb 1932 three-speed Aero Jap and rare pre-WW1 two-speeder?

David's beautifully restored 1932 trike is one of just 15 to 20 constructed during a transition period at the Malvern works from the vintage two speeders to the later Super Sports models. It's original, tamer, side valve JAP engine was stolen, and David acquired the chassis in a fairly sorry state. Fortunately he had the makings of an OHV JAP which better suited his requirements. The transmission, with a cone clutch behind the engine and a long propshaft to a bevel gearbox, drives twin chains to the rear wheel and is brilliantly simple.

Although a post Vintage machine, this Aero has all the charisma of the earlier models with its swept up tail, Morgan foot plates, split screen, nickel-plated rad' shell and Hispanoesque stork mascot. Quite often these machines look over-restored, but keen use of black enamel paint rather than plating greatly improves this ones looks.

It's a long time since I've looked forward to driving a vehicle so much. The style of this cheeky design calls you to have a go. Although its all action, it looks intimidating with the throttle and ignition on the

Right: Cornering hard, the Triking will become a two-wheeler but mostly handling is surefooted. Note remnants of muddy puddle over screen and editor. Below left: David Pittuck and wife at speed in Morgan trike race at VSCC Oulton

steering wheel spokes: David assured me it's actually very user friendly. I imagined bowling into a corner at speed, realising I was going too fast, forgetting where the throttle was and gripping the wheel rim as the trike headed for the hedge. In reality the throttle is set fairly constant once up and running, but you can never let your attention relax, planning for the road ahead.

The back-fire is like some demented poacher if you throttle down too quickly when racing up to junctions

Starting is simple. With the ignition retarded to save breaking your thumb or arm, one swing of the handle and the JAP barks eagerly into life. A sprint back to the cockpit to advance the ignition, adjust the throttle and climb aboard, doing the splits to get your legs under the wheel. The steering rim is bound in cord in true vintage sporting tradition and the view forward is wonderful, with the tappetts working frantically poking out in front of the rad, and the mascot flying high as you settle into the deep padded seats. Instruments are basic on the black dash with a drum speedo and ammeter in a central cluster.

Naturally it takes a while to co-ordinate hand throttle with foot clutch and floor change, confusing the characteristics of car and motorbike, but once on the move the experience is rivetting. It has to be otherwise you're heading for an accident.

Like all vintage gearboxes, the linkage requires familiarity to change smoothly and silently. The trick here is to let the revs fall off before you engage, and feel carefully with the selector. Once on the open road the big JAP is very torquey, and is quite happy to thump away in top with a lively performance.

Forty miles an hour has never been so dramatic, rolling down hills with the overrun popping and banging. The back-fire is like some demented poacher if you throttle down too quickly when racing up to junctions.

The steering is light and balanced while the handling is sure footed and I'm sure superior to most four-wheeled cars of the period. It's easy to see why the likes of Stuart Harper and David Caroline mix it with VSCC front runners.

I could have driven the Aero all afternoon around the Sussex back lanes, but travelling in convoy as David does with a group of trikes across France to cyclecar meets must be brilliant fun. He also very kindly allowed me to drive in his rare 1913 model. Extra controls include an oil pressure hand pump on the dash and an exhaust valve lifter to build up compression before the engine is started. The handle fits directly into the bevel box in front of the back wheel, while the gearchange and handbrake sit outside the chassis to the driver's right.

You could almost count the long strokes of the elderly 8hp JAP. It's delightfully simple to drive but producing a very spirited performance for a pre-WW1 machine. This survivor is in fine fettle and a regular runner in the Pioneer run for veteran motorbikes, and will easily keep pace with solo machines. Wet weather driving is a little unnerving with extra attention required to the brakes as the wet bands have no grip: constant application to the handbrake soon helps to warm them up! My short run around the Amberley Chalk Pits museum was much like riding an untamed horse, slowly giving it more rein as you become confident.

The refinement of Tony Divey's Triking greatly impressed David Pittuck. Its ride and performance for him took the trike concept into the modern age but losing none of the appeal. He meant it as no condemnation when he suggested it would make perfect transport for his wife to join him on continental rallies with the Morgan Aero.

Thrilling as the Triking is, I couldn't resist the rawness of the original. The Aeros charm and character make it essential for my ideal collection. What other vintage machine can you take the wife or girlfriend racing, dressed in black leathers? What a shame good ones are now so priceless. Either that or I'd have Tony Divey build me a demon all black Triking with a full house racing Guzzi engine just to out-drag Lotus Seven and Escort XR3 owners. That would stop them sniggering at traffic lights.

ACKNOWLEDGEMENTS

If your tempted by the brilliant Triking, contact Tony Divey at Barford Road, Marlingford, Norwich, Norfolk. Tel: 084 421 5555. Our thanks to David Pittuck and the Chalk Pits Museum, Amberley for their help.

MORGAN SUPER SPORTS

John Shapley tries a 52-year-old vee-twin powered three-wheeler. When Geoff Sturges bought it in Bristol for everyday transport , Moggies were fairly common. Now it's a distinguished survivor...

1909 when HFS Morgan built a car ...orts, it was more to find a use for a ...geot V-twin he had acquired than to ...nd one of the world's most enduring ...ts car marques. This vehicle, built in ... Malvern Link garage, was the first ...gan Runabout three-wheeler and it ... the beginning of a long line of ...dedly successful three-wheel sports ... that would continue until the early ...0s.

...y 1910 Morgan was exhibiting his ...le-seater equipped with either a single-...nder 4 hp or V-twin 8 hp JAP engine. ...ear later, the "Standard" two-seater ...del was launched, with the cheapest ...the range sporting a price tag of a ...dest 85 guineas. This "Standard" mo-...was powered by a 986 cm³ JAP twin. ...hese early models conjured up at ... dawn of motoring history, might ... been mechanically simple, but they ...e anything but crude. Even by its ...t recent standards, the Morgan can ...lly be regarded as sophisticated, al-...ugh the company now seems to be ...ding in that direction with their V8-...vered Plus-8 two-seater.

...Ir Geoff Sturges of Cape Town, who ...s one of the few Morgan three-...elers in the country, recently re-...hed our memories on the mystique ... has made the marque such an en-...ng phenomenon. In the acquisitive ...ety of veteran and vintage vehicle

collectors Geoff Sturges is something of an odd ball, for his interest lies not so much with relics of a bygone motoring era as it does with things mechanical. His purchase of the 1933 Morgan Super Sports came about more as a fortuitous necessity than out of a desire to acquire a distinctive old motor car.

An affair with Fenella. . .

At the time when Geoff bought the Morgan off a showroom floor in Bristol, Britain in 1965, he needed it for transport to commute to the technical college every day. "At the time there was nothing all that unusual about owning such a car — they were fairly commonplace about the city," Geoff recalls. Besides, he was intensely involved in an affair with "Fenella" who soaked up all his spare time.

Fenella was a 1926 Aveling Porter steamroller. As its name suggests, it was steam-driven and fired by a coal burning furnace and — a big attraction for an impecunious student — it was road tax free! There was also a pair of sickly Morris Eights that shared any crumbs of spare time that fell from the Sturges' cluttered table.

At the time of acquiring the three-wheeler for about R420, it was decked out with all manner of unoriginal bits and pieces. Tarted-up by an enthusiastic salesman, it had a fancy Austin steering

wheel, chromed hubcaps, electric wipers, traffic indicators and a rich assortment of paint jobs. Over the years, these have all been stripped off and, where necessary, replaced by original parts.

To prove to himself that the Morgan was more than just a commuter Geoff took it on a round-England trip, a long haul in those days. Considering the vehicle has no doors and requires a gymnastic feat just to enter its cockpit, it is amazing to learn that Geoff slept in the car for the journey. But as he says, he was thinner in those days. . .

Water-cooled twin

Geoff's '33 Moggie was one of the first to be fitted out with the water-cooled 986 cm³ Matchless o-h-v engine which developed 31 kW. This particular vehicle has turned in a best speed of 134 km/h over a timed quarter mile — going some, in a three-wheeler that is reminiscent of a child's pedal car and, to the uninitiated, feels about as secure.

In its day the Super Sports model was claimed to be capable of holding its own with any sports car on the road, and to offer "perfect stability at all speeds". The manufacturer even offered to paint the "low, coach-built body" in any reasonable colour of the customer's choice. The British price at the time was £135 and the road tax, £4.

From the front, the Super Sports

With many English miles behind her — and many kilometres of the Western Cape — this 52-year-old Moggie is now used only on special runs, usually with other oldies. When it was built in 1933, the advance/retard lever as well as the accelerator were mounted on the steering wheel (inset). This, of course, necessitates very direct steering, with just one turn of the wheel, lock-to-lock.

looks rather like a four-wheeled "Plus-four" with similar radiator, curved and louvred bonnet and coil-sprung suspension, with the hubs sliding and pivoting on "extended king pins": ingenious but fragile. The rear wheel is chain driven and sprung by underslung leaf springs.

When Geoff Sturges decided in 1969 that South Africa was the place to live he brought his car along with him. So far as he has been able to ascertain, there are only five three-wheelers in the country and this is the only one in Cape Town.

Before anybody goes anywhere in Geoff's Moggie, there is a comprehensive "pre-flight" check to be covered first. The cock of the fuel tank must be opened so it can gravity feed the Amal carb. The choke and advance/retard levers on the steering wheel have to be set to the start position. The valve mechanism of each cylinder has to be lavishly oiled, for the oil from the sump-mounted pump only reaches the cylinder heads a few minutes after the engine has been running.

Next you tickle the carb prior to cranking the motor over a few times, just to ensure all is sweet before firing it up. Now the moment has arrived — you switch on the ignition and get to work on that crank handle. A few lifeless chuff-chuffs, then it suddenly erupts into life with an unmistakable off-beat sound that only an unsilenced Vee-twin can produce. It will stir the pulse of any motor-

ing buff, but it is doubtful if the rest of the neighbourhood appreciate it.

Pulsates into life

With the motor going, the whole vehicle pulsates with life. The crank wallah dashes back to the cockpit and resets the controls to the "run" position. With all this palaver successfully executed, the Super Sports is prepped-up and ready for its next jaunt. . .

Getting into the cockpit is easiest if both driver and passenger climb in through the passenger side. But it's more easily said than done.

Even in the cockpit and settled on the hard seat it's quite a squeeze. Then of course there are no luxuries such as nicely contoured bucket seats or necessities as seat belts and never have I felt that I would appreciate one more even if it was to do nothing other than to hold one in place as you jog along the byways.

Before you is a large steering wheel with its three controls mounted on the two lower spokes. These are your controls for the choke, advance/retard and a long fluted lever for the accelerator. The dash has, at some time in the car's life, been vinyl covered and it houses a centre mounted speedo and ignition switch and dial gauges for the ammeter and fuel and there is a clock. There are warning lights for the ignition and oil pressure and there is a "twist on" dash light above the cubbyhole. There is barely sufficient room in this for more than a road map, a pair of gloves and cloth cap.

Stretching ahead of the "V" wind-

shield lies a long tapering bonnet that houses no more than a few electrics, coolant for the motor and the fuel tank. Mounted at the front of this and on either side are a pair of magnificent head lamps.

To set off, you disengage the clutch, nudge the selector lever forwards into first and gently edge home the clutch. There are no theatricals. The drive takes with a smooth progression that would rival any modern car.

The Moggie rolls up her sleeves and gets down to work with a gusto that lets you know she is no spent elastic band. Perhaps it was a result of being more out of the car than in it, but the rate at which the old girl picked up speed felt quite alarming. A brisk declutch and you are through into second gear.

There is no time to check on the road speed at which you change gear, for you are too busy trying to master the reverse "H" gear stick movement, but in no time at all the Matchless twin seemed to be hunting for another gear.

Mindful of the fact that you are in charge of a rare example of an endangered species, you go carefully and swop the cogs neatly into top. There is quite a jump between second and top gears, with a major drop in engine revs.

Despite being a three-wheeler, the Moggie felt remarkably stable, but keeping her on the straight and narrow at speed is clearly an acquired skill. Her steering is unusually direct and dauntingly heavy. The Super Sports is fitted with

194

Fragile as these early Morgans may seem (top left) the marque has proved to be one of the world's most enduring and the company recently celebrated its 75th anniversary. Above left — the simple rear suspension system and chain drive. The "Moggie" is powered by a water-cooled 986 cm³ Matchless engine that idles remarkably slowly and evinces surprisingly little vibration. A 50° V-twin, it puts out 31 kW at 4 000 r/min.

Although we were not able to try the Moggie at speed, this particular three-wheeler has clocked over 134 km/h. Geoff Sturges is at the wheel in this picture, with his daughter Pippa in the passenger seat. Direct steering makes the car a handful but it's exceptionally rewarding to drive.

a 1:2 reduction steering box, which yields just under one turn of the wheel, lock-to-lock.

The tar strip slicing through some of the Cape's oldest vineyards seems inadequately narrow and fearfully rough. Every little bump seems to send the Moggie hunting off in a new direction, every irregularity that catches the wheel's attention is picked up with relish, magnified in the works and transmitted to the crew. . .

Hi-rise exhaust

But after a few kilometres, you become attuned to the characteristics and begin to relax. But the gleaming hi-rise exhaust pipe skirting the cockpit edge stingingly reminds you it is not there for passenger support or for resting your elbows on. Despite the lack of shockabsorbers, the ride was not bouncy, nor was there any noticeable body roll around corners — due to the Morgan's low centre of gravity and that unique front suspension system that was only recently dropped from favour.

The front brakes were originally cable operated but have been modified to use Morris hydraulics. The handbrake, mounted between driver and passenger, operates the rear drum by cable. Both systems worked passably but their performance — poor by current standards, has to be allowed for in the way you drive.

Unfortunately I had no opportunity to try the Moggie at full stretch. "With a vehicle of this age, one seems to spend more time on maintenance than actually driving it" says Geoff. "But then I find it quite as fascinating." The next task he intends undertaking is to renew much of the frame and bodywork, but the problem at present is to locate a supply of ash timber. ●

The broad spread of the front wheels gives the dashing sportster a surprisingly stable feel through corners, even at relatively high speeds. The high-rise exhaust system looks impressive but passengers are warned to keep well away from it.

Trial by trike

Racing at Oran Park in a three wheeler Morgan.

by Ian Lee

THE starting lights were flashing yellow as we gridded on the second row at Amaroo Park. The marshal lifted his hand with fingers outstretched, five seconds to red. He ducked off the track and red came on; five more seconds and the green lit up.

Phil had the big JAP V-Twin blipping to 3500 rpm. He savagely dropped the clutch to get the Morgan's single rear tyre spinning. If the tyre bit too early the engine would stall. Too much wheelspin and we would just sit there.

Morgan three wheelers are notoriously slow starters and the two sidecar outfits in front of us darted away. Half way up Bitupave Hill we caught them. Phil jinked right, left, right looking for a way through. We nearly nudged both of them but there was no gap. Out of the corner of my eye I saw a blue flash as a big Vincent outfit got a dream run up the outside and scrabbled past the three of us into the lead.

What was I doing in borrowed leathers, clinging on for dear life in the passenger seat of a 1934 Morgan three wheeler in the middle of a motor bike and sidecar race? The story began just a fortnight before, with an invitation to ride in a race in one of the Morgan three wheelers that had come from Britain for two Bicentennial historic race meetings.

The diminutive three wheelers can race against cars or sidecar outfits. The Oran Park race was the first time that a Morgan three wheeler had ever raced in car and sidecar races on the same day at the same meeting! My invitation was for the following weekend at a bike-only Historic Meeting at Amaroo Park.

One of the spectators at Oran Park was Charles Morgan, grand-son of H.F.S. Morgan who began building his three wheelers in 1910. Charles is production manager at Morgan and his mission is to double production to about 80 Morgans a month. This will reduce waiting time to an acceptable average of five years instead of the 10 that some people now wait before taking delivery of their hand-crafted relic from the days when genuine sports cars were built.

Unfortunately today's buyers must be content with four wheelers — the last three wheel Morgan left the factory in 1950.

Australian Morgan enthusiast Terry Wright made the pilgrimage to the Morgan factory at Christmas 1987. While in England he invited the owners of the two fastest, racing Morgan three wheelers to bring their cars to Australia for the Bicentenary race. Back in Sydney he organised a committee to make the visit a reality. They secured sponsorship from British Airways to bring over the drivers and their wives, and from the Scotpac division of P&O to bring out the cars in a container.

The newer of the two cars was hand built in 1969 by Stuart Harper from a collection of genuine parts. It is a faithful replica of a car raced in the 1920s by E.B. Ware who was chief engineer of the JAP company. Morgan has never produced its own engines. Instead it has relied on engines purchased from several companies

photo by Clayton Lee

photo by Ian Lee

Left and top, Philip Spencer and Ian Lee crammed into the Morgan for the spin at Oran Park. Above, Stuart Harper (red overalls) and helpers push the E.B. Ware replica back from a test run. Right, Charles Morgan (left) and Cyril Hale with three wheeler.

photo by Ian Lee

...luding JAP which is named ...er its founder, John Arthur Pre-...ce. In recent years Morgan has ...rchased engines from Ford, Fiat ...d Rover.

The second of the two cars ...ited to Australia had been ...ught new in 1934 by Cyril Hale. ...'d been inspired to purchase the ...organ by a race at Donington ...rk. He says the cars looked ...wer than he drove on the road ...d he thought he could beat ...m. He bought his Morgan with ... standard V-twin Matchless ...gine and in his first race finished ...distant last! Race tuning did not ...lp so Cyril went back to the ...organ factory to see what could ... done.

He was sent to the JAP factory with a letter of introduction so that he could be interviewed to see if he was a suitable customer for one of the engines. Cyril ended up with a JAP 8/80. The numbers did not refer to the capacity but to the rated eight horsepower and the engine developed 80 bhp.

Cyril raced the car with much success until 1957 when he was severely injured in a crash. He made a full recovery but decided not to race again and he left the Morgan's wreckage in his garage. Some years later, Philip Spencer became interested and worked with Cyril to rebuild the Morgan. Phil was on the point of retiring from international solo and sidecar motorcycle racing and was looking for something to satisfy his con-

tinuing lust for power and speed.

Eventually Cyril sold the car to Phil on the condition that it continue to be used in competition rather than being wrapped up in cotton wool and placed in a museum which has been the fate of many other great racing cars. To make the Morgan more competitive, Phil increased the power of the JAP. "We really don't know

what its output is," Phil says, "but it used to produce about 100 bhp on 7.2 to 1 compression ratio on low octane, post war petrol and now we have it running on methanol at 13 to 1 compression ratio and we've increased the

photo by Philip Aynsley

capacity from 1100 cm³ to 1300 cm³!"

The only other change is to modern Pirelli motor cycle racing tyres.

At the age of 86, Cyril accompanied Phil and the beloved Morgan to Australia and rode as a passenger in one event at Oran Park. After the ride he delightedly exclaimed that the Morgan was ... "getting around the corners better and going faster than when I owned it!"

A week before Oran Park I went to have a look at the two Morgans and I marvelled at their simplicity. Phil calls it a victory of engineering over design. All they are is a collection of three wheels, a rudimentary frame and the giant V-twin engine which dominates the vehicle. The engine sits right between the two front wheels which are attached, via the stub axles, to collars which slide up and down vertical pillars.

The geometry of the front suspension never changes. The wheels go up and down in a vertical plane. Sliding pillar suspension was fitted to the first Morgan in 1910 and today's cars use the same system. A motorcycle style trailing fork with leaf springs controls the single rear wheel. Connecting the front and rear of the car are three parallel steel tubes and that is all the chassis you get.

The driveshaft runs in the centre tube to the three speed gearbox and from there the rear wheel is chain driven.

An aluminium body on an ash wood frame turns the assembly into a rudimentary but surprisingly stiff monocoque. Under racing conditions there was no body flexing that I could detect.

Driver comfort is minimal. In the front is a low perspex screen that you look over rather than through. At the side, the bodywork does not come up to the driver's waist and the car is so low you can put your hand down flat on the track.

The gear stick and hand brake are outside on the right and a thin, vinyl mat separates the driver from the wooden floor. The passenger isn't so lucky ... there is little room, nothing to hang on to and your legs are stretched out over the fuel tank. You have to wedge your feet firmly to prevent the centrifugal force from flinging them across to join the driver's feet on the pedals!

When I accepted the invitation, I expected a pleasant, sedate ride in a slow old car that the owner was desperate to preserve ... after

The big JAP V-twin — with weight of 362 kg and power output of 74 kW, the Morgan is very quick. Below, the cramped, spartan cockpit. Note the fuel tank filling the passenger footwell.

photos by Ian Lee

all, Phil's Morgan is worth something like $80,000! The Morgan club members quickly set me to rights ... they told me that with a weight of 800 pounds and a power output in excess of 100 bhp, the Morgan is very quick.

Recently, in Britain, Phil's car recorded times that were similar to those recorded by a Cosworth Sierra. The Sierra was not a Group A rocket ship but a production class saloon running on road tyres, but still a very fast car. Becoming a little nervous, I asked Phil whether he wasn't worried about breaking such a priceless antique? His answer did little to dispel my fears: "If we break them we fix them," he said.

When owners of Morgan three wheelers need a part they tend to machine up a batch so they can swap with other Morgan owners. This means that getting parts for a rebuild is generally not a problem. I needed two things for my ride in the Morgan ... a licence and protective gear. The Morgan Club rushed membership through and the Auto Cycle Union issued me with a competition licence after I had handed over the $30 fee and passed an examination on motorcycle racing regulations.

I already owned a helmet and Kelly Ashton lent me a set of leathers that just managed to contain my ample proportions. I got

out to Amaroo to find gloomy faces in the Morgan camp. Phil's car had blown a piston. He'd brought a spare but found that the JAP's bore had been badly scored by the dust and grit of Oran Park.

With the engine back together we went out for the practice session. Phil took things quietly as grid positions had already been allocated and times were not important. The Morgan three wheeler driving style is unique. The steering is incredibly heavy and is basically only used to point the car into the corner. From there on, it's all throttle control ... power on and the rear wheel drifts out, power off and the nose tucks tighter into the corner.

Phil changed gear only three or four times each lap. His Morgan has a three speed gearbox. First is used only for starting, third is used around most of the circuit and second is used occasionally to help the rudimentary brakes slow the car.

It quickly became apparent that the sidecar outfits would be a problem in the race. They braked a lot better but were much slower in the corners. This meant that they were hard to pass on the straights and, with passenger leaning out and doubling their width on Amaroo's mainly right hand corners, impossible to pass in the bends!

Phil gave my instructions:

"Don't act like a sidecar passenger just sit still so that you don't change the balance of the Morgan and don't get your feet mixed up with mine on the pedals."

I was a bit disappointed with my ride. I was able to appreciate the Morgan's handling, and Phil's skill was obvious, but it had all seemed a bit slow and tame. I hadn't realised that Phil had been driving quite slowly to preserve the damaged engine. The race was another matter!

Phil's intention to drive conservatively evaporated as the three sidecar outfits in front inflamed his racing instincts. We took Dunlop Loop and the back of the circuit through to Mazda Corner in a series of power slides. I was overwhelmed by the power and speed, the rasping racket of the JAP and the beautiful smell of the Castol R that blew back in a fine mist from the exposed valve rockers to coat my helmet.

Phil's driving had changed from smooth to brutal as he crouched forward on to the wheel and flung the Morgan into each corner in a desperate attempt to get past the outfits in front of us. Through the corners and down Amaroo's short straights we gained ground but the bikes were able to leave their braking later and re-open the gap. Halway through each corner we'd be right on their rear wheels and Phil would have to back off to avoid hitting the wallowing sidecars. A quick glance back showed that the rest of the field was out of sight.

All too quickly it was over. The flag came out to end our five laps and we hadn't lost or gained any positions. We'd actually finished third as one of the outfits in front of us was post-vintage and not in our class.

I've driven a lot of fast cars and ridden on race tracks with top drivers including several world champions, but never before had I experienced the sheer thrill of power and speed as in that 50-year-old racer that can't decide whether it is a car or a motorbike and sidecar. More Morgan, please!

chain to the rear wheel has the advantage of being easily changed to effect different ratios for road, racing and trials.

Perhaps surprisingly, Morgan were right in the vanguard of independent front suspension, using an innovative sliding pillar/coil spring arrangement in 1910. It might also be argued that the rear suspension was also independent – there being only one wheel, connected by swinging arms and quarter elliptic springs to the chassis. Dampers were deemed optional equipment by the men at Malvern, but Super Sports models sported ineffectual telescopics, which have now been replaced with Spax, and John thinks that period Hartford friction discs at the rear transform the handling *in extremis*.

John reckons his Morgan, which weighs only 834lb dry, is good for 80mph flat out using an 18-tooth sprocket – and he's lapped Oulton Park at nearly 60mph.

So what is a three-wheeler Moggie like to drive today? Many first-time Morgan owners come via motorcycles, or else learned to drive afresh on three wheels. That's quite an advantage because it removes preconceived ideas of how things should be. Any knowledge about driving a car should be promptly jettisoned. Indeed it is likely, on first acquaintance with a Morgan, that all instinctive reactions from driving a conventional car will serve only to confuse.

The first problem is getting into such a tiny vehicle. John suggested stepping in over the doorless sides and resting on the tail. He then brings his feet together and slides down neatly behind the wheel in one easy action. A driver, however, who unlike the svelte, tear-drop-shaped Morgan, has an unwanted excess of avoir-dupois arranged around his middle may find it altogether easier to enter from the passenger side, sliding the right leg under the wheel and finally insinuating the other leg over and around the upright handbrake and gearlever.

Once in, one is forced to admit that legroom is far better than you would ever have believed possible – though toes must be lurking in dangerous proximity to the radiator. And the two pedals you have just discovered are not quite what they seem, either.

The right one is the brake not the accelerator, though you will undoubtedly spend your first Morgan driving lesson trying to make it work as one, with the inevitable kangaroo consequences of the cartoon strip learner.

And the brake pedal, dear friends, is only for the back one, while the accelerator (you hardly dare ask) is operated from one of three levers on the steering wheel; where else? Now do please pay attention! The other two operate the ignition advance and retard, and the choke; it's all perfectly simple really.

That just leaves the handbrake. This is not a parking brake – simple-minded soul that you are – but the mechanism whereby the more effective front brakes are operated. The gearlever, looking like some escapee from a blacksmith's forge, has first where fourth would normally be, reverse where third would be, second

where first should live, and third – you've guessed it – where second usually resides.

Easy really, until you try to change gear with the handbrake.

Synchromesh? You must be joking. But yes the lefthand pedal is indeed the clutch. Where would you expect it to be?

And even given all those complexities, theory is easier than practice. As John patiently admitted, on first acquaintance the Morgan seems designed for an octopus – you simply run out of arms trying to operate the thing.

The accelerator lever, connected by Bowden cable, seems particularly alien. It operates over a wide arc, crudely opening and shutting off the engine. John avows that it's almost impossible to over-rev, but he isn't terribly convincing. Then of course, when you turn the steering wheel, the wretched thing disappears altogether, either up your coat sleeve, or in the more ample driver's case, into the nether regions of the stomach – probably never to appear again.

This is particularly irksome when you are trying to manoeuvre, because even when you find the thing, the lever then operates in the opposite direction. Gear changing was not particularly hazardous, but braking had its moments. John said that the rear brake is quite capable of locking up the wheel, even in the dry. So the drill, on a steep descent, is to lock the front brake lever onto its ratchet to slow down, shut down the throttle, apply the back brake with the pedal and, preferably, change gear. Oh and don't forget to give a hand-signal to other drivers at the same time, if you're contemplating turning.

Now you will understand the need for extra arms. Yet it's amazing how stable the little trike actually seemed through bends. Driver nervousness was the only real limiting factor. And though it bucked and weaved over coarse surfaces, the ride was really quite impressive given the design's antiquity and your closeness to the action. Only the razor-sharp steering, at two-thirds of a turn lock to lock, needed watching as the Moggie writhed over the bumps and adjusted to all attempts to rein her in a bit.

The engine really is amazing. You can potter gently along with the exhausts emitting cute, putt-putt noises that echo off the hedgerows, and then it will slog up even the steepest incline like a tractor. But it's probably best to keep the Moggie moving and, providing you've enough practice and confidence this low-flying bedstead is more than a match for many a modern. Matchless indeed!

With Morgan maestro Rowland back behind the wheel, the ride home was exhilarating, the twin exhausts running straight along either flank barking out a deafening, staccato note like a World War I fighter's machine gun. And – yes – I'm developing withrawal symptoms. Despite my not altogether convincing first attempts, and trying hard to forget the soaking endured for the sake of photography, I need (oh dear, yes, *need*) another go in a Morgan soon, to try to gain mastery of the beast. There must be uncharted depths of masochism left in me after all.

Three's Company

Morgan Three-Wheeler 1937 Super Sport

The Matchless Morgan

UK Special Issue

Beetling about on three wheels with its engine exposed, the Morgan defines the fun factor in early motoring.

One of the more stirring sights in the world of vintage or classic motor cars is a three-wheeler Morgan. Even more stirring is seeing a gaggle of them in action.

The first time I saw this spectacle was in Britain in the '60s, at a Vintage Sports Car Club race meeting on the twisty Oulton Park circuit. My Dad had said to me before the race "You'll enjoy this" and he was right.

The staccato bark of well-tuned V-twin motors, and low-slung little cars, with their engines exposed, beetling round corners with the drivers moving around in their cockpits as the cars took the bends, and a vivid impression of speed, has stayed with me through the years.

The chance to get close to one of these wonderful little cars came when *NZ Classic Car* found a 1937 Super Sport with Matchless V-twin motor.

We're not quite sure how many three-wheeler Morgans there are in New Zealand – estimates vary from half a dozen to more than twenty, and there are, of course, some Morgan lookalikes built in more recent times. But this 1937 Super Sport is quite definitely the real thing!

Visually, these vehicles are stunning. The engine in this car, a 990cc V-twin Matchless MX-2 (you may find JAP or Blackburne engines in other cars), dominates the front view. It's all business, completely exposed and totally purposeful.

The front suspension is the next thing to catch your eye. With long kingpins, exposed springs, and top and bottom links, once again it is completely different to anything you'll normally meet on the road.

Prominent headlights set high on the skimpy mudguards, a brightly chromed radiator, and exhaust pipes curving round on to the body sides complete the picture from the front.

Side on, the wee car has a short and stumpy body, broadly cigar-shaped, with the tail cut off and finished by the angle-mounted spare wheel. This particular configuration is known as the 'barrel-tail' body.

The front wheels are set well forward, and the single rear wheel nestles inside the rear body. The wheelbase is around 85 inches.

Small silencer

The exhaust pipes run along each side, with a pretty small silencer, towards the end of each pipe, making a half-hearted attempt to silence the engine's bark. No wonder the cars sound so

Chromed radiator and exhaust pipes curving round on to the body sides complete the picture from the front

purposeful, with the motor so exposed and not a great deal of exhaust silencing!

The body lines are set off on this car with a very nice paint job, done by

Muscle test – cranking over the engine

Derek Atkinson, NZ Morgan specialists, in Henderson, Auckland.

It's a very cosy two-seater, quite a struggle to get in, and you have to watch where your feet go as you thread yourself in – people new to these cars have been known to catch their size 10s in the cabling coming from the steering wheel-mounted throttle!

It is definitely not a car for big people and it is reputed to be impossible to get into the car with the hood erected, unless you are an eel!

Once in, you'll find there are only two pedals, for brake and clutch, and a hand throttle on the steering wheel modulates the go department.

Some owners have fitted a normal throttle pedal, to make the cars a little more like a normal car to drive, but

owner John Williams prefers to keep the car original – he has had so many years of driving them that he has no trouble settling back into driving the Mog after spells with normal vehicles.

Upholstery is very basic. The cars were originally fitted with pump-up seat cushions (Moseley "float-on-air") set on plywood, with such creature comforts designed with lightness rather than comfort in mind, one suspects! Since the seat cushions were usually punctured, one commentator wryly notes it was "float-on-wood" rather than "float-on-air".

Our present car has been upholstered with something approaching proper seats, as it no longer has to meet the 8cwt weight limit that at original build time dictated the fitting of lightweight componentry.

A classic-style windscreen is fitted (built from scratch by John to match the original), and in this very basic car, one is surprised to find a windscreen wiper, double-action, vacuum operated from the inlet manifold.

A small luggage grid is mounted atop the tail – John thinks these were fitted to most cars, as there is no luggage room in the tail.

This 1937 car was imported from the UK in 1981. Its present owner actually owned the car when he was 16 ("many years ago," he comments). His reason for buying the three-wheeler? He "just liked trying something different"! Finally, he sold it to a friend.

He kept in touch with the new owner, and bought it back from him on a trip to Britain, in much the same state as he had sold it. After shipping it out to NZ, John set to and did a full rebuild job on the car (taking around ten years).

Prominent headlights set high on the mudguards add to the insect-like look

The short and stumpy body, broadly cigar-shaped, with the tail cut off and finished by the angle-mounted spare wheel configuration is known as the 'barrel-tail'

Regular use

The job was completed in 1990, and since then the car has seen regular use, as John loves driving it. He has done much of the work on the car himself, building up his own fittings, when required in some cases, such as the exhaust pipes and windscreen, rather than trying to search out parts from Morgan specialists overseas.

One of the bonuses of the Morgan's simple design and construction is that it is very easy to work on. Access is not much of a problem – the engine is right out in front, easily got at, and removable from the car in just a few minutes anyway, says John – and most parts are lightweight and easily handled.

You want to work on the underside of the car? Sure, you tip it over onto its side!

Over the years, most owners, especially those with a motorcycling background like John Williams, would have done their own maintenance. It also means that restoration is less of a problem than in some cars, with labour a lesser component of the bill.

Design and construction

In technical terms, this model Morgan has a V-twin 990cc Matchless engine, available in side-valve or overhead-valve configuration, also either air- or water-cooled. It was a little more civilised in its sound and behaviour than the very vigorous JAP engine, which could be a bit awkward to start.

This car uses the final design of chassis frame, which went through several stages of evolution. These later models used a chassis of rather lower build to improve stability and roadholding. Steering had been by now geared down, though it was still very direct (by any

other car's standards). The transmission on these later cars comprise a friction clutch, a prop shaft running along the chassis centre line, with an intermediate bearing, feeding the drive into a gearbox input shaft on a three-speed and reverse gearbox, which in turn drives through a worm gear/wheel to turn a cross-shaft with sprocket, connected by a single chain to the single rear wheel. Phew!

On the other end of the cross-shaft is the generator drive. This car has been converted to a 12-volt electric system.

There were brakes for each wheel but not coupled, with the pedal actuating the rear drum and a lever (beside the gear lever) working the two front drums. The brakes are small, around 7″ drums, and do no more than an adequate job, says John.

It is essentially a twin-tube frame, with a central tunnel housing the prop shaft, and in fact not greatly different from the earlier models. By this time, the cars were considerably heavier, though

There are only two pedals (brake and clutch)

The front wheels are set well forward, and the single rear wheel nestles inside the rear body.

1937 Morgan Three-Wheeler Super Sport

Engine:
Matchless V-twin, 990cc,ohv, air cooled, 85.6 x 85.6mm, c.r 6.2:1, 39.1bhp at 4600rpm, torque c.50ft.lbs at 2400rpm

Transmission:
friction clutch, rear-mounted three speed plus reverse manual gearbox, rear wheel drive by chain, 19/48 teeth on final chain sprockets

Body/Chassis:
two-seater sports, tubular steel twin-rail chassis

Running gear:
ifs by coil springs, above and below stub axles sliding on a pillar, rear (single) wheel by quarter-elliptic, no shock absorbers at either end, direct steering by drop arm and drag link, drum brakes

Wheels/Tyres:
18" Dunlop Magna bolt-on wheels, 18 x 4.00" tyres

Dimensions:
L n/a, w/base 85.0", track front 49.5", kb weight 896lbs

Performance:
Performance: Max sp 85mph, 0-50mph 9.6secs, 0-60mph 14.0secs, st quarter m 18.5secs, economy 40-55mpg

Production:
n/a for this model

Notes: alternative engines available at this time, Matchless ohv or sv, air- or water-cooled, and JAP. Performance figures above from Autocar refer to similar 1939 model, should be quite representative of 1937 car.

Owner John Williams restored his Morgan during the '80s

Still quite a nippy car

The front suspension has long kingpins, exposed springs, and top and bottom links

engine outputs had also increased, so the Morgan was still a performance car in anybody's terms.

Airborne wheels

The rear wheel is sprung, but only just, by a quarter-elliptic spring, and the independent front suspension has limited travel – around two inches, John reckons, so on bumpy roads the Morgan can spend a fair amount of time with wheels airborne. Exciting stuff!

The rear wheel was fork-mounted, two forged tapered blades with phosphor-bronze trunnion bearings and a tie bar, and a quarter-elliptic spring at each side.

The independent front suspension is an interesting design, comprising essentially tee-shaped stub axles lying on their side, with the stem of the tee forming the wheel spindle or axle and the cross-piece sliding vertically up and down on a pillar forming the kingpin. Above and below the stub-axle cross-

piece, coil springs provide the springing action. It is simple, light and effective, though movement is limited, and has been used by Morgans since the start of production in 1910-11.

You will sometimes see the springs covered up, but on this car they are left exposed. John tells us he has widened the track slightly, by about 2", a trick used on racing Morgans to improve stability. It does not affect suspension geometry.

The steering is very direct, heavy to operate when the car is stationary, but lighter on the move. A drop arm comes out of the steering box, working on a drag link to the right wheel, which is track-rod connected to the left wheel.

In keeping with the Morgan's general movement towards more equipment in the late thirties (it now had to be seen to be making some show of keeping up with the MGs, Singers etc that were setting the pace for the four-wheeler

small sportscar market), a self-starter was fitted, considerably more effective on these Matchless engines apparently than on the JAP-powered cars.

A valve lifter is a useful adjunct to the self-starter, and a starting handle too is provided, engaging directly on to the crankshaft nose rather than the camshaft as on the JAP engines, says John.

Earlier cars

The early models, through to about 1930-31, used a frame of twin steel tubes, and the front assembly likewise; the engine was mounted to the main frame tubes at the front.

The suspension was independent at the front, with coil springs and sliding axles, with little movement, and a quarter-elliptic leaf spring looked after the rear wheel. Steering was extremely direct.

A leather-faced cone-type clutch took the drive back along a prop shaft to a bevel box, with a cross-shaft carrying on each

A car built for two

The various engines

The archetypal vision of the three-wheeler Morgan is that marvellous V-twin motor up front. It appears in various states of dress or undress, with more or less pipes attached depending on being air- or water-cooled, and could be either side valve or overhead valve.

The most frequently encountered motors were the Blackburne, the JAP and the Matchless that we see in our feature vehicle. These were usually in 1000 or 1100cc versions, but 750s and single-cylinder motors could also be fitted for special purposes.

Other V-twin motors from Anzani or MAG could be found. The most powerful of these V-twin engines would have been turning out an easy 40bhp, and some as much as 50bhp, enough to give very brisk performance in a car that was weight-limited by law to eight cwt.

Torque output – remember these were big, long-stroke cylinders – was very solid indeed.

Power output of the water-cooled engines was reckoned to be slightly more than the air-cooled ones – through better control of the cylinder-head temperature, for example the 1937 Matchless MX-4 990cc ohv water-cooled motor gave 42.1bhp, with the air-cooled Matchless MX-2, as fitted to this car, giving 39.1bhp.

luggage grid is mounted atop as there is no luggage room in *the tail*

A beautiful finish on this car

When is a Morgan not a Morgan?

When it is a Darmont, or even a Sandford. Darmont was the nameplate of the French licence-built Morgan, almost indistinguishable in appearance. These first appeared in 1924, and were available in various versions with side or overhead valve motors, and they even built a supercharged version (the Darmont Speciale) which was near enough a 100mph car!

The engines were French-built versions of the Blackburne.

The Sandford was built by an Englishman, Malcolm Sandford, living in Paris. His Morgan-inspired creations were somewhat re-engineered to use mainly in-line small four-cylinder engines like the Ruby – they had a more refined air to them generally than the British cars.

side a dog-clutch and chain sprocket, each side supplying a different gear ratio, through a chain and sprocket each side of the rear wheel.

Either gear was engaged via a central cockpit lever, and it was bad luck if you wanted to reverse – you had to get out and push – no great hardship, mind you, when the whole unit weighed only around 4 or 5 cwt.

Very brief history

Some 30,000 three-wheeler Morgans of all types were built, including some built under licence in France. Production began just before World War 1, around 1910, and continued to the beginning of World War 2, with a few special order cars built after the war, and shipped to Australia.

When this car was built in 1937, three-wheeler production was tapering off, as the comparatively recently introduced four-wheeler cars were proving notably more successful in the marketplace.

Morgan's most productive year for the three-wheeler was 1927, when over 1700 were sold.

The sporting element was uppermost in most people's use of the Morgan, as the three-wheelers weighed around 8cwt and the big V-twin engines, with plenty of power and torque, could really shift the Morgan along.

40bhp in 8cwt gives a power-weight

Alternative body styles

We show a few small pictures of different body styles available on the three-wheeler Morgan over the years, including the French Darmont. A family model could be bought, with just about seating for four, but most people's ideas of the Morgan encompass the various sporting configurations, the Aero, the Super Sports, the cigar-shaped body or the barrel-ended body we see on our feature car.

All have the sense of style that seems to be inherent in the Morgan body. It is carried right through to the present lusty four-wheel sportscars – a style that comes from being designed for a purpose – to make a light and efficient vehicle.

A classic-style windscreen (built by John to match the original)

Handy storage space behind the seat

211

ratio of 100bhp/ton, enough for very lively performance. Specially-prepared examples were successful in record-breaking and racing.

On the road

The Morgan is still quite a nippy car and, when driven in earnest by someone who knows the car well, can cover the ground very smartly indeed. A glance at the specification figures on our centre-spread shows that the Mog could cut out a standing quarter in around 18.5secs. It is very swift off the mark and in acceleration generally, with the combination of a torquey engine and light weight working well.

Drivers need to be familiar with the car's handling, ride and braking before it can be driven with confidence but once that is achieved this car is clearly great driving fun, an archetypal sports car.

It is ironic that what was in its time a very cheap car, offering fantastic performance for the price, is now a very expensive car indeed.

Surviving examples of Morgan three-wheelers are rare and very highly prized these days.

It is no surprise to find that modern recreations of the Morgan three-wheeler are proving successful, offering a cheaper alternative to the originals, as the one thing that has not changed over the years is the fun factor.

Morgans of this type clearly still offer a unique and fun-filled driving experience. A short drive is no more than a taster for this, and the full experience comes with ownership and regular driving.

DAVID CASS
PHOTOS STEPHEN PERRY

Our thanks to John Williams for allowing us to experience and photograph his delightful 1937 Super Sports.

It's a very cosy two-seater, quite a struggle to get in

The rear wheel is sprung, but only just, by a quarter-elliptic spring

The subtle arts of driving – and passengering!

Driving a three-wheeler, in earnest, is rather different from normal driving. There are several important factors to keep in mind. One is the road surface. Morgans are noted for rock-solid "suspension" and one is reminded of this every time you hit a bump – and with three wheels each following a different track, you hit a bump more often!

A Morgan driver soon learns to read the road surface ahead, and try to avoid the worst of the bumps. Three-wheeler neophytes tend to manage to get the bump nicely between the front wheels, forgetting that the central rear wheel then hits it square on – its minimal suspension ensures you are instantly and painfully reminded you got it wrong. You aim to get the bump underneath driver or passenger.

Second, when cornering in earnest, the balance of the vehicle is important. In a three-wheeler, roll effects are magnified. To prevent the vehicle overturning, it helps to balance the car with driver and passenger bodyweight working against the weight transfer caused by body roll.

It is, of course, the same effect that sidecar riders and passengers have to counteract, and Morgan drivers and passengers quickly learn to move to balance the car as it takes corners.

Thirdly, with only a single rear wheel, the car is very responsive to throttle input. It pays to have power on through a corner, which in turn can lead to oversteer.

A press-on Morgan driver soon becomes used to this effect, in much the same way as a 'chain gang' Frazer Nash driver does – it is just a fact of life. Counter-steering into a slide is very easy in both cars, fitted with extremely direct steering as they are. Power-off cornering gives the reverse effect, a tendency to understeer.

Why three?

It is probably a combination of two factors: one the vogue towards cycle cars evident in the earlier years of motoring, and two, the fact that in Britain, three-wheeler cars enjoyed a considerable tax advantage over four-wheelers.

Quite simply, three-wheelers were cheaper to put on the road, and in perennially cash-strapped Britain, this was a factor of some importance.

The one drawback to this was that a three-wheeler had to weigh less than 8cwt, so all sorts of weight-saving design stratagems were used – when applied to Super Sports Morgans, this gave them their performance, but when applied to family saloons (Reliants, Bonds et al) it gave an air of fragility!

A small coterie of three-wheeler enthusiasts have been reproducing the Morgan formula on and off for some 70 years. We've noted how the French, with their leaning towards cyclecars, produced two contemporary three-wheelers, the Darmont and the Sandford. More recently in the eighties and nineties, enthusiasts in the States and the UK produced Morgan-like vehicles such as the Triking, powered by a Moto Guzzi V-twin motor.

Here in NZ, there are a few around, one powered by a Fiat Bambina-type 650cc motor, others by V-twin bike engines such as Hondas, Guzzis or Harleys.

Clockwise from Left:

• 1913 Runabout
• 1922 model
• 1934 Super Sports
• 1929 Aero
• Two recent NZ – built lookalikes
• Driving and passengering – in earnest!

Morgan three-wheeler

It's crude, but John Evans has a special reason to appreciate it

The name's Morgan. John Morgan Evans. At school they called me Organ Morgan, and I hated it. It was only when I was flicking through mum and dad's honeymoon photos that I understood where the Morgan bit had come from. Stap me if that wasn't pop at the wheel of a restored 1937 Matchless-engined Morgan three-wheeler. His Morgan three-wheeler, he told me.

And here I am at the wheel of another – a 1933 Sports two-seater. It's like stepping into that old family photo and sharing some of the old man's excitement. The two-seat cockpit is a tight fit. You sit with legs stretched out, hands

THANKS TO JOHN HOAR OF MORGAN THREE WHEELER CLUB: TEL 0181 311 7282

Mid-lane bumps can set 1933 Morgan's single rear wheel squirming alarmingly, but it still rides remarkably well

Three speeds plus reverse in H-gate

clamped to a large steering wheel. Ahead is an oval wooden dashboard framing vital instruments. At your feet are a clutch and a footbrake, to the

side a handbrake and a three-speed plus reverse H-gate gearchange.

Owner and Morgan Three Wheeler Club member John Hoar crank-starts the water-cooled 42bhp 990cc Matchless vee-twin engine. It comes alive in a way no modern tinbox ever could. The engine's exposed valves bob like pecking hens, vibrations attack the car's floor and the slightest misapplication of throttle or ignition lever threatens to snuff out the lot in a moment.

I do a few circuits to practise

Evans named after honeymoon car

juggling the hand throttle, ignition advance/retard lever, clutch and gearchange. Torque comes by the shedload from zero revs, but the Moggy isn't as quick as I'd been told. I have to take one hill in second. The steering is just three-quarters of a turn from lock to lock, so you lean into a bend rather than steer. Alarmingly, mid-lane humps set the rear end squirming, but you get used to it. For all its primitive sliding pillar front suspension (still used on Morgans today) and quarter elliptical rear suspension, it rides over gently undulating B-roads surprisingly well.

But how mum and dad toured Cornwall in AFH 955 I'll never know. Of course, things were slower, then,

the roads quieter, and the Morgan must have cut a bit of a dash. But it's a crude device and Hoar's story of an American couple who were flung out of theirs and killed a few weeks ago only confirms my worst fears.

Sadly, mum and dad had to call a halt to their honeymoon tour when a wheel cracked. Morgan called a halt in the late '30s when production went over to four-wheelers. I'd like to say it was a good thing, too, but a little black and white photo of happy days stops me. ●

Matchless vee-twin produces 42bhp

Massive steering wheel has only three quarters of a turn from lock to lock

Menace à Trois

1928 Morgan Aero

With the current Aero 8 gracing this month's cover, what better vintage car to look at than the original, three-wheeled Morgan Aero?

WORDS & PHOTOS PENN MCKAY

These three-wheelers are definitely an acquired taste and for me a very tentative one. This view came about because of my recent search for a ride-on mower. I test-drove a locally built three-wheeler. It got away on me and threw me off, causing this *pennsioner* to display astonishing agility as he leapt clear of the still moving cutting blades.

Consequently, my view on three-wheelers was, I thought, permanently warped – anything equipped with a tricycle under-carriage is viewed with great suspicion.

Labour of love

The story of this car, and its incarnations, is an example of the amazing history of many vintage cars. Peter Alderdice, the present owner, carried out the latest rebuild over a lengthy period – as most restorations are, being labours of love carried out by men now taken off the hunting trails and needing therapy to counter the stresses of work.

Getting the car was the first task: "My dream started to be realised in late 1991, when a work colleague (Rob Hennin) mentioned that his father-in-law owned a derelict Morgan three-wheeled car. On his next trip to Wanganui, Rob enquired on my behalf if the car might be for

PETER ALDERDICE ON THE EARLY HISTORY OF HIS CAR

"The car left the factory on October 19 1928, delivered to Mann & Sons, agents in Coventry. During the 1940's Roy Lowe located the car in bits at the Holmes Bros Garage in New Plymouth. He told Joe Robinson, who subsequently purchased it. Joe recalled there being JAP water-cooled barrels, but the alloy crankcases were missing. Joe started reassembly and completed painting the chassis and fitting the Lucas sidelights to the alloy cycle guards.

Before reassembly was completed, Mark Edward Webb, an aircraft engineer, purchased it in 1951. He assembled the car using a JAP air-cooled side-valve motor, ex-sawbench (# 71460). When I spoke to Joe

Robinson in October 2000 (Joe was 87 then), he recalled Mark Webb turning up and giving him a ride after the car was completed.

Chas Withers purchased the car on June 16 1952 from Mark Webb. It was garaged in a hangar at the New Plymouth airfield at Bell Block and after a few minor repairs he drove it home to Wanganui. The ownership papers show it was re-registered in New Plymouth in December 1951.

"Between then and 1977, Chas Withers used the car extensively, so it must have broken his heart when a shed fire almost put an end to this great little survivor in 1977."

le, but was met with a firm rebuttal, as the wner (Chas Withers) still intended to restore "

has had campaigned the car for many years d it had been a very significant part of his life. ere's something about vintage cars that gets to an owner's bloodstream so man and achine become deeply attached. Well, the uman does anyhow. Trouble is humans are ortal, unlike the machines, which are nearly

immortal thanks to humans who keep reincarnating various heaps of bits.

Well, as it turned out mortality caught up with Chas – as it will with every one of us.

"Chas passed away in February 1992, and I considered myself very fortunate to be able to purchase the car. I gave Janet (Chas' wife) an undertaking the car would be restored. It had been stored in a farm shed, but had deteriorated very badly after a fire in the shed. For instance

MORGAN

When you think of the great British marques that have come and gone, you have to look at Morgan with huge respect. It's the survivor and one of the last of the numerous marques that constituted 'Best of British' when that phrase meant something. Morgan was always a low volume builder compared to everybody else, being drawn steadily towards the sporting end, a position they totally occupy today. Morgan is now known for hand built, expensive and iconic cars – if you've got one you must be rich! In fact, they were originally mainly builders of inexpensive three-wheelers that gained a reputation for being sporty and reliable.

They saw the writing on the wall and went over to making four-wheelers in the MG-type from about 1935 – if you can't beat 'em, join 'em. This they have done extremely successfully, finding a market niche that is entirely Morgan. If you want one you have to order and wait, I'm told.

the intensity of the fire had melted the aluminium front cycle guards to appear just as small blob of aluminium affixed to the top of the front brake drums."

Peter got lucky meeting a trio of similarly focused nutters: Mike Shepherd, who wanted to build a replica, having owned a Morgan years previously; and Richard Hudson, who owned a completely disassembled 1929 Morgan Aero and assisted greatly by allowing Peter to borrow various bits

for castings to be made. Finally, there was Chris North, who lived less than 5km away and was engaged on a similar restoration. All of this occurred during 1992-93.

Mike jumped at the chance to use Peter's chassis as a master to build two new chassis from – using the correct tubing and many of the original bits, of course

Peter obtained the drawings of the wooden frame from Martyn Webb via the Three-Wheeled Morgan Club (TWMC) in the UK. These plans went to Bob Coggan, a retired boat builder, and he completed the frame in March 1993.

Chris North has considerable engineering expertise, so it was a real stroke of luck to have him engaged in a similar project just down the road.

There was a lot of work in all of this, much of it complicated, including casting various replacement items that had not survived the fire. Peter vividly remembers watching the 1995 Rugby World Cup while threading and soldering

new radiators from copper tubing and 11,000 washers.

On The Road.

The Morgan has a great power-to-weight ratio with an 1100cc side-valve, air-cooled JAP V-twin engine, transversely mounted in a tubular frame. It has two-speeds using dog clutches and chains on two cycle-type gear wheels. Add independent

The Morgan has a great power-to-weight ratio with an 1100cc side-valve, air-cooled JAP V-twin engine, transversely mounted in a tubular frame

front suspension, with sliding pillars and coils and you're looking at something very advanced for its period. No wonder they sold a lot for such a small firm.

Try it out on a brisk sunny winter's morning, on a swooping rural road and you've got something very sporty – not to mention scary. It sounds like a vintage motorcycle, scoots along at motorcycle

speeds and makes your eyes water just like any motorcycle does if you don't wear goggles.

Peter lives in rural South Auckland and has an exciting private test run outside his property: a series of switchback ridges, one succeeding the other with Peter's house at the end of the road. It's true what they say about these Morgan three- wheelers: the closest thing to flying without taking off.

The torque from the 1100cc JAP twin is amazingly strong, heightened of course by the very lightweight body – which they had to be, to maintain their registration advantage.

In either of the two gears, at any speed, there is a powerful response when you advance the hand throttle lever mounted on the steering wheel. Even at speed, it's astonishingly stable. There's no hint of the roll I expected sitting over only one wheel thanks to the broad base of the two wheels and independent suspension, out-riggered up front.

Peter is a total enthusiast for these sorts of blasts from the past – he's also got a gaggle of vintage Harleys tucked away, some in full running trim (with sidecars) and some under restoration. ∎

THREE-WHEELERS

You might think of these as a sort of aberration produced in dribs and drabs. Well you'd be wrong, because Morgan had them in serious production from 1910 to 1930 and sold over 18,000 of them! They came out in two and four-seat versions and in racing guise as well. They were by far the most successful of the various three-wheelers, particularly in motor sport where the power to weight ratio was usually in their favour. All of this was enhanced by a variety of optional engines – sv or ohv, water-cooled or air – with Blackburne, JAP, Precision, Matchless and Ford all getting a run.

Morgan's sporting record included 115mph by a woman in 1929, and in 1925 they were the fastest un-supercharged 1100cc car in the world, at 104.68mph for a flying kilometre.

The thought of those sorts of speeds in these tiny craft causes me to blanch just writing about it, but as it turned out the real experience was both exhilarating and terrifying – just the kind of thing we need to jolt us out of our complacency.

There were other three-wheeler makers, but none as successful, or as determined as Morgan. They were of course, simply a step in the transition from two-wheels to the small four-wheelers, and on that path, the Austin 7 was the decisive stumbling block.